TOOLS FOR TRANSFORMING SCHOOL CULTURE

leveraging the six elements for positive change

ALEXANDER McNEECE | BO RYAN

Foreword by Anthony Muhammad

555 North Morton Street
Bloomington, IN 47404
800.733.6786 (toll free) / 812.336.7700
FAX: 812.336.7790

email: info@SolutionTree.com
SolutionTree.com

Visit **go.SolutionTree.com/schoolimprovement** to download the free reproducibles in this book.

Printed in the United States of America

Library of Congress Cataloging-in-Publication Data

Names: McNeece, Alexander author | Ryan, Bo author
Title: Tools for transforming school culture : leveraging the six elements for positive change / Alexander McNeece, Bo Ryan ; Foreword by Anthony Muhammad .
Description: Bloomington, IN : Solution Tree Press, [2027] | Includes bibliographical references and index.
Identifiers: LCCN 2026006276 (print) | LCCN 2026006277 (ebook) | ISBN 9798893740776 paperback | ISBN 9798893740783 ebook
Subjects: LCSH: School environment | School management and organization | Learning, Psychology of | Educational change
Classification: LCC LC210 .M45 2027 (print) | LCC LC210 (ebook)
LC record available at https://lccn.loc.gov/2026006276
LC ebook record available at https://lccn.loc.gov/2026006277

Solution Tree
Cameron L. Rains, CEO
Edmund M. Ackerman, President

Solution Tree Press
Publisher: Kendra Slayton
Associate Publisher: Todd Brakke
Acquisitions Director: Hilary Goff
Editorial Director: Laurel Hecker
Art Director: Rian Anderson
Managing Editor: Sarah Ludwig
Copy Chief: Jessi Finn
Senior Production Editor: Miranda Addonizio
Proofreader: Charlotte Jones
Text and Cover Designer: Abigail Bowen
Content Development Specialist: Amy Rubenstein
Associate Editor: Elijah Oates
Editorial Assistant: Madison Chartier

ACKNOWLEDGMENTS

To all the leaders who have shaped my path and allowed me to discover my purpose of helping others—parents, principals, and priests: Your mentorship and modeling have been true gifts. Please know that your role in this book was fundamental.
—ALEXANDER MCNEECE

I would like to thank my family for all their love and support.
—BO RYAN

Solution Tree Press would like to thank the following reviewers:

ZACHARY ASHAUER
Social Sciences Teacher
Hortonville Area High School
Hortonville, Wisconsin

JEFFREY BENSON
Educational Consultant
Jeffrey Benson LLC
Brookline, Massachusetts

DOUG CROWLEY
Assistant Principal
DeForest Area High School
DeForest, Wisconsin

JOHN D. EWALD
Associate
Solution Tree
Frederick, Maryland

KIRBY A. MANESS
Principal
Ayden-Grifton High School
Ayden, North Carolina

PETER MARSHALL
Educational Consultant, Author, and Associate
Solution Tree
Burlington, Ontario, Canada

JENNIFER MCMASTER
Superintendent of Education
Northwest Catholic District School Board
Dryden, Ontario, Canada

GEORGINA RIVERA
Principal
Charter Oak International Academy
West Hartford, Connecticut

*Visit **go.SolutionTree.com/schoolimprovement** to download the free reproducibles in this book.*

TABLE OF CONTENTS

Reproducibles are in italics.

ABOUT THE AUTHORS

Alexander McNeece, PhD, is the founder of McNeece Consulting and the associate executive director of the Metro Bureau, an organization that supports Michigan-based executive administrators. Previously, he served as a central office director, award-winning principal, teacher, and coach. When he was principal at Douglas Elementary in Douglas, Michigan, he and his staff utilized the Transforming School Culture framework to successfully turn the struggling school into a high-performing, A-graded institution. As a consultant, McNeece has worked with districts around the United States and Canada to close the achievement gap, transform school culture, strengthen the school-improvement process, and develop pedagogy to help students love learning.

McNeece has written multiple children's books for kindergarten readiness support. His previous professional books, *Launching and Consolidating Unstoppable Learning* and *Loving What They Learn: Research-Based Strategies to Increase Student Engagement*, help teachers develop strong instructional cultures in their classrooms.

He holds both a bachelor's degree and a master's degree in curriculum and instruction from Michigan State University. He earned a doctor of philosophy in educational leadership from Eastern Michigan University.

To learn more about Alexander McNeece's work, visit www.alexandermcneece.com or www.linkedin.com/in/alexandermcneece.

Bo Ryan is principal of Ana Grace Academy of the Arts Middle School, a magnet school in Bloomfield, Connecticut. He has led two different schools to Model Professional Learning Community (PLC) at Work® certification: (1) Cromwell Woodside Intermediate in 2012 and (2) Greater Hartford Academy of the Arts Middle School in 2016, just four years after it opened in a factory in the middle of a city. In addition, he led Ana Grace Academy to High Reliability Schools level 4.

Bo has worked in education since 1994, having served as a teacher, coach, director, adjunct professor, principal, author, and consultant. He was also a graduate assistant coach at Syracuse University in 1992–1995 for a team that won two bowl games and the Big East Championship. He is author of *The Brilliance in the Building: Effecting Change in Urban Schools With the PLC at Work Process*, a collection of all his experience teaching and learning in urban schools over two decades, which in 2024 won an International Impact Award. He is also author of *Teachers Leading Learning: Empowering Educators Through Cycles of Instructional Improvement*, which won the same award in 2026, and *The Leadership 10: Building a Culture of Leaders*, a picture book for all ages that appeared in Amazon's Top 5 New Releases in teacher and student mentoring. He has contributed to the anthologies *Culture Keepers: Leaders Creating a Healthy School Culture* and *Culture Champions: Teachers Supporting a Healthy Classroom Culture.* In 2025, he was an International Impact Book Awards finalist for Author of the Year, and in 2026, he was named Marquis Who's Who in America.

To book Alexander McNeece or Bo Ryan for professional development, contact pd@SolutionTree.com.

FOREWORD

By Anthony Muhammad

In 2007, I left a very comfortable job as a middle school principal in Metro Detroit at a school that I absolutely loved. I left because my mentor, the late Dr. Richard DuFour, encouraged me to take a leap of faith and join him as a consultant training individual professionals, schools, and school systems in a school-improvement model he'd developed with Dr. Robert Eaker called Professional Learning Community (PLC) at Work. The satisfaction that I experienced as a principal was a direct result of my commitment to the core tenets of PLC, so I felt compelled to join him and others and spread the good work.

The PLC process involves a group of professionals who agree to focus on student learning, work collaboratively, and use evidence of student learning to guide their work. The process is so logical that I philosophically committed instantly upon exposure at a conference in 2001, and I was blessed to lead a staff that became PLC zealots along with me. Together, we achieved record growth in all academic areas as well as supported our students socially and emotionally. Little did I know that our optimistic view of professional improvement, collaboration, and relentless belief in students was not the norm—it was the exception.

My first year of consulting was an emotional roller coaster. I would bring my PLC bag of tools from school to school. Some schools showed an immediate magnetism to the concepts, and I left feeling fulfilled and inspired. But at many schools, where I would bring the same bag of tools, the educators responded with disinterest and, in some cases, overt hostility. I entered consulting with the naive assumption that educators and educational institutions were monoliths, and I thought that if I simply made a logical case for PLC, people would embrace the concepts and become immediate allies.

After the first year of consulting, I felt as if I had made a huge career mistake. I was even actively seeking ways to go back to my old job as the principal at the school that I loved. Then, I had an epiphany. *Maybe the obstacle to embracing good practice is not the practice itself; maybe the problem is the culture of the institution.* This simple thought sent me down a rabbit hole, and I started to intensely study the concept of school culture. I researched the work of Willard Waller, Roland S. Barth, Kent D. Peterson, and Terrence E. Deal. These pioneers of school culture research tried to analyze this construct and give it meaning. What I learned from these scholars was that all schools have a culture. The important distinction to consider is if your culture is productive (healthy) and primed for excellence, or if your culture is unproductive (toxic) and preventing growth and excellence. The gap I found that remained in the literature was a detailed understanding of why some school cultures become healthy and why some remain toxic. Additionally, I wondered, can toxic cultures be transformed into healthy cultures? These questions led me to publish the first edition of the book *Transforming School Culture: How to Overcome Staff Division* in 2009, and the second edition in 2018.

Alexander McNeece and Bo Ryan have stepped into the arena of school culture scholarship to advance school culture practice to the next level. My books are typically philosophical in nature because, at heart, I am a philosopher. I love to contemplate ideas and shift paradigms, but there is always a need for logistics, nuts and bolts, and specific strategies. This book fills that vacuum. Both authors are highly accomplished practitioners. In fact, Alex McNeece was an English teacher at that middle school that I loved so much in Metro Detroit. Bo Ryan has walked the walk of transformation as an award-winning principal at a high-achieving urban school in Connecticut.

This book breaks down all the critical aspects of healthy cultures. Some of those aspects include shared vision of excellence, professional growth and integrity, positive symbolism, and powerful celebrations of student and staff excellence. Alex and Bo not only give research-based insights but also provide the reader with practical tools, templates, activities, and ideas that can easily be implemented at any school. I cannot think of a better companion to my life's work on school culture than this book.

Finally, I want to encourage you to not just read this book but do some deep reflection on your own school culture. Experiment with some of the tools and techniques that this book provides and watch staff morale, engagement, and efficacy improve. I have been asked before to define, in one sentence, the essence of my school culture work. My response is this: "Any school can produce a healthy culture if they emulate the behaviors of a healthy culture." This book is a detailed guide for that journey.

INTRODUCTION

To transform school culture for the better, school leaders must develop systems that will help their students and staff learn more and achieve greater outcomes. In *Transforming School Culture: How to Overcome Staff Division*, Anthony Muhammad (2018) writes that leaders need to "stimulate conversation and inspire educators to analyze the impact of their belief systems on their practices and how those practices impact their students" (p. 153). Because you have chosen this book, we know that you have the core motivation to make this happen. Readers of this text will find tools, suggestions, and support from the latest research to empower their teams to accomplish the goals central to cultural transformation.

The importance of a healthy school culture should not be understated. Decades of research establish a reliable, positive link between school culture and student achievement. A 2024 study, for instance, quantifies this link, finding a highly significant and very strong positive correlation ($r = 0.812$) between school culture and student learning achievement (Santia, Astuti, & Syafitri, 2024).

This benefit is amplified when schools move from traditional isolation to a structured collaborative culture. In 2025, Texas schools found that this cultural shift yielded significant, measurable progress (Mansell & Kirksey, 2025).

- Overall, students averaged just over three months of additional learning in mathematics and two months of additional learning in reading compared to peers who did not learn in a structured collaborative culture.
- For traditionally underserved populations, the impact was even greater. Economically disadvantaged students gained approximately four months of additional learning in mathematics, while multilingual learners gained about three and a half months of additional learning in reading.

Furthermore, the impact of a healthy school culture deepens over time. The same Texas study notes that these learning gains grew larger each year following implementation, highlighting the compounding effectiveness of a healthy school culture (Mansell & Kirksey, 2025).

Everyone wants these outcomes, but this is challenging work. It's difficult to figure out where to begin. Our goal is to help you and your teams create a healthy school culture. This book serves as a practical guide to implementing key elements of school culture transformation. It is designed for teacher leaders and principals who are ready to move from theory to action. We have researched the newest advances and philosophies of school culture to bring them to you.

It is an honor that you have chosen this book to support your development of a healthy school culture. We take that opportunity very seriously. When we were school leaders, we were driven by the same motivation—to transform our teams and create a healthy school culture to support students—and were guided by the core principles identified in *Transforming School Culture*. Because of that experience, we want to share the tools we used and support principals and teacher leaders in having the critical conversations necessary to change culture—and lives. We'll begin by defining a healthy school culture, introduce the roles that teachers fit into within a school culture, relate our own experiences with healthy school cultures, and preview the six elements of a healthy school culture as defined by Anthony Muhammad, the author of *Transforming School Culture* and the foreword of this book.

Healthy School Cultures

Educational leadership expert Kent D. Peterson (2002) defines healthy school cultures as characterized by educators who do the following.

- **Believe in student potential:** Educators in healthy school cultures possess an unwavering belief in the ability of all students to achieve success. They actively communicate this belief to others in what they do in the classroom and what they say in the staff lounge every day.
- **Collectively support student success:** Educators in healthy school cultures create and support the development and implementation of policies, procedures, and practices that align with a belief in universal achievement.

This definition establishes that while a strong belief in student potential is essential, it's not enough. Educators within healthy school cultures take proactive steps to address challenges. They identify problems, develop solutions, and work collaboratively to implement them.

Beyond his years as a teacher and principal in schools that operated as professional learning communities (PLCs), Alex has spent fifteen years doing school culture audits and has often observed similar school leadership focuses during these visits. As a visitor to a school, it takes less than an hour to discern the true difference between a healthy school culture and a toxic one. If a school collectively supports student success, the behavioral norms of the staff are immediately noticeable. Teachers and administrators celebrate student learning, both on the school walls and in their daily communications. Engaging teaching strategies are evident in classrooms from the first bell. Finally, and critically, the master schedule routinely builds in extra time for students to learn essential standards.

One of the biggest misconceptions Alex encounters during these audits is that school climate, specifically how well the adults get along, is the center of school culture. To be clear, we value collegial and bonded staff relationships. However, a healthy school culture is defined by the collective effort to help students achieve grade-level success or beyond. Some schools prioritize maintaining staff relationships over implementing what students need; they avoid critical conversations for the sake of preserving harmony. They are afraid to address how they celebrate students, how they can adjust classroom instruction, and how they can modify their daily practices to give students more time to learn challenging concepts. We need to be totally clear: This fear of interacting on a meaningful pedagogical level restricts schools' growth.

In *Transforming School Culture*, Muhammad (2018) describes the different roles that educators play in school change. We believe that no school will be able to change its culture without addressing how these roles interact and the critical events that happen in the organization every day. This book and its tools are designed to support principals and leadership teams before, during, and after those interactions.

These analyses, conversations, and reflections won't be easy, but they are essential for transforming your school's culture. Adult drama hinders student success; this is a reality familiar to anyone who has worked in schools. At the same time, educators should remember that resisting change doesn't make the resister a bad person. Treat all members and their voices with respect, but never avoid necessary conversations. The catalysts for change are conversations about "how we do things around here."

With this in mind, the tool you find most daunting in each chapter of this book is likely the one your school needs most. Principals and teacher leaders might shy away from the most impactful tools to maintain a pleasant climate, but please understand: Using these challenging tools, engaging in these discussions about your culture, and making necessary changes to school policies, procedures, and practices will ultimately create the best climate you've ever experienced. Adults who choose to work in schools, though sometimes stuck in their ways, genuinely want to make a difference for students. When you adjust your culture and see improved student outcomes, you fulfill a fundamental human need. The school becomes more than a collection of adults working side by side. It becomes a place with a systematic and schoolwide focus on learning that empowers everyone: teachers, students, principals, and parents.

The School Culture Players

If school improvement were as simple as sharing a definition, this book and the tools within it wouldn't be necessary. While some members of the school community are likely eager to implement change, others may resist those efforts.

Transforming School Culture holds a mirror up to the roles people play in the change process of a school. Muhammad's (2018) text helps readers understand four educator roles in the development of healthy or toxic cultures. As a prereader of *Transforming School Culture*, Alex was struck by how accurate the role descriptions were. When he began using the book in school trainings, he found the audiences were similarly shocked by the accuracy. Alex is a bit of a Shakespeare nut, and for him, the roles various educators fulfill brought to mind a timeless line from *As You Like It*: "All the world's a stage, and all the men and women merely players" (Shakespeare, n.d.). He started using the term *school culture players* due to how amazingly the behaviors of the four archetypes matched the various schools (or stages, if you will) he visited. Essentially, the usage of school culture players helps schools see the behavioral roles that people play in the change process.

Readers of *Transforming School Culture* will know these already, but here is a short summary of the four roles we will refer to as *school culture players* throughout this book.

1. **Believers:** These educators believe all students can learn, and they adopt change to make that happen. They are dedicated individuals who believe the goal of students' success is worth trying strategies and activities that are outside the norm. They participate in, and even sometimes lead, school-improvement efforts.
2. **Fundamentalists:** These individuals resist change. Their motivation is to maintain the status quo. This group dominates the school's informal communication networks. Their interactions generally focus on defaming, disrupting, or distracting to derail change initiatives that are being developed or implemented. These individuals generally don't have malice toward schools, communities, or students, but sometimes their rhetoric sounds like they do when they are trying to convince others to maintain the status quo.
3. **Tweeners:** These are new team members who are being socialized into the culture of the school. Their goal is to learn the expected culture. Many times, they are new to the teaching profession, which adds both a layer of idealism and a lack of real classroom experience. These individuals will have a *moment of truth* when a negative event that sits outside their expected experience makes them pick a side within the culture.
4. **Survivors:** This was a statistically rare group when *Transforming School Culture* was originally written. We would opine that this group is larger after COVID-19. This group's motivation is to survive the day, the week, the month, or the school year. They show no growth in professional practice and don't participate in building change initiatives.

It is important to dig deeper into the group of Fundamentalists, as they are the resisters to change. From the outside, all their resistance looks similar, but their motivations to resist can vary greatly. Understanding these motivations to help staff come together is one of the cruxes of this text. To get everyone on the same page, figure I.1 diagrams all the school culture players with a particular focus on the different levels of Fundamentalists.

Starting at the bottom of the diagram, all individuals enter into your organization as Tweeners. Educators join schools with positive intentions and a desire to help all students. Through multiple factors or missing factors elaborated on in chapter 3 of this book, Tweeners have a moment of truth (Muhammad, 2018). This moment of truth in the organization and the culture's response determine to which side of the school culture paradigm they will go. To the right, they can take the Believer's path. To the left is the Fundamentalist's path.

Once someone is on the Believer side, their path is not permanent. As illustrated in the figure, leadership actions (or the lack of them) can cause Believers to slide over into the Fundamentalist path. Plenty of individuals have been members of a team only to have

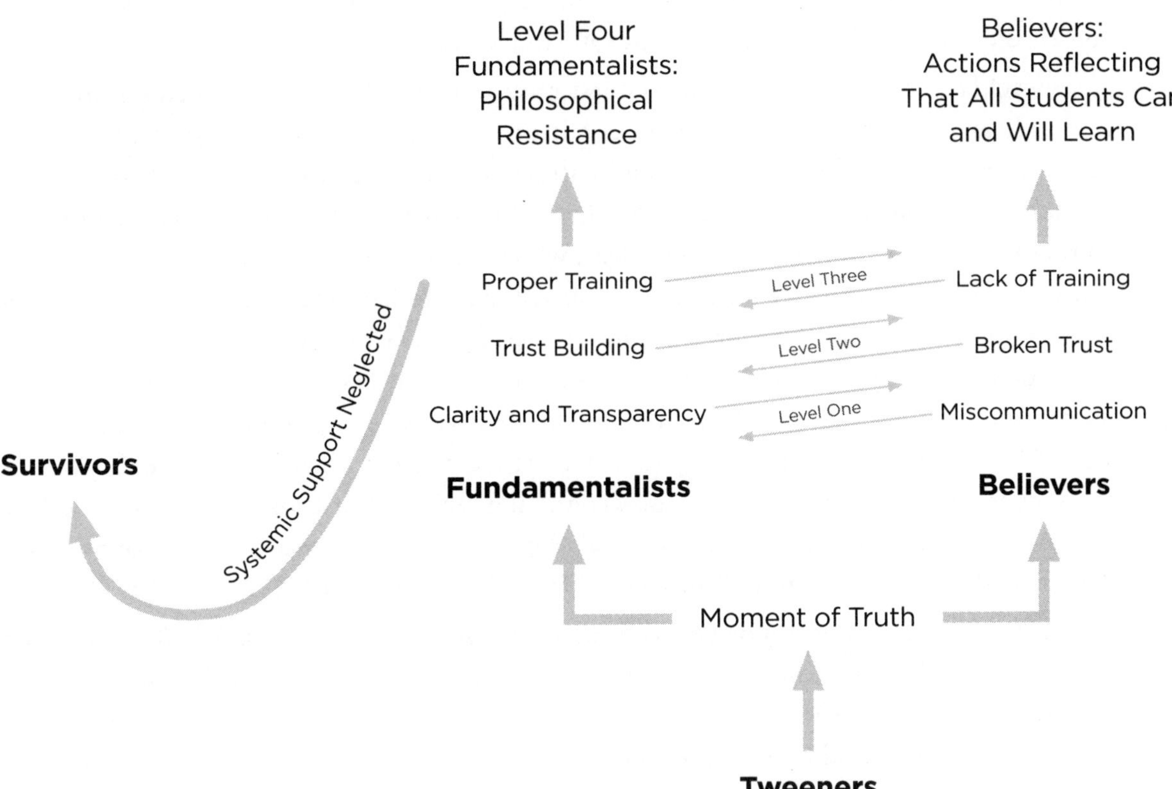

Figure I.1: *The school culture players.*

their organizational aspirations derailed by a district, school, or teacher leadership change and a coinciding clouding of communication. What they believed was best for all students and students' learning became fuzzy due to multiple other messages and initiatives (Level One Fundamentalists). Or, more personally, some people may have felt crushed when a change initiative that they poured their hearts and souls into was derailed because of a lack of grit among those in leadership positions; these leaders did not support the change or, even worse, kowtowed to a small but vocal group in the school that resisted the change. There is a deep and sad irony there: These individuals became resisters because leadership lacked the wherewithal to stand up for them (Level Two Fundamentalists). Finally, those who believed all students could and would learn may have lost that belief if leadership didn't ensure they had support to implement the instructional necessities in the classroom. Staunch Fundamentalist thought will develop in a teacher who believed every student could learn but was constantly proven wrong because they lacked the classroom skills to make it happen (Level Three Fundamentalists). Very importantly, Level Three Fundamentalists are on the path to becoming Survivors when those skills are not being developed in a routine and coherent way. Leaders at all levels should learn that a lack of support and growth within a culture is what creates Survivors.

An important lesson readers need to take away from this is that most Fundamentalist behavior is created by poor leadership at the district, principal, or teacher level. Knowing the importance of your actions in relation to culture and using the tools in this book will help you ensure that you don't create resistance in your space.

Level Four Fundamentalists are the last group to consider. As the preceding information indicated, teachers on the Fundamentalist path potentially are very different in their motivations to resist. In a healthy school culture that develops the will for all students to succeed, Level One Fundamentalists will flip to the Believer side with clear and consistent communication. Level Two Fundamentalists, who have been hurt before, will flip when trust is properly built. Level Three Fundamentalists will need to have their skills developed. Level Four Fundamentalists are very different from those at the other three levels. These individuals don't subscribe to the concept that every student deserves success. They stake their identities on this concept and resist any change because, in their view, change to the system is unnecessary. Why should they expend energy to help all students grow when they believe that not all students are able to grow? These individuals don't align with the first basic premise of a healthy school culture. Additionally, these individuals adopt the persona of *negative focuser*, or one with a negative disposition toward new programs (McNeece & Sheppard, 2025; Snyder, 2017).

This group is just as important to bring on board as all the others. All educators start their careers with positive intentions. We believe culture creates Level Four Fundamentalists, and building a supportive, accepting, and accountable culture is the only way to support this group. You will find tools in this book that Level Four Fundamentalists may resist, but engaging them to participate is the only way to help them. They are worth bringing aboard, but for the sake of our students who need healthy school cultures to thrive and succeed, we will not be held hostage. This book will help you and your teams work on that.

Our Experience With Healthy School Cultures

As authors, we came across *Transforming School Culture* differently, but our stories have several similar elements. Both our leadership experiences were shaped by Muhammad's concepts, which changed the core of who we are and what we believe about the importance of what we do. He is a character in our soul stories, as defined by Timothy D. Kanold (2021). A *soul story* is a reflective but forward-thinking professional story that defines you and your purpose. It is meant to help educators navigate the challenges they face while maintaining their professionalism and well-being (Kanold, 2021). Consider your motivation and coherently develop your own soul story as we share why *Transforming School Culture* is so important to us.

Bo's Soul Story

I am fortunate to have a mother who went to great lengths to help keep me from getting thrown out of middle and high school and a father who had the insight to send me to a prep school after I barely graduated from high school.

My story starts in Meriden, Connecticut. My urban neighborhood in Meriden consisted of mostly two- and three-family homes. People in the house next door bootlegged alcohol, people in the house down the street sold drugs, and we lived half a mile from two housing projects. On one hand, I met some of the greatest people in the world in my neighborhood, and on the other hand, there were so many children in the neighborhood and so many ways to get into trouble. I chose to participate in all the ways I could.

The trouble I was getting into in the neighborhood carried over to school. I was suspended from middle school several times over the course of three years and received report cards filled with Ds and Fs. My mother changed her work hours from second shift to overnight to check on me in school. She visited the middle school weekly. To change my behavior, both in school and in the neighborhood, she organized her own version of a Scared Straight program. She had me meet with a police sergeant, a detective, and a few other police officers for a couple of hours. They discussed with me the legal consequences of my actions.

My father, through his coaching connections, got me into Cushing Academy in the small town of Ashburnham, Massachusetts. I did not graduate and walk on stage with my high school class because I did maintenance work at this prep school at the end of my senior year and then lived there for the summer. I thought of the kids I grew up with in my neighborhood who did not have this opportunity. Only three of those kids graduated from high school. Several ended up in prison. A few died at an early age. Prep school changed my life. I owe my parents for sending me to this amazing place. I also must pause here to thank Coach Wayne Sanborn, a coaching friend of my father's and one of the leaders of the school, who fought to get me accepted into the school.

At the prep school, there was a belief that all students would succeed, and that belief was visibly evident in the staff's actions. The teachers refused to see their students fail. For example, I was enrolled in a precalculus class. Knowing that I had minimal success in mathematics in high school, I tried to drop the course. My teacher, Mr. Burke, said that I would stay with the class and earn an A, but I must see him every day at study hall. Also, Mr. Sanborn took on the role of mentoring me during my year at Cushing Academy. That year, the school's belief in me was so powerful that I not only thrived academically but also was recognized for being a kind and supportive member of the community.

My teaching career started in the city of Hartford, Connecticut, which is one of the poorest cities in the United States (World Population Review, n.d.). Honestly, that was the greatest job of my entire career. In my first principal job, I thought that all staff were Believers but learned this was not true. Even though I had a copy of *Transforming School Culture* in 2012 and the second edition in 2017, it wasn't until 2021 that I started to really understand what Muhammad meant about transforming school culture. At that time, I also clearly understood that my challenges with staff had a name (the War of Paradigms) with four different players: (1) Believers, (2) Fundamentalists, (3) Tweeners, and (4) Survivors. The book, quite honestly, saved my career, as did the mentorship of Anthony Muhammad, which I am forever grateful for. I knew that I was doing the right work. The tools that I created aligned with the right work.

My *why* has guided every step of my career. I wanted to work with people. I wanted to make an impact on students who were Black and Latine, like the kids I grew up with in my neighborhood. I wanted to make an impact on students who grew up in urban neighborhoods. Actually, I wanted to help *all* students from *all* walks of life. My soul story brings me to my dream of working with the Transforming School Culture team. Anthony Muhammad (2018) describes a healthy school culture as this: "Educators have an unwavering belief in the ability of all their students to achieve success, and they pass that belief on to others in overt and covert ways" (p. 20). I would not be writing this book if not for the many people who had an unwavering belief in my ability.

Alex's Soul Story

My first year of teaching was nothing short of magical. I started the school year afraid of not meeting the needs of my fourth graders. I had read Alfie Kohn (2018) and Nel Noddings (2005) when I was a preservice teacher and was dedicated to the pursuit of developing a classroom where care comes first. At the time, this was an atypical approach.

I brought multiple animals and plants into the classroom to support the students to learn about care through the responsibility of taking care of these life-forms. We had a classroom vivarium of an active food chain from crickets to lizards to turtles, a guinea pig, and even a rabbit that was free to hop around the room. I blocked the room with a wooden board (short enough for a fourth grader to step over but tall enough to contain the rabbit). Many of our classroom rules revolved around the animals, like no running or quick movements because of the classroom rabbit. The caring structure was working well, and a strange event enriched it.

One winter morning, a parent showed up to my open classroom door holding what looked like a baby wrapped in a towel. I said hello, and she responded, "I hear you have animals in your room, and I brought you another." She then revealed she was carrying a rabbit as she bent over to release it onto the classroom floor.

As usual, my classroom rabbit was out, and it took less than a second for these two animals to acknowledge each other's presence. They both sprang from different sides of the room and mated so rapidly that if you blinked, you would have missed it. I, of course, freaked out, being a brand-new fourth-grade teacher who just had rabbit intercourse occur in my classroom. I quickly scooped up the other animal and returned it to its owner, stating that one rabbit was all we needed. I played it off, and I made it through the day as if I was not afraid of getting fired because of a display of animal coitus that morning. By the following week, I stopped thinking much of the event—that is, until I started seeing some changes in the classroom rabbit's behavior, appetite, and physical appearance. She was pregnant!

I decided to make lemonade out of lemons. I pointed out the change to the class (and even had to connect it back to the event that happened some weeks before). We researched what to do, what the rabbit needed, and the extra supplies we would need for her and the babies. We all waited with anticipation, and one morning, we came into the room to find her nest was filled with a litter of baby bunnies. It was a magical morning with the class, and over the next few days, my students handled and cared for these new babies. The entire school heard about them, and each class set up a time to visit. My students acted as proud docents, introducing all the classroom animals and finishing with the baby bunnies.

Whenever we finished work early or had free time, my students put the bunnies out on the carpet. They wrote essays about what to name the bunnies as well as why they should take the bunnies home at the end of the year. I lived in my school's community, and I heard about these rabbits at the grocery store for years after these students matriculated. Even better, that first year of teaching, with all its typical challenges, was amazing for the students. We created a strong community, and I'm convinced the animals helped drive student success through multiple adjacent connections.

As my second year was approaching, I was set to have students experience something similar; however, the school had a new principal. I didn't know her, but she did come with a reputation for being tough. As a former athlete who experienced many different types of coaches, I had no issue with toughness, especially when it was about accomplishing our shared mission and goals.

My Tweener moment of truth was the first time I met her. It was shortly before the school year began when I came in to set up my room: the library, the bulletin boards, and the animals. When I was nearly done, she showed up at my room. I was eager and happy to meet her. She walked in and asked, "What's all this?" I started to recount the connection between the animals and the curriculum, the focus on care, and the impact it had on the students. She cut me off while I was explaining and said, "We don't have animals here. Get them out." She turned and walked out.

I knew those animals were great for students, and banning them with no rationale seemed incomprehensible. This was my first experience that leadership, along with the attending policies, practices, and procedures, is often not about what is best for students but about power-hungry or insecure leaders. At the time, I was devastated. Under what felt like tyrannical leadership, I lost the love for teaching students and creating a classroom environment that engaged them.

At the end of the school year, I was planning on leaving the profession, but a football-coaching job opened at the high school. With my background in the sport, I took the job and then began looking for any other job in the district that I was qualified to do and that would get me onto the field at the proper time.

By what seemed divine intervention, I ended up taking the seventh-grade English language arts (ELA) position at Levey Middle School in Southfield, Michigan, the same year that Anthony Muhammad started as the principal. I was a lost educational soul, but in the first staff meeting, he rekindled in me why I got into teaching: I wanted to make the world a better place. I certainly was not the most skilled instructor, nor was Levey considered to be a good school at the time. Through the collaborative leadership of Muhammad and all the critical elements shared throughout this book, the team at Levey started to change our trajectory and the success of the students. This process was about communicating clearly, building trust, growing together, and developing collective teacher efficacy. The chapters in this book reflect both what happened at Levey and what happened in other schools that were part of Muhammad's study. It is my highest professional honor to have been part of the Levey staff and changed the lives of the students who attended there. With this book, I hope to help you and your team replicate our success and transform your school's culture.

Six Elements of a Healthy School Culture

In addition to knowing your own why, you have to know your teachers' why. All school cultures must grow policies, practices, and procedures to help them accomplish their mission. Teachers need to connect themselves and their experiences to the students they guide. Finding your and your teachers' soul stories is the first step.

Essentially, you must help the adults of the organization be introspective as part of your yearly routines so they can find their internal motivation. Education is a vocation. People are drawn to careers in schools because they want to help children and society and impact the future. You have to help teachers and other members of the school community reflect on their motivation. You need the group to share an understanding of why the changes you will make are important to those core principles.

Additionally and very importantly, this is a trust-building activity. Trust is key to how your school views change (Muhammad, 2018). You and your team will have tough conversations when using the tools included in this book. Sharing your why and helping your team develop their why are critical to building team members' trust in the changes that will be asked of them. A foundation of trust allows you to have tough conversations, work through disagreements, and come out the other side as a team.

The process of identifying your why with your team consists of two tools: (1) "Tool I.1: Identifying Your Why" (page 13) and (2) "Tool I.2: Three-Step Interview" (page 14). This may be a lengthy activity due to the essential conversation involved, but it may be the most important activity you do this year, so set aside a good amount of time, such as half an in-service day, so that you can do both tools in one session. Ideally, schools should start every year with this activity. This activity was key to how the team at Levey built its healthy school culture.

We developed this book to help your team engage in the productive struggle required to transform your school's culture into a healthy one. Plainly, you should approach culture work with open eyes because nothing about this is going to be easy. Plan to have hard conversations, but understand that through those conversations, a new and healthier culture will develop to address the needs of your community's students. In those tough moments, remember that the pressure and stress you feel will equate to better outcomes for your students today and a clearer, more positive trajectory for their lives. We specifically developed the information and tools in this book to help you transform your culture.

To assist you, this book is organized into chapters based on the key elements of healthy school cultures that Muhammad (2018) identified in his initial research. Each of these critical areas of action can be found in chapter 8 of *Transforming School Culture*. In forming these chapters, we used our experiences as teachers and leaders, exemplars from school sites we visited, and the latest research. We created tools for each chapter to support your development.

In chapter 1, we discuss universal academic goal setting and the need for a systematic and schoolwide focus on learning. Chapter 2 looks at key celebrations that healthy school cultures need in order to grow. Chapter 3 addresses how schools support their new staff throughout the entire year to socialize them into a healthy culture. Chapter 4 supports teams in evaluating levels of collaboration so that they can build a healthy school culture and remove the walls of isolation. Chapter 5 guides teams in analyzing their current system of capacity building to make sure their culture provides intensive professional development. Chapter 6 is about evaluating the level of collaborative leadership and mutual commitments to ensure schools foster consistent accountability. Finally, chapter 7 helps teams evaluate their overall growth or determine where to begin.

Figure I.2 illustrates how all these healthy school culture elements come together.

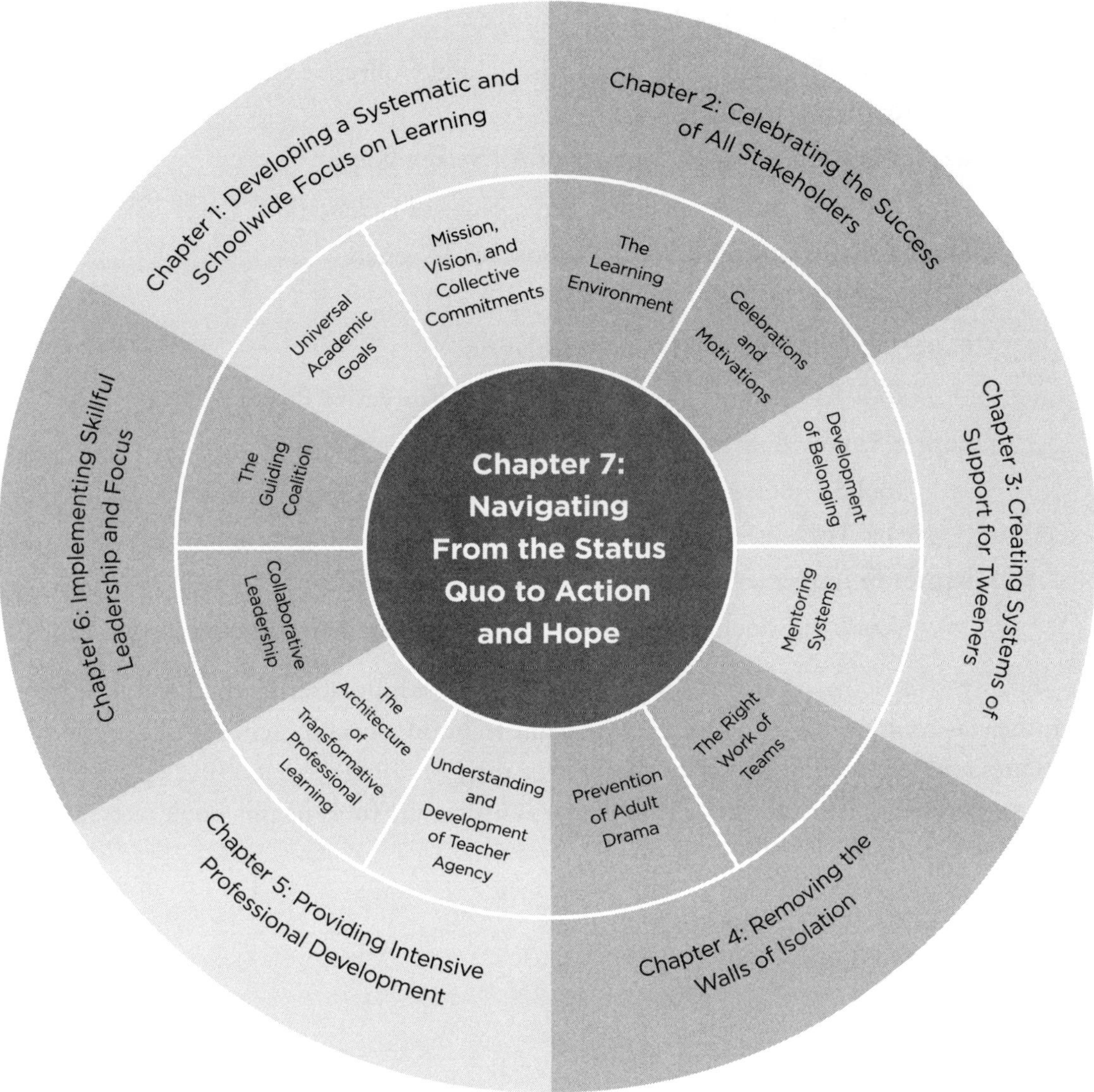

Figure I.2: *The heathy school culture elements.*

You can read this book front to back or skip directly to the element that your school culture needs most. The tools in this book were created with the understanding that you won't need to use all of them at once. As you move through multiple cycles of improvement, you can pick and choose which tools to repeat and which to implement anew.

You will probably know right away where to begin based on the following chapter and tool summary, but if you are uncertain where to begin, we recommend administering chapter 7's "Tool 7.1: Transforming School Culture—Diagnostic Survey" (page 240) to your entire staff. This tool provides a comprehensive overview and helps you identify which chapter to focus on first. All the other chapters have survey tools that can prompt collective understanding of where your culture stands in the critical areas of action.

- **Chapter 1:** Developing a Systematic and Schoolwide Focus on Learning
    - "Tool 1.3: Survey—Universal Academic Goals That Frame (or Don't Frame) All Activity in Our School" (page 37)
    - "Tool 1.5: Survey—Mission, Vision, and Collective Commitments Analysis" (page 42)
- **Chapter 2:** Celebrating the Success of All Stakeholders
    - "Tool 2.2: Survey—Student Perceptions of Celebration" (page 72)
- **Chapter 3:** Creating Systems of Support for Tweeners
    - "Tool 3.1: New Teacher Survey" (page 107)
- **Chapter 4:** Removing the Walls of Isolation
    - "Tool 4.1: Survey—Analysis of Our Collaborative Practices" (page 146)
- **Chapter 5:** Providing Intensive Professional Development
    - "Tool 5.1: Survey—Dissonance of Traditional Professional Development" (page 181)
- **Chapter 6:** Implementing Skillful Leadership and Focus
    - "Tool 6.1: Principal's Collaborative Leadership Self-Assessment" (page 218)

Finally, this book is not just for principals or site administrators. It is for all leaders, from the classroom to the boardroom, who want to build a healthy school culture for their colleagues and meet the needs of the learners in their building. The job of shaping culture belongs to everyone. It is our hope that you will utilize the tools in this book to transform your school's culture.

Tool I.1: Identifying Your Why

Purpose

Why are you here? Why did you show up today? The everyday rigors of working in a school can sometimes cloud or redirect your thinking. It is important that you reflect on your purpose and the reasons you decided to work with students.

Instructions

Brainstorm reasons why you decided to work in education and give your professional time to students, schools, and the community. These will raise complex feelings, so take your time. Here are some questions to help you reflect on your why.

What personal experiences or challenges have shaped your decision to serve students, schools, and the community?
Who are the mentors or role models who have influenced your journey, and what lessons have they taught you about leadership and service?
How has your connection to the community shaped your perspective on the importance of your work?
What moments or relationships with students, families, or colleagues have deepened your commitment to this profession?

Tool I.2: Three-Step Interview

Purpose

Coming together as a school and talking about our purposes and motivations are key to our work together. The purpose of this tool is to facilitate structured sharing of personal motivations among staff. Let's create deeper understanding, connection, and trust by hearing from each other.

Instructions

Partner with a teammate who is from a different grade level or department. Using what you both filled out on tool I.1, complete the following process.

1. Have your partner take five to ten minutes to explain their why. Take notes.
2. Now it is your turn. Take five to ten minutes to share your why. Your partner will take notes.
3. Like a news reporter, share publicly what your partner told you. Everyone will do this.

Discuss the following questions after step 3.

How does your why align with the legacy you hope to leave for your students, colleagues, or community?
In what ways does your work today reflect the values and passions that define your life's purpose?
What lasting difference do you hope to make in the lives of the students and staff you serve?

CHAPTER 1

Developing a Systematic and Schoolwide Focus on Learning

PRINCIPAL LEWIS WAS A veteran educator who believed deeply in the learning potential of every student. As a teacher, he had led various programs to support students, and when he transitioned into the role of principal, he assumed that his staff would share his commitment to student success. However, he quickly realized that not everyone saw their role in the same way he did.

During the interview process, he had heard concerns about the lack of a collective focus on learning within the school. Many staff members did not prioritize student learning or professional learning. The biggest challenge was the shift in instructional practices necessary to create a systematic and schoolwide focus on learning. Some teachers had been using the same methods for years and resisted any attempt to change. The result was an inconsistent approach, with teachers doing whatever they wanted in terms of instruction and professional development and having no unified sense of purpose.

Many of these educators had been successful students themselves. They questioned the need for change. If it worked for them, why should they do something different?

To address their concerns, Principal Lewis reviewed student achievement data with the staff, highlighting a stark reality. While some classrooms demonstrated strong learning outcomes, others did not. He reinforced a core belief that all students can learn, but some need more time and support to do so. He also made it clear that, moving forward, every policy and practice would be evaluated based on its impact on student learning.

Working with a group of teacher leaders, Principal Lewis and his leadership team developed a plan to improve student outcomes. The schoolwide initiative had two key action steps.

1. All classrooms would follow a structured, consistent schedule for focused instruction in reading and mathematics.
2. The school would implement a thirty-minute intervention block twice a week to provide additional time and support for students who needed help mastering grade-level standards.

Principal Lewis and his leadership team fully committed to these changes. In a healthy school culture, adults align their practices with their belief in student learning. To build credibility, the team not only shared school data but also emphasized the importance of ensuring that all students reached grade level and beyond. The leadership team was well prepared with clear tools to support staff learning. This allowed teacher leaders to take ownership of and facilitate their own meetings using these resources. Collaboration and collective responsibility became the expectations.

Resistance, however, was inevitable. Some staff members openly opposed the changes. A few even left the school. Others actively worked to undermine the new initiative, clinging to past routines and contractual loopholes. Some resorted to subtler forms of defiance, spreading rumors, filing complaints, and challenging administrative decisions over minor details.

In the teachers' lounge, concerns turned into whispered criticisms.

"Did you hear that he thinks our teaching is the problem?" one veteran teacher asked.

"He's just trying to make a name for himself," another said.

During implementation, one teacher chose to teach an unrelated lesson, despite receiving clear instructions on the new reading block. When confronted, she smiled and said, "Oh, I thought you meant creative reading time."

During a faculty meeting, a teacher interrupted Principal Lewis's presentation with a series of pointed questions. With arms crossed, they disrupted the discussion and tried to change the direction of the entire initiative.

"The real problem is that students are not quiet enough at lunchtime! I spend valuable teaching time getting them back under control. Fix that problem before we make all these adjustments in our schedule."

Meanwhile, the central office received an influx of complaints from a small group of teachers, such as "The new math schedule violates my contract" and "If we take this time for intervention, we'll never finish the year's content. Students will have missing skills."

One of the barbs was also sent to the superintendent, who was the school's former principal: "Principal Lewis is not an intervention guru. If you were still the principal in this building, we wouldn't have this problem. He is destroying our climate!"

Each complaint seemed designed to overwhelm the administration and slow progress.

Change was never going to be easy, but Principal Lewis knew that lasting transformation required persistence. Despite the resistance, he and the leadership team remained steadfast, and over a few months, the staff began to invest in the schoolwide focus on student learning because of the way the leadership team supported their professional growth. Leadership provided tools and resources to ensure these meetings remained centered on meaningful instructional improvements. Educators received ongoing coaching and guidance. Teachers were given time beyond their prep periods to collaborate with their teams. When the teachers began to see more students achieving success, the school celebrated. Most importantly, every staff member was expected to align their practices with a single goal—student success—and the principal and leadership team lived that expectation as well.

To achieve these outcomes, the leadership team and Principal Lewis relied on tools outlined in this chapter to guide their leadership.

- They clearly articulated the reasons for the changes and connected them to the purpose of the school.
- They built trust with the staff through deep knowledge of instructional practices, transparency, and modeling of the work.
- They empowered teachers through conversations on this chapter's tools, building their capacity to guide the process.

As the culture shifted, the school moved closer to its true purpose: ensuring that all students had the opportunity to learn and thrive.

If you are a teacher leader or school principal, has your experience been similar to Principal Lewis's? How can you tell if your school has a systematic and schoolwide focus on learning? At the core of this book, we give you a way to analyze your culture and develop the most important changes. We will not shy away from the resistance you will experience, because it's coming. Using the opening vignette as a starting point, this chapter explores some of the barriers that leaders may encounter as they implement a schoolwide focus on learning. We will consider how you begin the work of implementing this focus and how the school culture players' roles work with this element.

Barriers to a Focus on Learning

In the opening vignette, the staff did not accept the implementation of intervention time as a critical practice. Even though the principal brought in staff to help plan that time in a collaborative manner, staff members wanting to preserve the traditional culture of the school—who Muhammad refers to as Fundamentalists—fought back. They began a resistance campaign. These actions follow a predictable pattern of resistance referred to as the *three Ds* (Muhammad, 2018).

1. **Defame:** When team members attempt to rule by intimidation, change agents (such as principals and teacher leaders) become the focus of personal attacks on their background, culture, vocabulary, dress, or typical leadership behaviors. Can you identify the defamation behavior from the opening vignette?
2. **Disrupt:** If bad-mouthing the change agent doesn't work, Fundamentalists' next step is to focus on the policy, practice, or procedure. This is the disruption or delay tactic. Fundamentalists may try to create obstacles that make the change seem so overwhelming that staff lose confidence in its implementation. Can you identify the disruption behavior from the opening vignette?
3. **Distract:** If the preceding tactics to derail the policy, practice, or procedure don't work and many staff are moving forward, Fundamentalists may try individual or

small-group tactics. These can erode collective teacher efficacy if the change agents allow the culture to accept distraction behaviors. Sometimes, the behaviors are minor, like being on a personal technology device during a meeting, but other times, Fundamentalists might fail to come through on an important activity. Can you identify the distraction behavior from the opening vignette?

These three D tactics hurt, especially the personal attacks of defamation. They may make you question your efforts and even your place in the school. So, when these happen, who do you go to?

First, lean on your fellow Believers and your guiding coalition. They are your immediate allies who can offer validation, perspective, and support. Don't carry the weight of these attacks alone; share what's happening. If the three Ds take place within the guiding coalition, address and discuss them (see chapter 6 for a much deeper dive into what the guiding coalition is and isn't). Second, if you are a teacher, bring the issue to your principal. An effective leader needs to be aware of these undermining behaviors so they can protect the change process and, most importantly, the people driving it. Remember, these attacks are not reflections of your worth but predictable reactions to positive change, and your support system is there to help you weather the storm.

The opening vignette also highlights an important point that all readers must understand: Why do people resist? The concept of *apprenticeship of observation*, introduced by Dan Lortie (1975) in his influential work *Schoolteacher: A Sociological Study*, essentially helps explain why most people don't perceive systemic advantages and disadvantages as problems. Educators, parents, and even policymakers are unwilling to change a system that they don't believe is flawed or to prescribe fixes that are just repackaged causes of the problems and dig deeper holes.

The thinking behind this concept delves into the deeply ingrained nature of education practices; Lortie (1975) argues that both educators and the general public are shaped by their extensive firsthand experience as students. For roughly thirteen years, individuals are immersed in the school environment, observing teachers, administrators, and the overall culture. This prolonged exposure creates a powerful, often subconscious, framework that influences how they perceive and approach education, which explains why ineffective school practices persist despite calls for reform.

Apprenticeship of observation helps you understand why Fundamentalists, who are not bad people, will push back on important changes that they don't believe are necessary. Reasons for this pushback are as follows.

- **Limited perspective:** Educators often struggle to innovate because they've experienced only one system.
- **System reinforcement:** Successful former students (teachers) tend to defend the system that benefited them.
- **Bias and expectations:** Teachers' expectations can be skewed by their own positive experiences and can potentially disadvantage students who don't fit a typical mold.

How to Begin the Work of Focusing on Learning

All students can learn, but some require more time and support. To create a systematic and schoolwide focus on learning, schools must reflect on their current reality. Systems of additional time and support will vary across schools, but some core elements will remain consistent.

What would a school culture expert observe in your building in the first hour? What systems of learning would be evident or missing? "Tool 1.1: Transforming School Culture Standards" (page 33) is designed to help a guiding coalition understand staff perceptions of existing norms and practices. Use it to prompt staff conversations and generate data for the guiding coalition to reflect on as they determine what to celebrate and what needs to change.

Bo, who was a principal for over twenty-one years, learned the crucial importance of maintaining a laser-like focus on students' essential standards and structuring extra time in the school day through collaborative team meetings and educational books. Now, his school is thriving because a culture of student learning permeates everything his team does, from working on common assessments and student data analysis to providing extra time for students to meet expected grade-level outcomes.

Cultures have artifacts that show what they value. Do your school's artifacts around a systematic and schoolwide focus on learning show that you value having students meet grade-level standards? If your building exhibits the artifacts of a healthy school culture, celebrate your successes and use a selection of tools from this chapter to further improve your culture. If your school lacks most or many of these artifacts, use the tools in this chapter to establish a foundation for achieving the characteristics of a systematic and schoolwide focus on learning.

As you begin strengthening or rebuilding your systematic and schoolwide focus on learning, two fundamental questions that drive adult behavior will be critical to address.

1. **What are our universal academic goals?** Effective schools establish clear, measurable goals that all members of the school community understand and embrace. These goals provide a road map for teaching and learning and serve as benchmarks for measuring progress. They should be the focus of intervention time. Furthermore, clear academic goals are a hallmark of a PLC (Eaker, Hagadone, Keating, & Rhoades, 2021) and a healthy school culture (Bayar & Karaduman, 2021). See how the school celebrates when students meet these goals.
2. **Have we built a collective focus on purpose?** A shared sense of purpose is essential for creating a cohesive and high-performing school. One person shouldn't unilaterally decide what the mission and vision are; all voices must collaboratively build the school's purpose. If everyone understands the school's mission and their role in achieving it, they are more likely to work together effectively and support each other's growth (DuFour, DuFour, Eaker, Mattos, & Muhammad, 2021; DuFour et al., 2024; Eaker et al., 2021). When a school has had conversations about its core purpose and unified that focus through conversations, the system can move forward and adapt to the unique challenges that the school faces yearly.

The following sections cover these concepts while also giving you tools to hold and evaluate conversations to build the foundation of your healthy school culture. Some leaders and teachers feel these types of activities are frivolous, but if you want to intentionally build a healthy school culture where educators believe all students can learn and they act on that belief, you simply cannot skip this step.

Universal Academic Goals

Why start with goals? Chapter 8 of *Transforming School Culture* (Muhammad, 2018) explores the most common traits of a healthy school culture. The chapter begins by discussing the critical role of developing universal academic goals. This emphasis underscores a profound truth: Goals are where theory and practice meet; they are reflections of what the school values and believes about its students. This claim is supported by psychology studies that cite goal setting as one of the most powerful tools humans use to change behaviors and organizations (Hemi, Madjar, & Rich, 2024; Smith & Smith, 2015).

Consider this: The definition of a healthy school culture essentially states that the adults in the culture must believe all students can and will learn *while also acting on that belief.* Without clear, tangible goals, your team may get stuck in the belief side of the definition.

To be clear, goal use is nothing new in schools, but that does not mean schools always do it well. Probably every school in the world that has some level of government funding has goals that it must submit in a report at some time. Obviously, compliance with state or provincial and federal grants does not mean those goals were developed properly or that they are a centering point within the building. Additionally, goals are viewed differently at different levels of a K–12 organization. Due to the fundamental nature of elementary schools, it is typical that these schools have at least one shared literacy and numeracy goal, but in secondary schools, goals are more challenging; due to the departmental or subject-area separations of these organizations, a literacy and numeracy goal doesn't always have a clear connection to other content areas (Bendikson, Broadwith, Zhu, & Meyer, 2020).

At the classroom level, teachers use goals all the time (Newman, 2012). These goals can apply to an entire class or be individualized for each student. In some of the most successful classrooms we have visited, teachers have students develop personal goals, giving them both ownership and motivation (McNeece, 2020). Traditional classroom examples of goals are important, but the goals that truly help schools create healthy cultures blend the school's universal academic goals and coherently connect those to classroom goals. This connection fosters a culture where goal setting becomes a norm in all classrooms. During school culture audits, seeing this type of alignment is special and tells us that classroom values reflect a belief in student growth.

Universal academic goals go beyond just classroom practices (Smith & Smith, 2015). These goals should be reflected in all the school's artifacts, such as its hallway displays, websites, and social media posts. The universal goals connect to the collaborations and conversations the teachers have both formally and informally (Grant & Drew, 2024; McNeece & Sheppard, 2025). When a school defines universal goals, these goals are evident and impactful. Teachers will grow more in their effectiveness when their collaborative teams develop goals, regularly assess progress toward meeting them, and express confidence in them (Grant & Drew, 2024).

Are you interested in seeing what your school's artifacts say about your universal academic goals? You can use "Tool 1.2: Finding Artifacts That Show How We Value (or Don't Value) Our Universal Academic Goals (Building Walk)" (page 35) to do that.

Secondary teams may feel that this tool about posting student progress toward the goals is slightly elementary. However, that feeling is really just the socialized belief that middle and high school classrooms don't post exemplary student work, which is contrary to our experience with the adolescent mind. Furthermore, secondary schools post and celebrate all types of non-goal-related artifacts (and many for good reason), like content related to participation in sports or extracurricular teams. Teams also need to show that they value the universal academic goals of students in the artifacts they share.

Creating transparency around universal academic goals is essential for building clarity and fostering meaningful conversations within your school. Shared understanding of the why behind your goals and how they connect to daily instruction strengthens collective ownership and drives purposeful action. Transparency ensures that goals are not just top-down mandates but shared commitments that empower teachers to collaborate, reflect, and refine their practices. By openly discussing progress, challenges, and next steps, your team can create an action plan that is both strategic and sustainable, leading to real growth for both educators and students. Consider these four different levels of universal academic goals.

1. **Absence:** There is no clear academic direction. Teachers work independently, leading to inconsistent student experiences and frustration.
2. **Flit:** Goals exist but lack clarity and follow-through. Initiatives start but fade without support, causing confusion and limiting progress. New goals constantly emerge before the team has a chance to implement current goals.
3. **Direction:** Goals are collaboratively built and connected to strategies, but alignment across departments is inconsistent. Progress is tracked, but efforts lack full coordination.
4. **Clarity:** Everyone understands, believes in, and actively works toward shared goals. Collaboration, data tracking, and teacher leadership drive continuous improvement.

So, which level would your school's culture fall into for its academic goals? "Tool 1.3: Survey—Universal Academic Goals That Frame (or Don't Frame) All Activity in Our School" (page 37) provides a view of teachers' perceptions of goal setting and implementation within the school, focusing on key elements like communication, celebration, collaboration, and shared commitment.

Reflecting on your school's alignment with universal academic goals is a crucial step in fostering clarity and collaboration. To make this reflection more impactful, analyze the survey results from tool 1.3 by calculating the mean and mode for each question. The mean provides an overall sense of staff perception, while the mode highlights the most common response, revealing areas of consensus or division. Presenting these statistics to staff can spark rich discussions about differing perspectives and areas for growth. Consider using one of these activities or something similar.

- **Gallery walk discussion:** Print survey data charts, including mean and mode statistics, and post them around the room. In small groups, teachers rotate through stations, discussing key trends, surprises, and areas of agreement or disparity. Each group records insights on sticky notes to share in a whole-group debrief.
- **Four corners reflection:** Label each corner of the room with a response category (for example, absence, flit, direction, and clarity). Read out key data points and have teachers move to the corner that best represents their experience. Groups discuss why they chose that category and then share takeaways to identify common themes and areas for growth.
- **Data carousel:** Organize large chart paper stations with different data points from the survey. Groups rotate, adding reflections, questions, or possible action steps. After completing the rotation, groups review all contributions and highlight key takeaways to inform next steps in schoolwide goal setting.

These interactive approaches to looking at academic goals encourage engagement, shared ownership, and collective problem solving. Consider how they will positively impact Level One and Two Fundamentalists.

After engaging in reflection and discussion on schoolwide survey data, the next step is to connect these insights to best practices in universal academic goal setting. While the survey highlights staff perceptions and reveals patterns in alignment, "Tool 1.4: Universal Goals Self-Evaluation Rubric" (page 40) provides a structured way to assess where your school currently stands and what moving up the levels looks like. This tool helps translate broad reflections into specific, actionable areas for growth.

To be clear, schools can choose to use either tool 1.3 (the survey of universal academic goals) or tool 1.4 independently, but using both in this order builds a deeper level of clarity. The survey results offer a big-picture view of how the entire staff perceives goal alignment, while the rubric provides a detailed road map for progress. Together, they create a natural progression from identifying schoolwide trends to evaluating best practices, allowing teams to action-plan with a clear vision for improvement.

Are you ready to transition to action planning that is data driven, strategic, and aligned with growth-oriented practices? See tool 1.4.

A Collective Focus on Purpose

Sadly, we are at a precarious and deeply cynical moment when it comes to solidifying the why for educators. A quick scroll through social media reveals "influencer" educators openly mocking the concept of defining their why, often through short videos where they parody an administrator's response to a teacher who is struggling with student behavior. These clips, while seemingly lighthearted, reflect growing skepticism toward a practice that was once deeply personal and professionally affirming.

At the same time, we must acknowledge two critical realities: (1) the often-clumsy implementation of efforts to help teachers find their collective purpose and (2) the unfortunate trend of some principals (and leadership teams) abdicating responsibility for supporting their staff. Let us be clear: That is a recipe for developing Fundamentalist behavior in your school.

Brilliant Voice From the Field

BRIG LEANE

Author and National Presenter; Former Principal, Fruita Middle School, Fruita, Colorado

Our guiding coalition determined who was on what team and who our singletons were; then it directed all teachers to determine the essential knowledge and skills that all students would be required to learn. We used a common template for every educator to complete and document their progress through the PLC process, which was captured in our simple PLC Dashboard—a visual scoreboard identifying who had completed the template. We treated teacher teams and singletons who were behind—as identified in the dashboard—as being undersupported. We frequently celebrated two specific things at staff meetings and in weekly Friday emails to staff: (1) students who didn't learn at first but did after in-class reteaching and (2) teachers who had learned and implemented new instructional strategies as a result of this process. Those gave all of us the evidence that we were making progress in the very worthwhile work of ensuring student learning of the essentials and growing as educators. (B. Leane, personal communication, September–October 2025)

To find a better way forward as a leader and school-improvement team, let nothing in the discussion be about merely going through the motions. Furthermore, if you, as a leader, feel discomfort in your personal commitment to helping all students succeed, or if you are unwilling to engage in open and honest conversations with your staff about purpose, then you are not the right person for the job. The same standard applies to teachers serving on the guiding coalition or school-improvement teams. If you rely solely on the principal to establish and reinforce collective purpose without taking personal accountability, you are failing to lead in your current role. True leadership, at all levels, requires both shared vision and individual responsibility. Failed leadership at a school is devastating for student outcomes.

If any of these statements made you wince, there is no better time than right now to chart a different direction. In the following sections, we review how to attack the issue of building the collective why and how to evaluate your current reality. We blend in what the research says schools should have been doing all along.

Building the School's Why

As noted earlier, goals are a core hallmark of a PLC. A school must also collectively develop the other three pillars of a PLC—its mission, vision, and collective commitments (DuFour et al., 2024). These components are the foundation of a PLC culture, representing the school's purpose, future, values, beliefs, and focus on results, and they provide the framework for all decision making within a school (DuFour et al., 2021). Let's define those pillars and their impact on the thinking of a culture.

Mission

A mission statement or mission work involves defining the core purpose of an organization and how to achieve that purpose (DuFour et al., 2021; Eaker et al., 2021). It is essential for creating a positive school environment. It helps guarantee that all students acquire the knowledge, skills, and dispositions that will prepare them for their future. This includes providing equal access and ensuring high achievement.

The mission clarifies why the organization exists (DuFour et al., 2021, 2024; Eaker et al., 2021). This is not a new concept, as Terrence E. Deal and Kent D. Peterson (1994) highlight the importance of sharing core values in *The Leadership Paradox: Balancing Logic and Artistry in Schools*. Leadership must effectively communicate these values and emphasize the deeper mission of the organization (Bayewitz et al., 2020).

Developing a mission statement is a collaborative activity. Teacher teams must work together to define the school's purpose, sharing and refining their ideas in a collective process (Eaker et al., 2021). Without this collaboration, a mission statement risks becoming hollow words that fail to reflect the school's true values and goals (Gruenert & Whitaker, 2019). For mission statements to have a real impact, they must be taken seriously, with adequate time given for staff reflection and input (DuFour et al., 2021).

Vision

A clear vision outlines a school's desired future state (DuFour et al., 2021; Eaker et al., 2021). It answers the question "What different future are we working toward?" and serves as a critical step in laying the foundation for a new school culture (Eaker, DuFour, & DuFour, 2002; Eaker et al., 2021). In other words, a vision statement describes what a school wants to become. The vision statement provides direction and defines how the school will grow to meet the needs of its students (DuFour et al., 2021; Eaker et al., 2021).

Creating the vision statement, like creating the mission, is a collaborative process in which teams define their aspirations for the school, share their ideas, and refine the document. This step ensures alignment with the school's goals and culture-building efforts. Leaders must connect this statement to actionable strategies to avoid the pitfall of misalignment. The vision should be not a mere formality or just words on a page but something that all stakeholders take seriously with adequate time for staff input and reflection. A vision statement should be tied to practical changes and clear belief statements. It should also be used to guide a school's actions.

Collective Commitments

Once the mission and vision are established, it's critical to reflect on whether policies, practices, and procedures align with staff behaviors. Collective commitments represent the promises staff members make to each other about their work and the changes they hope to see in students (Eaker et al., 2021). Without clear commitments outlining specific actions for teachers, support staff, and principals, success will remain elusive.

These commitments translate theory into action by fostering collective efficacy, the belief that teams can positively impact student learning through their collective efforts (Eaker & Marzano, 2020). Here are some key questions to answer when creating collective commitments (Bayewitz et al., 2020; DuFour et al., 2021; Eaker et al., 2021).

- What pledges are you prepared to make to your fellow educators that will help everyone achieve the school's mission and vision?
- How do you envision your students having grown or changed by the end of their time with you?
- What foundational beliefs define your role in ensuring all students achieve at high levels?
- If your school or district truly acted on its stated values and goals, what would the school, team, and classroom learning environments look like?
- What concrete steps can you expect to see that would demonstrate the school's priorities?

Evaluating Your Current Reality

Why are these important elements to collaboratively build? Healthy school cultures develop in part from the interactions that teammates have with each other. All cultures also grow from finding solutions to the problems they encounter (Schein, 2004). Teams can use the tools and processes in this chapter to shape their conversation around change.

Teams must intentionally assess whether their mission, vision, and commitments are understood as well as reflected in daily decisions and actions. To do that analysis with your team, use "Tool 1.5: Survey—Mission, Vision, and Collective Commitments Analysis" (page 42). This tool categorizes schools into four levels.

1. **Harmony:** Strong alignment and consistent implementation of core values are evident.
2. **Structure:** A solid foundation exists, but there are areas for growth.
3. **Fragmentation:** Gaps and inconsistencies suggest the need for focused improvement.
4. **Chaos:** Little alignment exists, signaling an urgent need for intervention.

Once the data is collected, the goal is not just to analyze numbers but to spark meaningful conversations that drive action. Teams should first look for patterns across the categories. Rather than jumping to solutions, they should ask what they notice, what surprises them, and where perceptions align or differ.

This process builds shared understanding of artifacts and values around the school's collective focus. It creates space for team members to process concerns and recognize areas of success. By engaging in honest reflection and discussion, school teams can use this feedback to identify strengths, confront barriers, and take the necessary steps toward building a collective purpose, one where the mission, vision, and collective commitments are not just words on a page but living principles that drive meaningful change.

Once your team has discussed the current reality, celebrate if you have alignment or plan how to redeploy your collective purpose. The research suggests that this may not be as easy as it seems. Educators may lack a real grasp on the reasoning behind the mission, vision, and commitments of their school, and due to that lack of understanding, they often struggle to take concrete steps that lead to actual change (DuFour et al., 2021). To counter that, all collective purpose conversations should begin with the data. Your team needs to see and understand the needs of your students.

Putting together the right data is highly important. For extra support while you develop your data, use "Tool 1.6: Preparing the Presentation for Staff—Solid Data, Empirical Evidence" (page 45), which guides school-improvement teams in preparing data-driven presentations by focusing on key checklists and questions.

Data helps educators identify where they need to improve and make changes to alter outcomes. These educators should ask, "What specific actions do we take daily to bring the needed changes to life? What's one concrete step we could take to move from words to actions?" Some individuals with deep ties to the existing culture may appear to support change while subtly maintaining outdated practices (Gruenert & Whitaker, 2019).

Furthermore, some of the data points we share in tool 1.6 could be considered controversial, so talk them out in your leadership team first. We believe transparency is always best. The data may be hard to think about, but by talking about it, you can identify a problem and prescribe a solution in a proactive way.

Brilliant Voice From the Field

ANDY BAUMGART

Former Principal, Bullen Middle School, Kenosha, Wisconsin

At Bullen Middle School, our mission, vision, and collective commitments are not static statements but the dynamic foundation of our culture. This foundation is intentionally reviewed and reaffirmed annually by the principal, guiding coalition, and full faculty. Our goals are in alignment to create a shared purpose.

This purpose is visibly embodied by a framed poster, displayed prominently in the hallway by the entrance and signed by every staff member, symbolizing our universal accountability. It reflects a rigorous consensus-building process we have established, with our annual surveys showing overwhelming and enthusiastic support from our staff for the school's direction. These collective commitments guide our adult behaviors and professional learning as we focus on relationship building, culturally relevant instruction, and understanding of diverse student experiences to close data-identified gaps.

Though we do not claim perfection, the results of this unwavering focus are tangible. You can feel and see it in our building when our students and teachers are interacting. Academically, our students consistently demonstrate growth, and the achievement score rose ten report card points. Behaviorally, our outcomes are unprecedented. We had to completely re-norm the data for what were once considered highflier, medium, low, and no behavior instances, as the categories no longer applied to our student population. By living our mission and vision daily, we demonstrate a powerful model where our collective commitments drive results for every student. (A. Baumgart, personal communication, October 18, 2025)

The School Culture Players

How do the concepts and tools of this chapter impact the different school culture players? Throughout the chapter, we have identified the impact these strategies and tools have on different groups. This section further breaks that down by Believers, Fundamentalists, and Tweeners. Survivors are rarer and not necessarily part of every staff; thus, this chapter's and other chapters' content does not apply as strongly to them.

Empowering Believers

Fundamentalists will rule and Fundamentalist behavior and adult drama will thrive if you don't intentionally build a positive, systematic focus on learning and discuss research-driven solutions and current practices. However, if you do the opposite, you will empower the Believers. When a school builds its foundation with time and collaboration around its mission, vision, collective commitments, and universal academic goals, conversation naturally aligns with a Believer's thought process: All means all. More importantly, in schools where the norms of formal communication networks help meet the challenges of every student's learning, Believers are in control. Open dialogue and structured goal setting within a school's culture empower Believers. Clear structures, consistent expectations, and dedicated time for collaborative talk reinforce their belief in what schools should be doing for students (Muhammad, 2018).

Supporting Tweeners

Tweeners—educators who are still finding their place in the school culture—must be intentionally socialized into the shared mission. Schools that integrate mission and vision work into new teacher onboarding, rather than simply rushing new educators into classrooms, set the foundation for long-term success. Using structured tools at key points in the year, such as tool 1.5 (the survey on mission, vision, and collective commitments, page 42) at the start of the year, can help ensure ongoing alignment and reflection.

Every school has teams at different stages of success with the PLC process. Leaving socialization of new staff to chance can create gaps in commitment and practice. Proactively engaging new team members ensures that a school's systematic focus on student success remains strong. For more details on supporting Tweeners, refer to chapter 3.

Flipping Fundamentalists

Just as aspects of this chapter empower Believers, these activities also flip Fundamentalists into the Believer category. Addressing resistance from Fundamentalists requires a structured approach. Let's address why that is for all the different levels of Fundamentalists.

Level One (Need Clarity): Gaining Clarity

Cooperation develops from understanding the rationale behind change (Muhammad, 2018). Real-time discussions that include concrete evidence and data help educators see this reasoning. Ensure that the mission, vision, and expectations are crystal clear because these help your team identify why the change is important (Muhammad & Cruz, 2019). Without clear communication about change, resistance can stem from confusion rather than opposition.

Importantly, some school leaders will feel the need to finish important conversations in the time frames defined by meetings, but leaders will have to accept that these conversations can take longer. You can make conversations more efficient through collaborative planning, but the humans in your organization will need processing time. Resume a conversation at the next meeting, rather than keeping people later when they have lives to attend to. Never make anyone decide between staying at a meeting about your mission and vision that is running long and attending to their family. Teachers are very passionate people who have decided to devote their lives to the betterment of students; don't force them to choose between the kids they love at school and the kids (or family) they love at home.

Level Two (Need Trust): Building Trust and Dialogue

Trust is a more abstract concept than clarity. When a principal and a leadership team demonstrate a level of consistency and belief in the process, they create a much higher level of reliability (Muhammad & Cruz, 2019). Encourage honest reflection, challenge assumptions, and focus on collective responsibility to ensure your school's mission and vision translate into meaningful action. You create feelings of trust when you use these tools and have these conversations.

The first time someone says something like "I'm not sure an extra intervention block is going to help when the kids still won't do their homework," use that openness as an opportunity to identify additional issues that need to be addressed. If they are posing that question genuinely, it deserves to be addressed. If they aren't, still acknowledge the need and time for future problem solving and pivot back to the team purpose and plan. If you ignore a distraction question (from the three Ds) during a meeting, the Fundamentalist will pose that same question in the informal setting of the staff lounge and will use that adjacent issue as a rationale to refute the entire change.

Another important piece of trust is credibility (Muhammad & Cruz, 2019). Reviewing and discussing all the tools outlined in this chapter as a leadership team before you use them with staff will prepare those who are guiding conversation. Talk about the different personalities and school culture players in your school related to what you believe their responses will be. Plan together what to say to help everyone grow. We are not suggesting preparing statements to shut down Fundamentalists of all levels. Instead, determine what Fundamentalists need to hear as part of the information you are developing and how to make sure that open dialogue remains the norm. Even though it is related to Level Four Fundamentalists, be ready and knowledgeable to debate as a collective, using data, the current reality, and the collective focus you identified with this chapter's tools.

Level Three (Need Capacity of Skills): Experiencing Guided Implementation

Some Fundamentalists resist not out of defiance but because they don't know where to start. Educators may understand the mission, vision, collective commitments, and goals but struggle to take meaningful action, so real change can't occur (DuFour et al., 2021). Receiving tools and collaborative support can help them take the required actions for supporting the implementation of the new culture. This is why the action plan at the end of the chapter ("Tool 1.7: Creating a Systematic Plan for More Time and Support," page 48) is an important activity. If you develop what needs to change and how the staff need to grow but you don't support that with action, the Level Three Fundamentalists will be lost in the implementation. Chapter 4 expands on this, emphasizing that PLCs offer the best opportunities for professional development.

Level Four (Resistant to the Core Mission): Recognizing Non-Negotiables

The mission and vision must make it clear that opting out, from either student supports or systemic improvements, is unacceptable. These guiding principles help all educators understand what the team collectively stands for.

The tools and activities outlined in this chapter are multifaceted in their impact on different staff. One of the most important concepts of *Transforming School Culture* is understanding perceptual predetermination and the negative impact it has on students (Muhammad, 2018). *Perceptual predetermination* is the concept that student achievement has a strong correlation with the level of belief a teacher has in their student's ability to succeed or likelihood to fail. When your team uses this chapter's tools, this thinking is pushed into open discussion, publicly revealing the bias that "those kids can't learn." These types of comments are usually reserved for smaller conversations in the informal networks, where opportunities to challenge such ideas are very limited. But when these comments are fully on display, the principal, teacher leaders, and Believers have opportunities to challenge these ideas and address Level Four Fundamentalists' views that run contrary to the expected values and beliefs of the group.

In our experience, when a Level Four Fundamentalist realizes that their beliefs misalign with the norms of the group, it triggers them either to reevaluate their perspective or to detach from the school and seek work elsewhere. It is very challenging for a Fundamentalist to continue their protests once the collective of the school has deemed the basis for their resistance unacceptable, but sadly, they can transfer to many other schools and sour informal communication networks there.

Chapter 1 Tools

The goal of this chapter is to give all stakeholders in the school shared knowledge of the expectation to create a systematic and schoolwide focus on learning. After you have used the tools in this chapter (listed in figure 1.1), the action plan in tool 1.7 will help you and your leadership team develop and refine the next steps for meeting the element of this chapter. You and your guiding coalition can use this tool to reflect on where you are in the quest to master a systematic and schoolwide focus on learning. The tool can be used multiple times during the school year as needed.

Tool Number	Title of Tool	Purpose
Tool 1.1	Transforming School Culture Standards	Assess and improve the implementation of key school culture standards for student learning and support.
Tool 1.2	Finding Artifacts That Show How We Value (or Don't Value) Our Universal Academic Goals (Building Walk)	Help staff identify how universal academic goals are reflected in the school environment, foster shared understanding of these goals, and connect classroom practices, hallway displays, and staff collaboration to the school's mission.
Tool 1.3	Survey: Universal Academic Goals That Frame (or Don't Frame) All Activity in Our School	Gather teacher feedback on how academic goals are collaboratively built, communicated, celebrated, and supported by a shared commitment and culture.
Tool 1.4	Universal Goals Self-Evaluation Rubric	Encourage collaboration, reflection, and a shared commitment to improvement.
Tool 1.5	Survey: Mission, Vision, and Collective Commitments Analysis	Gather teacher feedback on how the mission, vision, and collective commitments are collaboratively built, communicated, supported, and implemented.
Tool 1.6	Preparing the Presentation for Staff: Solid Data, Empirical Evidence	Ensure you are planning and preparing data for a staff learning event that will clarify the guiding coalition's purposes and the students' needs.
Tool 1.7	Creating a Systematic Plan for More Time and Support	Create a systematic and schoolwide plan to give more time and support to all students who need it.

Figure 1.1: *Chapter 1 tools.*

Tool 1.1: Transforming School Culture Standards

Purpose

Assess and improve the implementation of key school culture standards for student learning and support.

Instructions

Complete the following process.

1. For each standard, rate the school's current implementation level (1 = not yet implemented, 4 = exemplary).
2. Document specific observations or examples supporting your rating.
3. Create an action plan to improve standards rated below desired levels.

A Systematic and Schoolwide Focus on Learning					
The Transforming School Culture Standards	**Current Level of Implementation**				**Thoughts and Visible Indicators**
Staff guarantee learning in their classrooms by ensuring all students have access to grade-level assignments that align with academic standards.	1	2	3	4	
Staff ensure that all students who need more time and support in their learning receive it during the school day.	1	2	3	4	
Staff guarantee all students have access to grade-level curriculum, and the pacing allows enough time for teachers to teach and students to learn.	1	2	3	4	
Universal academic goals are collectively understood and connected to grade level, subject-area team, or singleton academic goals.	1	2	3	4	
The school has a common vocabulary related to its collective mission, vision, and commitments.	1	2	3	4	

page 1 of 2

Staff monitor student learning data with a balanced assessment system based on the priority standards used to create the guaranteed and viable curriculum.	1	2	3	4	
Staff use the results to drive problem-solving conversations, reflect on practice, improve professional practice, and identify students who need more time and support.	1	2	3	4	
Professional learning focused on staff learning, data analysis, and collaboration is embedded in the daily schedule.	1	2	3	4	

What is the school's current level of implementation?

Wonderings and Next Steps

Need	Goal	Action Plan With Follow-Up

page 2 of 2

Tool 1.2: Finding Artifacts That Show How We Value (or Don't Value) Our Universal Academic Goals (Building Walk)

Purpose

Help staff identify how universal academic goals are reflected in the school environment, foster shared understanding of these goals, and connect classroom practices, hallway displays, and staff collaboration to the school's mission.

Instructions

Schedule your building walk for a time when you are free, preferably during the regular school day. During the walk, look for evidence of universal academic goals in these areas.

- Hallway displays
- Classroom environments
- Conversations with colleagues

Observe displays inside and outside the school. Check social media. Visit classrooms and focus on charts, displays, and materials that are out in preparation for future lessons. Join conversations and listen for talk about teaching, collaboration, and goals.

Tips for Success

- **Think objectively:** It is hard to remove yourself from the culture when you are studying it. Push yourself to view the artifacts you find as a stranger would see them. This is a reflective activity, not an evaluation. Focus on noticing connections, not critiquing practices.
- **Keep the goals in mind:** Review the school's universal academic goals before you begin. Reflect on how these might look in tangible artifacts, teaching strategies, or interactions.
- **Be respectful:** Ask for permission before entering classrooms or joining conversations. Share the purpose of your artifact walk with colleagues.
- **Ask questions:** If something is unclear or intriguing, ask colleagues for insight.

Once you collect all the data, bring your observations to the full team but allow for anonymous input on the observation data. You can accomplish this with a technology tool, like Google Forms, or with a poster activity where observers write their notes for the different areas onto several posters.

Once the data is up, do a gallery walk to see what the team thinks. Talk about strengths, opportunities to improve, and any paradoxical opinions. This is also a good time to ask if anything in the school is celebrated more than academic goals (like sports championships, positive behavior, or social activities). Celebrating other elements of your school is not bad, but if your team is truly about learning first, academics should be found in greater numbers than other elements. This activity will be important for ensuring that universal academic goals are not just aspirational statements but visible elements within the school's culture.

page 1 of 2

Area	What to Look For	Examples	Your Notes
Hallways	Posters or bulletin boards reflect schoolwide academic goals.	A display shows student progress on academic goals or highlights achievements.	
Places Outside of School or Online	People see messages about your academic goals outside your school environment. Information is posted on the school's website and social media accounts.	Celebrations of students' accomplishments relate to the academic goals.	
Classrooms	Teaching practices include evidence of your academic goals, like anchor charts, or student work is displayed.	Anchor charts titled Writing Strategies align with the school's writing-improvement goal. Posted student work directly connects to a universal academic goal.	
Conversations	Teammates talk about teaching strategies or goal progress outside of formal meetings.	A teacher discusses a new method for improving reading comprehension with a colleague.	
Other observations related to the academic goals:			
Other artifacts related to sports championships, positive behavior, or social activities:			

page 2 of 2

Tool 1.3: Survey—Universal Academic Goals That Frame (or Don't Frame) All Activity in Our School

Purpose

Gather teacher feedback on how academic goals are collaboratively built, communicated, celebrated, and supported by a shared commitment and culture.

Instructions

Take this survey privately. Your answers will be collected for discussion and remain anonymous.

Survey

1. How clearly are the school's academic goals communicated to the staff?

4	3	2	1
Very clearly	Somewhat clearly	Vaguely	Not at all

2. How well do your fellow teachers implement strategies to meet the academic goals of the school?

4	3	2	1
Very well	Somewhat well	Not well	Not at all

3. How frequently does the school acknowledge and celebrate achievements linked to academic goals?

4	3	2	1
Frequently	Sometimes	Rarely	Never

4. Do you agree that achieving academic goals is a meaningful and celebrated part of the school culture (in the classrooms, in the hallways, and online)?

4	3	2	1
Strongly agree	Agree	Disagree	Strongly disagree

5. To what extent are teachers involved in setting the school's academic goals?

4	3	2	1
Fully involved	Somewhat involved	Rarely involved	Not involved at all

page 1 of 3

6. How often do leadership and teachers work together to align academic goals with classroom practices?

4	3	2	1
Frequently	Sometimes	Rarely	Never

7. Based on evidence in their classrooms, how committed are your colleagues to achieving the school's academic goals?

4	3	2	1
Very committed	Somewhat committed	Minimally committed	Not committed

8. How confident are you that the school's academic goals are supported and shared by staff?

4	3	2	1
Very confident	Somewhat confident	Minimally confident	Not confident

9. How often do you collaborate with colleagues to implement or achieve academic goals?

4	3	2	1
Frequently	Sometimes	Rarely	Never

10. Do you agree that the school fosters a collaborative culture to support and achieve academic goals?

4	3	2	1
Strongly agree	Agree	Disagree	Strongly disagree

Scoring

The preceding questions provide a view of teachers' perceptions of goal setting and implementation within the school, focusing on key elements like communication, celebration, collaboration, and shared commitment. Calculate your scores for each category using the following chart.

Category	**Questions**	**Score**
Communication and Understanding	Add your scores for questions 1 and 2.	
Celebrations for Achievement	Add your scores for questions 3 and 4.	
Collaborative Construction With Teachers	Add your scores for questions 5 and 6.	
Shared Commitment	Add your scores for questions 7 and 8.	
Collaborative Culture Around Goals	Add your scores for questions 9 and 10.	

page 2 of 3

Interpret your scores for each category.

- **Clarity (score of 7–8):** You have strong alignment in this area.
- **Direction (score of 5–6):** You have some room for improvement.
- **Flit (score of 3–4):** You have significant gaps in this area.
- **Absence (score of 2):** You have a critical need for improvement.

Team Reflection and Discussion

As a school team, reflect on the anonymous staff results and discuss patterns or areas needing attention. Use these insights to identify next steps for improving the alignment and implementation of universal academic goals. Based on the data outcomes, use the tools from this chapter to support the team.

Tool 1.4: Universal Goals Self-Evaluation Rubric

Purpose

Encourage collaboration, reflection, and a shared commitment to improvement. This self-evaluation rubric helps school teams identify their current level of clarity and alignment with universal academic goals. Use this tool during a staff meeting and pair it with the related survey (tool 1.3, page 37) to compare perceptions and explore alignment.

Instructions

Complete the following process.

1. **Group discussions:** Divide into small groups, mixing grade levels or subject areas to promote fresh perspectives.
2. **Rubric review:** Read the descriptions of each level shown on the rubric—absence, flit, direction, and clarity.
3. **Self-assessment:** Reflect as a group on your current practices. Discuss where your team aligns with the rubric and why.
   - How do our current goals reflect clarity and alignment?
   - Are our goals collaboratively developed and supported by clear strategies?
   - What evidence from classroom instruction or schoolwide practices connects with one of the rubric descriptions?
4. **Survey comparison (if available):** Determine whether anything jumps out at you in the rubric and survey tool data.
   - Do survey results align with our placement on the rubric? Why or why not?
   - What insights do the survey responses offer about areas for growth?

Tips for Success

Take notes on what the teachers say is their current reality. Those notes should go to the school-improvement team for analysis, planning, and possible celebration. Make sure the teams can articulate what missing elements may help them reach the next level.

Calibrate where your school aligns with the following rubric.

Source for rubric: Adapted from Bendikson, L., Broadwith, M., Zhu, T., & Meyer, F. (2020). Goal pursuit practices in high schools: Hitting the target? Journal of Educational Administration, 58*(6), 713–728; Lowry, K. L. (2021).* A case study of the leadership styles a highly effective principal employed to cultivate teacher collective efficacy *[Doctoral dissertation, Texas A&M University]. OAKTrust. https://oaktrust.library.tamu.edu/items/aec18f85-34f5-4a28-94a7-ff652b4a4fe6; Newman, R. (2012). Goal setting to achieve results.* Leadership, 41*(3), 12–16, 38; Smith, J. R., & Smith, R. L. (2015).* Evaluating instructional leadership: Recognized practices for success. *Corwin.*

	Clarity	Direction	Flit	Absence
Description	The school enjoys a high level of clarity and alignment in its academic goals. Everyone understands the goals, believes in them, and actively works to achieve them. Data on team success is celebrated in both the short term and the long term. Teacher leadership is part of the implementation process. Teachers collaborate effectively, share best practices, and monitor progress consistently. This shared commitment creates a culture of high expectations and continuous improvement.	The school has a sense of direction. Goals are built collaboratively and have strategies connected to their implementation. Academic goals are clearly defined, but there might be inconsistencies in how they are understood and applied across different departments. The school may lack full alignment and coordination. There is growth toward learning of relevant skills and an increased level of teacher persistence on related classroom activities. Goals are evaluated and celebrated.	In this school, goals are mentioned, but there is a lack of clarity and commitment. Initiatives are introduced but often abandoned before any real progress is made. This constant shifting of priorities can create confusion among teachers and hinder student growth. Sometimes, too many goals inhibit the success of one or two academic goals, or goals are ambiguous and not driven by strategies nor the ability to quantify progress. Goals are developed by leadership alone, without a collaborative process.	In this school, there is no defined direction for academic improvement. Teachers work independently with varying priorities, and collective efforts are minimal. This lack of a common focus often leads to mixed results and a sense of frustration among staff. Inconsistencies in student experiences and outcomes are the norm.
Example	Picture a school where the goal of improving student literacy is not just communicated but supported by dedicated professional development, shared resources and strategies, and regular data analysis to track progress and inform instruction.	An example of a school in this stage is one that sets a schoolwide goal to improve student writing but leaves individual departments to determine how to implement this goal. This could lead to varying approaches and levels of success.	A school in this stage might decide to implement a new reading program but fail to provide adequate training or support for teachers, leading to inconsistent implementation and limited impact.	In a school with no clear direction, academic goals do not impact classroom instruction. Teachers in this situation who read this rubric will think about how nice it would be to work in a school with direction and will ponder the years of their career they have spent without this critical alignment.

page 2 of 2

Tool 1.5: Survey—Mission, Vision, and Collective Commitments Analysis

Purpose

Gather teacher feedback on how the mission, vision, and collective commitments are collaboratively built, communicated, supported, and implemented.

Instructions

Take this survey privately. Your answers will be collected for discussion and remain anonymous.

Survey

1. How collaborative was the development of the school's mission and vision with input all stakeholders?

4	3	2	1
Fully collaborative	Mostly collaborative	Partially collaborative	Not collaborative

2. How often do you see the school's collective commitments reflected in the actions of staff members and administration?

4	3	2	1
Always	Often	Sometimes	Rarely

3. How often are decisions about school priorities made with collective input and transparency?

4	3	2	1
Always	Often	Sometimes	Rarely

4. How well do the mission and vision reflect a strong belief in the potential and abilities of all students?

4	3	2	1
Completely reflect belief in all students	Mostly reflect belief in students	Somewhat reflect belief in students	Do not reflect belief in students

5. To what degree were our students' strengths identified as part of our development of the mission, vision, and collective commitments?

4	3	2	1
Fully identified	Mostly identified	Partially identified	Not identified

page 1 of 3

6. During the development of our school's mission, vision, and collective commitments, how often was the potential for unconscious bias discussed and considered in our decision-making processes and the resulting documents?

4	3	2	1
Always	Often	Sometimes	Rarely

7. How frequently does your team use cycles of inquiry connected to the school-improvement process to assess progress and refine practices?

4	3	2	1
Frequently	Sometimes	Rarely	Never

8. How effective are the school's cycles of inquiry in driving meaningful improvements in alignment with the school-improvement process?

4	3	2	1
Very effective	Somewhat effective	Minimally effective	Not effective

9. To what extent do the staff challenge status quo practices that do not align with their mission, vision, or collective commitments?

4	3	2	1
Consistently challenge	Frequently challenge	Occasionally challenge	Rarely challenge

10. How often are myths or outdated practices addressed and replaced with evidence-based approaches?

4	3	2	1
Always	Often	Sometimes	Rarely

Scoring

Calculate your scores for each category using the following chart.

Category	Questions	Score
Mission and Vision Clarity	Add your scores for questions 1, 2, and 3.	
Belief in Student Ability	Add your scores for questions 4, 5, and 6.	
Cycles of Inquiry and Data Use	Add your scores for questions 7 and 8.	
Overcome Barriers to Change and Collective Responsibility	Add your scores for questions 9 and 10.	

Interpret your scores for each category.

Mission and Vision Clarity and Belief in Student Ability

- **Harmony (score of 9–12):** There are strong alignment and consistent implementation in this area.
- **Structure (score of 6–8):** A solid foundation exists, but there are opportunities for growth.
- **Fragmentation (score of 4–5):** Inconsistencies and gaps require focused improvement.
- **Chaos (score of 3):** There is an urgent need for intervention and support.

Cycles of Inquiry and Data Use and Overcome Barriers to Change and Collective Responsibility

- **Harmony (score of 7–8):** There are strong alignment and consistent implementation in this area.
- **Structure (score of 5–6):** A solid foundation exists, but there are opportunities for growth.
- **Fragmentation (score of 3–4):** Inconsistencies and gaps require focused improvement.
- **Chaos (score of 2):** There is an urgent need for intervention and support.

Team Reflection and Discussion

As a team, discuss the aggregated results of the anonymous survey. Analyzing patterns in scores allows for the identification of trends or disparities in responses.

- What should we celebrate?
- What should we work on?

Action Plan

Based on your reflection and discussion, develop an action plan.

- How should we address what the survey data tells the team?
- What do you want to change?
- What is the first step to move in that direction?

Source: Adapted from Bayewitz, M. D., Cunningham, S. A., Ianora, J. A., Jones, B., Nielsen, M., Remmert, W., et al. (2020). Help your team: Overcoming common collaborative challenges in a PLC at Work. *Solution Tree Press; Deal, T. E., & Peterson, K. D. (1994).* The leadership paradox: Balancing logic and artistry in schools. *Jossey-Bass; DuFour, R., DuFour, R., Eaker, R., Mattos, M., & Muhammad, A. (2021).* Revisiting Professional Learning Communities at Work: Proven insights for sustained, substantive school improvement *(2nd ed.). Solution Tree Press; Eaker, R., Hagadone, M., Keating, J., & Rhoades, M. (2021).* Leading PLCs at Work districtwide: From boardroom to classroom. *Solution Tree Press; Eaker, R., & Marzano, R. J. (Eds.). (2020).* Professional Learning Communities at Work and High Reliability Schools: Cultures of continuous learning. *Solution Tree Press; Gruenert, S., & Whitaker, T. (2019).* Committing to the culture: How leaders can create and sustain positive schools. *ASCD; Muhammad, A. (2018).* Transforming school culture: How to overcome staff division *(2nd ed.). Solution Tree Press.*

page 3 of 3

Tool 1.6: Preparing the Presentation for Staff—Solid Data, Empirical Evidence

Purpose

Ensure you are planning and preparing data for a staff learning event that will clarify the guiding coalition's purposes and the students' needs.

Instructions

As a school-improvement team or guiding coalition, use these key ideas, checklists, and questions to prepare your data presentation to staff.

1. **Form the presentation team.**
    - Checklist items:
        - ☐ Principal
        - ☐ Teachers
    - Questions to ask:
        - ☐ Does the presentation balance the voice of the principal and the voices of the teacher leaders?
        - ☐ Are the teachers who are presenting representative of multiple grade levels or department areas?
2. **Identify key data sources.**
    - Checklist items:
        - ☐ Academic performance data (standardized tests and grade data)
        - ☐ Behavior and attendance data
        - ☐ Collective student engagement data from surveys
        - ☐ Feedback from students, parents, and teacher surveys
        - ☐ Graduation rates, course completion data, and enrollment in Advanced Placement or other rigorous courses (secondary)
        - ☐ Average number of staff absences
        - ☐ Number of professional development hours
        - ☐ Number of teachers who have left the school within the calendar year
        - ☐ Number of new teachers hired this year
        - ☐ Teacher observation data (strengths and needs)

page 1 of 3

- Questions to ask:
    - ☐ What are the key trends in academic performance over the last three years?
    - ☐ How consistent are academic outcomes and student engagement levels across grade levels and subject areas?
    - ☐ How will the presentation team honor statements about needed actions on academic-adjacent outcomes and then refocus on academics? (While developing interventions for behaviors and attendance is positive, this activity is about developing academic goals and adjusting our classrooms to meet the needs of the learners.)

3. **Ensure data equity and disaggregation.**
    - Checklist items:
        - ☐ Disaggregation by race and ethnicity
        - ☐ Disaggregation by family income level
        - ☐ Disaggregation by disability status
        - ☐ Disaggregation by English language proficiency
        - ☐ Disaggregation by gender and other relevant demographics
        - ☐ Disaggregation by grade level
        - ☐ Disaggregation by department (secondary)
        - ☐ Other: ______________________________
    - Questions to ask:
        - ☐ Does the data show trends and gaps in outcomes among different groups?
        - ☐ Are there patterns of inequity that consistently affect certain groups?
        - ☐ How do academic outcomes compare across subgroups?
        - ☐ What current strategies were developed to address the needs shown in the data?
        - ☐ Are there areas where outcomes diverge from expectations?
4. **Review data representations and ease of understanding.**
    - Checklist items:
        - ☐ Ensure all team members can access and understand data visuals (graphs, charts, tables, and so on).
        - ☐ Verify that data presentation avoids bias or manipulation.
        - ☐ Provide summaries or snapshots for clarity during meetings.
        - ☐ Avoid information overload, but have additional data available upon request.
        - ☐ As part of the presentation plan, give first-time viewers time to process what they are seeing.

- Questions to ask:
    - ☐ Are the data visuals easy to understand and interpret?
    - ☐ How much time will team members need to understand and interpret the data?
    - ☐ Does the way we present data encourage discussion and reflection?

5. **Promote dialogue rooted in data.**
    - Checklist items:
        - ☐ Develop ground rules in the meeting to avoid subjective statements (*I think*, *I feel*, or *I believe*) and to root opinions in the data.
        - ☐ Use a protocol to make sure all voices in the room are heard and one or two individuals don't dominate the conversation.
        - ☐ Discuss alternative data sources that teachers might cite for pushback or support.
    - Questions to ask:
        - ☐ What evidence highlights or challenges the conclusions we are drawing from this data?
        - ☐ What additional data might colleagues use to refute our interpretations?
        - ☐ Do we anticipate any elements of perceptual predetermination or intrinsic predetermination to be revealed?
        - ☐ How will we respond if there is an open challenge to this data?
6. **Establish next steps.**
    - Checklist items:
        - ☐ Set a timeline for finalizing the mission, vision, and collective commitments.
        - ☐ Assign dates for this work to build to completion of the plan.
        - ☐ Remain flexible with the amount of time needed to talk about these concepts (it will be lengthy).
        - ☐ Recognize that this activity will be an ongoing process.
    - Questions to ask:
        - ☐ How will we make sure the team does not fail to act due to disruption or distraction methods of the Fundamentalists?
        - ☐ How will we develop a communication plan for sharing the final outputs with the school community?

Source: Adapted from Bayewitz, M. D., Cunningham, S. A., Ianora, J. A., Jones, B., Nielsen, M., Remmert, W., et al. (2020). Help your team: Overcoming common collaborative challenges in a PLC at Work. *Solution Tree Press; DeMatthews, D. E., & Wang, Y. (2023). How can principals lead in the school improvement planning process? Reducing biases in shared decision making.* The Clearing House: A Journal of Educational Strategies, Issues and Ideas, 96*(2), 43–51; Eaker, R., & Marzano, R. J. (Eds.). (2020).* Professional Learning Communities at Work and High Reliability Schools: Cultures of continuous learning. *Solution Tree Press; Gruenert, S., & Whitaker, T. (2019).* Committing to the culture: How leaders can create and sustain positive schools. *ASCD; Muhammad, A. (2018).* Transforming school culture: How to overcome staff division *(2nd ed.). Solution Tree Press.*

page 3 of 3

Tool 1.7: Creating a Systematic Plan for More Time and Support

Purpose

Create a systematic and schoolwide plan to give more time and support to all students who need it. This plan will reflect the current reality of the school and involve all staff in problem-solving conversations to build shared understanding of a collective focus on purpose.

Instructions

Complete the following process.

1. Give staff time to individually reflect on the current reality and write their thoughts in the following chart. Have them generate comments about strengths, weaknesses, or areas where their team does not support students.
2. Allow discussion time in grade-level or department teams. Staff should talk about and reflect on what the team does well and potential blind spots.
3. Have a group conversation about the current realities for each factor. Where supports are necessary, have a facilitator write down those needs. Brainstorm ways to build systems where there are gaps. Give staff additional time to complete the final Problem-Solving Needs and What the Guiding Coalition Needs to Know sections.

Tips for Success

- **Focus on student needs:** Keep the focus on how the current systems are impacting students and how they can be improved to better meet their needs.
- **Be solution oriented:** Move beyond simply identifying problems to collaboratively brainstorming and developing actionable solutions.
- **Follow through:** Develop a clear plan of action with assigned responsibilities and timelines to ensure the identified solutions are implemented effectively.

System of Supports for Learning
Grade Level and Content Area:
Goals:

Factors to Consider, the Current Reality, and Actions We Will Take to Improve Include the current reality in the left column and actions to improve in the right column.	
Student Learning Data:	
Use of Priority Standards:	
Grade-Level Assignments Aligned With the Standards:	
Space for Interventions and Enrichment:	
Available Resources:	
Time in the Day:	

Current Schedule:	
District Mandates:	
Building Space:	
Available Staff:	
Transitions:	
Cafeteria Coverage:	
Duty Coverage:	

Team Reflection and Discussion

Can we see a clear connection between our school's academic goals and the support we provide as well as how and when we provide it? If so, where do we see this connection? If not, where is our misalignment?

Options to Provide More Time and Support

- **Flex time:** There is time during the school day when the teacher does not teach new material but gives students more time and support or enrichment and extension based on the priority standards taught and assessed in the classroom.
- **Flex days:** Time is built into the schedule to give students more time and support or enrichment and extension after a common assessment. Support staff go to the classroom for this.
- **Time in the schedule:** Time (thirty to thirty-five minutes) is embedded in the schedule so students can travel to a classroom for more support, Individualized Education Program (IEP) support, enrichment, or extension during the day. This practice includes more staff members and more space. The collaborative teams decide where students need support based on common formative assessment data.
- **Combination of embedded time, flex time, and flex blocks:** Teams use a combination of these three practices.

Problem-Solving Needs

What the Guiding Coalition Needs to Know

Source: Adapted from Ryan, B. (2023). The brilliance in the building: Effecting change in urban schools with the PLC at Work process. *Solution Tree Press.*

page 4 of 4

CHAPTER 2

Celebrating the Success of All Stakeholders

THE STAFF LOUNGE AT Northwood Elementary often felt divided. On one side were teachers like Mr. Miller, a second-year teacher who still brought a hopeful energy to his work. On the other was Ms. Albright, a veteran whose cynicism was a regular presence.

"I think we finally had a breakthrough with Jamal," Mr. Miller said to a small group in the lounge one morning, quiet but pleased. "We used those new fraction tiles, and for the first time, he wasn't just guessing. He was explaining his thinking. It was great."

From across the room, Ms. Albright looked up from her phone and stepped into the conversation. "Jamal?" she said flatly. "I had him last year. Give it a week." She clicked her teeth. "The second it gets hard again, he'll be back to square one. Some kids just don't have the follow-through."

Uncomfortable silence ensued. The positive energy in the conversation dissipated. The other teachers in Mr. Miller's group smirked and rolled their eyes at the comment. Ms. Albright never seemed to miss a chance to talk behind a student's back. It was a familiar pattern: a small success shared, then immediately undercut by a general negative comment. Mr. Miller left the room feeling deflated and questioning his small victory.

Ms. Martinez, another veteran teacher, had seen this kind of exchange countless times. She was tired of the negativity that seemed to drain the life out of the building's most dedicated educators.

After school later that day, Ms. Martinez ran into Mr. Miller as they were both exiting the building. "I heard what you said about Jamal," she began. "That's a big deal. That's the kind of thing we should be sharing." He thanked her, and the two went their separate ways in the parking lot.

After getting into her car, Ms. Martinez thought about doing something more, both to encourage Mr. Miller and to push back against the negativity of the school's Ms. Albright–type teachers.

The next morning, a new small corkboard appeared in the staff lounge. On it was a single index card in Ms. Martinez's handwriting: "A win for Jamal in Mr. Miller's class! He explained his reasoning with fractions using the new tiles. Great teaching, great learning!" She hadn't asked for permission; she just put it up. She called it the wins board.

For a few days, the board held just that one card. Then, another appeared, celebrating a student who had shown kindness on the playground. A third note, written by a support staff member, thanked a teacher for helping with a difficult parent phone call. The board started to fill with small, specific moments of progress and appreciation.

The following week, Mr. Miller was in the lounge when Ms. Albright started to complain about a lack of student motivation. "They just don't come to school ready to learn," she said to no one in particular.

Before the comment could settle and sour the room's mood, Ms. Martinez, who was reading the wins board, turned and calmly said, "That's interesting, because this note says Ms. Tan's student, who has been struggling with attendance, has been here every day for two weeks straight. That sounds like he's ready to learn." She wasn't confrontational, just observant.

Ms. Albright rolled her eyes but fell silent. The board, covered in handwritten celebrations, offered a different story than the one she was used to telling. The adult drama hadn't disappeared, but it was no longer the only narrative. The simple, impromptu, and public act of celebrating small successes had created a counterbalance, a visible record of the good work happening every day. It gave teachers like Mr. Miller a place to feel validated and teachers like Ms. Martinez a tool to gently but firmly push back against toxic school culture players.

Consider one of the most important celebrations in your life. What did it symbolize? Was it a bonding between two people, like a wedding? Was it a milestone or a rite of passage, like a birthday or a graduation? Was it a community celebration, like a festival? You can learn so much about a culture and its values by looking at how groups celebrate meaningful events, milestones, and transitions (Deal & Kennedy, 1982, 1999; Schein, 2004; Trice & Beyer, 1993). These types of celebrations make people's home cultures or communities what they are and show everyone what they value. They keep individuals on track on good days and bad ones alike.

Celebration is just as important in classrooms and schools. School rituals transmit the shared values and beliefs of a school's students, staff, and community (Escobedo, 2012). When celebrations are meaningful and authentic in school, they help students develop a true desire to learn and grow (Aungst, 2016). This chapter gives you the tools to build (or enhance) a celebratory culture. In this chapter, we start with how different types of celebrations impact the learning environment and how you can use celebrations to achieve real motivation (to move beyond the carrot, so to speak). We next discuss how you can reboot celebrations in your school and how celebrating can impact the school culture players.

Celebrations and the Learning Environment

Every teacher should know that celebrations create a positive learning environment and are directly connected to students' learning and achievement. Celebration, recognition, and reward systems acknowledge, honor, and thank students for displaying positive social and academic skills, and they also help students perceive the school as a supportive place where they can try, fail, and succeed. Indeed, the power of recognition to foster student resilience is clear. A large-scale study involving over thirty thousand students found that those who received an excellence award showed a 10.9 percent overall lift in persistence compared to their peers, with the effect being even more pronounced (a 20.23 percent increase) for students in the lowest academic quartile (Bliven & Jungbauer, 2021). According to Douglas Fisher, Nancy Frey, and Ian Pumpian (2012), this is true for teachers as well; workplaces are better when they devote time to celebrating milestones and achievements. *Transforming School Culture* (Muhammad, 2018) clearly identifies the power and importance of celebration, which should permeate every aspect of a school culture in both institutional and impromptu ways. Let's look at the types of celebrations and how to move beyond the carrot (or an external reward) when it comes to motivation.

Types of Celebrations

Celebrations come in numerous forms, including institutional (academic and social or behavioral) and impromptu. *Institutional celebrations* are planned and scheduled events that occur regularly throughout the school year. These celebrations are typically visible to the entire school community and are often used to recognize student achievements, foster school spirit, and build relationships among students, staff, and families. They can be categorized as academic or social.

Examples of *academic celebrations* at the elementary and secondary levels include the following.

- **Student-focused celebrations:** These include end-of-year awards ceremonies, academic awards nights, science fairs, students of the month, student-led parent conferences, grade-level student awards, and arts showcases.
- **Teacher-focused celebrations:** These include academic assessment reveal meetings, end-of-year goal reflections, teacher of the month, teacher of the year, and academic fairs.

Examples of *social or behavioral celebrations* at the elementary and secondary levels include the following.

- **Student-focused celebrations:** These include back-to-school night, grandparents' day, winter holiday concerts, field day, homecoming week, spirit week, prom, graduation, no tardy parties, and perfect attendance celebrations.
- **Teacher-focused celebrations:** These include retirement parties, holiday parties, teacher appreciations, staff appreciations, and staff breakfasts.

Impromptu celebrations, as touched on in the opening vignette, are spontaneous events that recognize and reward students and staff for their achievements and efforts. They can be as simple as a verbal shout-out in a team meeting or as elaborate as a surprise party. Sometimes, schools have a cache of gifts for these celebrations, like free tickets to a school or local event or even vouchers for special treatment at a local business. Impromptu celebrations can be initiated by anyone in the school community, including teachers, students, administrators, and support staff. Believers can even use impromptu celebrations to push back against negative comments, as was shared in the opening story.

If a guiding coalition or principal wants to develop the concept of impromptu celebrations, they should initially model it by publicly recognizing staff and students for their efforts and achievements. This will help create a positive culture in which celebration is a normal and expected part of school life. Also, ensure students celebrate their peers with impromptu celebrations. Empower them to celebrate peers for academics, friendship, and teamwork. By doing this, they can make impromptu celebrations a regular occurrence in their school.

During school culture audits, Alex has found institutional celebrations are more common than impromptu celebrations. Consider using "Tool 2.1: Impromptu Celebration Ideas" (page 71) to add these to your culture.

Celebrations in schools encompass more than just students and teachers; they are vital for fostering a positive culture that includes support staff, parents, and the broader community (Hierck, 2017). Just as meaningfully and authentically celebrating students helps them develop a true desire to learn and grow, recognizing the contributions of all stakeholders strengthens the entire school community.

Celebrations also greatly push back on negative cultural elements (as you will see in the School Culture Players section of this chapter, page 66). As the opening vignette illustrates, celebrations in schools insulate newer teachers from adult drama. By understanding the power of celebration, principals and guiding coalitions can intentionally shape a school culture where growth, effort, and achievement are consistently valued and reinforced to the entire school community. Effective celebrations can also shift the focus from extrinsic to intrinsic motivation.

Motivations Beyond the Carrot

School celebrations should be meaningful and authentic. They must recognize the work, process, and effort of all stakeholders, not just the visible outcomes. Educators should ensure that celebrations focus on opportunities for growth for everyone. When the emphasis is on continuous learning and improvement, taking risks and embracing challenges become less daunting to everyone at the school.

Recognizing achievements, both big and small, encourages growth and sustains motivation (Aungst, 2016). However, consider the purpose behind these celebrations; it's crucial that you understand the realm of motivation, especially the distinction between extrinsic and intrinsic motivation. This understanding allows you to plan beyond basic rewards and help your school's entire community think about why you all are here and why what you are doing is worthwhile. While the allure of external rewards like prizes or accolades can initially spark action, true and lasting motivation stems from a deeper understanding of the impact and value of one's efforts, or intrinsic motivation.

Extrinsic Motivation

Extrinsic motivation includes rewards (or punishments). Educators know a lot about this. A piece of candy as a reward for finished work, recess time taken away for a lack of production, and even the grades teachers assign are extrinsic rewards and punishments. Extrinsic motivation can be a positive tool, and it works as a jumping-off point for many students. Celebrations are the positive side of extrinsic motivation.

Bo has witnessed the positive impact of recognizing achievements. He developed many celebrations in his time as a football coach. During his experience coaching at Syracuse University, he was tasked with motivating college athletes, many of whom were accustomed to being star players at their high schools but had to pay their dues as younger players in the program. He implemented daily recognition and an award he called "chocolate chip cookie player of the day." The players loved being recognized for their work.

After Bo was done coaching, he became a classroom teacher in Hartford, Connecticut. He continued to recognize and celebrate students. One way he did this was by creating an early open gym program for the students in the school. The program served hundreds of students a day for seven years. The program included daily activities, and Bo always found ways to recognize and celebrate all the students in the room. During this time, he also was the summer director of a local chapter of the National Youth Sports Program, which serves students in impoverished communities all over the United States. He took over a chapter that was very close to closing, which meant that more than five hundred ten- to fourteen-year-olds would not have a summer camp. He initiated systems to recognize and celebrate students on a regular basis. This change was so profound that the chapter was recognized nationally, but the real reward was seeing those students have a safe, positive, and celebratory place to be for the summer. Last, as an administrator, Bo routinely supported the development of many celebrations, his favorite being the principal of the day program for students. The day's principal was chosen by staff members, highlighted in the school, and recognized as the leader of the building.

Humans, both young and old, will initially engage in an activity to earn a reward (or avoid punishment). In education settings, this often manifests as students striving for high grades, teachers seeking recognition, or schools aiming for positive external evaluations. These behaviors are not bad, but moving beyond working for a reward is very important. Also, critically, every teacher has encountered a student whose motivation is retreating or who is no longer impacted by the extrinsic motivations of school (McNeece, 2019).

Celebrations tied solely to these extrinsic factors, such as rewarding only a few winners or focusing solely on achieving a certain score, can be problematic. As Mark Barnes (2015) argues in *Assessment 3.0: Throw Out Your Grade Book and Inspire Learning*, grades can be dangerous tools because these pervasive extrinsic motivators place a subjective label on students that says little about their actual academic achievement. Moreover, a system focused more on extrinsic rewards than on intrinsic motivation will develop students who chase a grade rather than pursuing deeper understanding (McNeece, 2019).

 **Brilliant Voice From the Field** 

RICHARD TOMKOWIT

Assistant Principal, Fred D. Wish Museum School, Hartford, Connecticut

For years, Fridays were our Achilles' heel—our most challenging day for attendance and a major contributor to our high rate of chronic absenteeism. We decided to tackle this problem head-on with the introduction of Free Time Friday. This system was designed to reward consistent attendance: Show up Monday through Thursday, and get a ticket for Friday's fun, which included popular physical activities like extra recess and open gym.

The change has been transformative. The students are now highly motivated to be in their seats all week to earn that Friday reward. Not only has our Friday attendance stabilized, but the overall consistency has allowed us to reduce our chronic absenteeism by 15 percent. Free Time Friday is a simple, effective, and fun solution that I would recommend to any school struggling with this issue. (R. Tomkowit, personal communication, September–October 2025)

Intrinsic Motivation

Intrinsic motivation is the desire to engage in an activity because it is interesting, enjoyable, or self-directed or because it provides a sense of accomplishment (McNeece, 2020; Ryan & Deci, 2000). This type of motivation is more powerful and sustainable than extrinsic motivation. It creates resilience (McNeece, 2020).

The power of celebration lies in its potential to bridge the gap between initial extrinsic rewards and the development of intrinsic motivation. While teachers might begin by celebrating the completion of a task that carries an external reward (like a grade), the true value of that celebration lies in shifting the focus to the learning, growth, and impact achieved. Teachers need to help students understand that their efforts weren't just about getting a carrot but had a greater impact on themselves and others. That may be a tough sell because traditional school cultures have focused almost entirely on extrinsic motivators (McNeece, 2019).

How to Reboot Celebrations

This section presents ideas for fostering the transition from extrinsic to intrinsic motivation for stakeholders in need of motivation. For students, consider doing the following to reboot celebrations.

- **Celebrate growth and effort:** Acknowledge improvement over time, the use of new strategies, and perseverance through challenges, not just final grades (Aungst, 2016). A teacher could share positive feedback with a student's parents, guardians, or administrators about how the student doesn't give up even when the work is challenging. Schools that post proficiency scales or rubrics in classrooms celebrate students' growth up those rubrics or scales. This growth needs to be celebrated and recognized on a regular basis.
- **Showcase learning processes:** Create opportunities for students to explain their thinking, share their problem-solving approaches, and reflect on their learning journey (Aungst, 2016). For example, during cooperative learning time, while supporting students' thinking in groups, the teacher could share with the entire class the excellent insights they've heard from the various groups. Student-led conferences are also a great way to showcase student work.
- **Connect learning to real-world impact:** Celebrate how students can apply their knowledge and skills to make a difference in their lives, communities, or future aspirations. Highlight the value of schooling and its relevance (McNeece, 2020). Teachers could have students help decorate the classroom with items that have some bearing on their futures, like pictures and information from colleges, career path artifacts, and exemplary report cards, to focus on connections to what is relevant. Staff can also celebrate students' number of articles or books read, words read, or minutes read. All these things improve students' literacy skills.
- **Provide opportunities for self-celebration:** Encourage students to identify what they are proudest of in their work and to share it with others (Barnes, 2015). It's important to have a daily routine of reflecting on how far the students have come. An example of this is a short exit ticket that the teacher collects at the end of each class period or day to see and validate the students' growing understandings. Self-grading using a proficiency scale or tool is a great way for students to monitor their progress, chart their learning, and celebrate their success. Robert J. Marzano (2017) states that using proficiency scales and tracking students' progress on those scales allows for the celebration of status and growth. *Status* refers to a student's score at a particular moment, and *growth* refers to the difference between the student's current and first scores on the topic.

Do you want to find out what your students think about your current system of celebration in the classroom and the school? You can use their honest feedback to drive the needed changes talked about later in this chapter. To find out your students' perceptions of celebration, use "Tool 2.2: Survey—Student Perceptions of Celebration" (page 72).

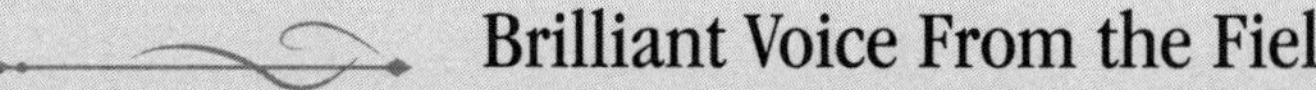

Brilliant Voice From the Field

KELLY J. BREWER
Former ELA Teacher, Northeast Middle School, Midland, Michigan

Celebrating success is a powerful way to create community and culture within a classroom. As a middle school teacher, I regularly celebrated students from day one. We began with a "fireworks" celebration to recognize achievements both big and small, and soon, students began celebrating one another with our fireworks hand motions. Celebrating success became ingrained as part of our class routine and culture. With our proficiency scales, we set a goal for every student to be solid with level 2 ELA vocabulary by the end of October. Each student was celebrated individually with a short but meaningful ceremony as they achieved their level 2s, and we celebrated the entire class when we all made it. We measured success as a class when everyone achieved level 2 status, which encouraged students to support one another, increasing class camaraderie. We celebrated reading success by keeping a running tally of books read collectively. Each time we hit a hundred mark, we celebrated with a read-in, a blissful hour dedicated to reading and snacking. Students were very motivated by this class goal and its celebration. Setting individual and class goals and authentically celebrating these milestones helped foster a supportive and encouraging class environment! (K. J. Brewer, personal communication, September–October 2025)

For teachers, consider the following.

- **Celebrate innovation and risk taking:** Acknowledge teachers who try new strategies or adapt their practices to better engage students (McNeece, 2020). When you have monthly celebrations for your teachers, make sure these celebrations are connected to a strategy or behavior that is impacting students in a positive way.
- **Focus on the impact on student growth:** Celebrate stories and data that demonstrate the positive influence of their teaching on student learning and well-being (Nohe-Dirk, 2024). When reviewed as a group or individually, data should not just be used for analysis. Make sure that every time you review the learning outcomes, you find a celebration that connects to the students.
- **Foster a culture of shared success:** Recognize collaborative efforts, peer support, and collective achievements among the faculty (DuFour et al., 2024). Teams can receive awards for the work they put into a special function or event that led to positive student outcomes.
- **Provide opportunities for reflecting on and sharing effective practices:** Celebrate moments of professional insight and growth gained through collaboration and reflection (Scoresby, 2024). Many teachers don't take the time to process the impact they have made on students. Give them that time. At a staff

meeting, consider having them write a short note to themselves about a difference they have seen in a student because of their work.

- **Acknowledge dedication and commitment:** Regularly appreciate the hard work and passion that teachers bring to their profession (DuFour et al., 2024). Consider developing a wall of growth for your teachers. Throughout the year, collect samples of students' work and post them on the wall in an adult space of your school. Make sure that before-and-after samples from roughly one student per class are there to highlight how the students have grown due to the teachers' efforts.

Do you want to celebrate teachers for their excellent instructional process and outcomes? Consider using "Tool 2.3: Academic Fair for Culture" (page 75) to allow staff to visit classrooms and celebrate the excellent artifacts of the instructional culture. An academic fair is almost like an instructional round, but it can be done when students are not in the building. It give teammates a chance to see the artifacts of a classroom.

For support staff, consider the following.

- **Highlight their vital contributions:** Celebrate how the support staff's work supports the overall mission of the school and directly impacts the learning environment (DuFour et al., 2024). For example, create a support staff spotlight on the school newsletter or website, highlighting specific examples of how their work has made a difference.
- **Recognize positive interactions with students and staff:** Acknowledge support staff's role in fostering a welcoming and supportive school climate (DuFour et al., 2024). For instance, implement a "caught being kind" board where students and staff can publicly recognize support staff for their positive actions. One easy way that leadership in the building can connect with support staff is to help in the cafeteria. They can build relationships with the cafeteria team and custodians during this time by serving meals, monitoring students, or cleaning the cafeteria after meals. This will greatly increase positive interactions with the support staff in the building.
- **Celebrate their dedication and commitment:** Appreciate their efforts in maintaining a functional and positive school setting (DuFour et al., 2024). One idea is to organize a surprise appreciation breakfast or luncheon for support staff and provide personalized thank-you notes from students and staff.

Parents need to be celebrated. Bo's school does something very special to write its story; it harnesses the tools of social media to celebrate staff, students, and, importantly, the parents. Make sure to write your own story about your students' successes. An amazing event the school holds to celebrate parents is called *power hour*. During this time, the staff develop a sheet of student names and phone numbers. The administration spends one hour making positive, celebratory calls home, during which they talk about the success of the students and connect that to the effort of the parents. They even write down the parents' responses, which are shared with the staff at a later time.

For parents, consider the following.

- **Educate them about the learning process:** Help parents understand the value of effort, growth, and intrinsic motivation instead of solely focusing on grades

(McNeece, 2020). Encourage them to focus on their child's development and perseverance, not just final outcomes (Barnes, 2015). Create a short video message that gives them the rationale and tools to do this.

- **Showcase the impact of their effort and support:** Highlight, in multiple public ways, how their involvement and encouragement contribute to their child's success and to the school community (Barnes, 2015). Move beyond events like a once-a-year PTA thank-you lunch; have a routine way to celebrate the parents who contribute to the success of all the students at the school, such as newsletters and social media.
- **Celebrate their raising of expectations:** Some of the most powerful tools for parents to use are raised expectations (Simms, 2024). Parents of struggling students need help communicating and celebrating expectations. Focus on daily attendance or attendance to each class. Celebrate parents for fostering open communication and give them the strategies to do so by suggesting they ask questions like "What did you learn today?" and "Did you complete all assignments?" Help them reflect on behavior with their child by asking, "Did you interfere with the learning of others?" When parents use these tools, celebrate them in a private meeting or phone call.

Figuring out when to celebrate parents and the community can be a challenge. One of the best ways to celebrate your community and families is to celebrate *with* them. Get a team together and get into the community.

Staff members can create a plan to visit homes and the community during the summer or at other times when students are not in the building. This is a great way to celebrate the community and connect with families. Look for ways to create community partnerships. As an assistant principal, Bo connected with students from Trinity College to have them come support students in classrooms. As a principal, he created partnerships with the local high school to have its students serve as mentors and tutors. In addition, his team created a partnership with the local college football team, who came to the school on Fridays to participate in recess with the students.

Alex's school wrote and published a children's book for kindergarten readiness and delivered it to homes in the community, whether or not the residents had students attending the school. The book's art and setting revolved around the community and its landmarks. Not only did the book dramatically drive up the rate of readiness, but it also connected former parents, future parents, and other residents with the school's mission. The book was the talk of the town and was one of the essential elements that shifted the culture.

For the community, consider the following.

- **Share stories of student and school success:** Communicate the positive outcomes of the school's work and its impact on the community (DuFour et al., 2024). Have students present at local city council meetings and to organizations like Kiwanis and Rotary, and make sure local businesses are recognized when they help your students.
- **Involve community members in meaningful ways:** Create opportunities for community members, including local organizations, businesses, and government entities, to contribute to student learning and school events (McNeece, 2020;

Nohe-Dirk, 2024). This will make an impact on students and connect the process and outcome in a way that builds the community's intrinsic motivation to support the students of your school. You could have community members come help with in-school celebrations. Ana Grace Academy of the Arts Middle School, for example, partnered with the Hartford Yard Goats, a Minor League Baseball team, to throw a no tardy party that celebrated students for getting to class on time.

Brilliant Voice From the Field

HEATHER SILVIA

Former Principal, Donlin Drive Elementary, Liverpool, New York

We start every meeting with celebrations. At first, it was awkward, as this wasn't a common practice. However, when there is much work to be done to achieve high levels of learning for all, we need to celebrate the small wins to ensure we don't burn out. As the principal, I often had small, cheap, or free treats—a chocolate bar, a pack of gum, a piece of fruit, a "leave early" pass, a recess coverage pass, and so on—to spur on the staff members complimenting each other's wins. And teachers love celebrating their teammates! As a brave soul shouted out a celebration, they were tossed a treat, and it caught on! Not only did the clapping for the staff member and tossing of a treat to the one who shared the good news add laughter and levity to the meeting, it also made it fun to celebrate. Years later, it is an established practice to start every meeting with celebrations. And, leaders, don't be fooled that you don't have time . . . You don't have time not to do it! (H. Silvia, personal communication, September–December 2025)

By consciously designing celebrations that emphasize learning, growth, impact, and community contribution, educators can move beyond the limitations of purely extrinsic rewards and cultivate deeper, more sustainable intrinsic motivation in all stakeholders. This shift not only enhances individual engagement and achievement but also fosters a more positive and purpose-driven school culture. Every school needs an easy way to celebrate specific staff members to remind people about the school's purpose and priorities. DuFour and his colleagues (2024) offer four suggestions to those who face the challenge of incorporating celebration into their school culture:

1. *Explicitly state the purpose of celebration.*
2. *Make celebration everyone's responsibility.*
3. *Establish a clear link between the recognition and the behavior or commitment you are attempting to encourage and reinforce.*
4. *Create opportunities to have many winners. (pp. 258–259)*

As you reflect on your school's celebrations, utilize "Tool 2.4: Celebrating the Success of All Staff" (page 79). Educators can use this easy tool to make sure staff members specifically have a culture of celebration in their school or district. The suggestion that we offer is to have awards for all staff: the nurses, cafeteria team, custodians, office team, teachers, and noncertified staff. Also, have staff recognize other staff with some type of award that can be passed from one staff member to another. Figure 2.1 offers some ideas.

Name of Celebration	Criteria for Recognition	Award
Student Champion	• They have a relentless belief in students. • They have a never-give-up attitude with students. • They connect with students daily. • They bring joy to teaching and learning. • They make all students feel like they belong.	Student Champion
GOAT	• They display a high level of personal commitment. • They maintain an unwavering expectation of student learning. • They refuse to see students fail. • They believe that all students will learn because of what we do, and they support the school's initiatives. • They refrain from negative talk about students or gossip about adults.	GOAT Greatest of All Time
MVP	• They support a safe and orderly environment. • They ensure the basic needs of the students are met (health and food). • They make sure the building is clean and safe. • They advocate for student well-being. • They celebrate the following staff members: the nurses, security guards, cafeteria team, and social workers.	MVP
Learning Leader	• They are a model educator for staff in the classroom, in the art room, or in the office. • They model exemplary practices focused on the learning block and proficiency scales. • They ensure daily effective instruction in the classroom. • They support instruction across the building.	

Star Teammate	• They maintain great focus on the collaborative team process. • They relentlessly advocate for student learning during team meetings. • They view collaboration as the engine that drives school improvement. • During meetings, they maintain focus on the issues that are most significant to improving student achievement.	Star Teammate
High-Five Award	• This staff member is making a positive impact on the staff and students. • They bring great energy. • They live the motto: "Love wins." • They are a valuable member of the culture.	Great Job!
People's Champ	• This staff member or community organization makes or distributes award-winning meals for our staff and students. • They greet our students and staff.	W

Figure 2.1: *Example institutionalized celebrations.*

This shift begins with and requires making the purpose of celebration explicit. Instead of merely applauding a final product, educators should celebrate the process, the skills developed, and the journey of learning. Gerald Aungst (2016), author of *5 Principles of the Modern Mathematics Classroom: Creating a Culture of Innovative Thinking*, sums it up well:

> *Celebration events tend to place value on the products that students create. When they exhibit in a more meaningful way, they showcase specific processes or skills. They share in order to reflect, debrief, and help others learn, often from imperfect works in progress. When students share their growing expertise, they begin turning to one another for support rather than relying exclusively on the teacher. (p. 130)*

At Bo's school, teachers follow a systematic process focused on student learning called the *learning cycle*. During the cycle, teacher teams and singleton teachers take the following steps.

1. **Plan:** Study the curriculum, plan a block of time, and create an instructional focus.
2. **Assess:** Create, administer, and score assessments to measure learning of the curriculum.
3. **Take action on data:** Analyze the data and take action to support learning based on the results.

Learning cycles can occur as many times or for as long as schools would like in order to maximize student learning. Schools that are focused on learning should create tools for all three steps to allow teams, including singleton teachers, to do the work. The tools are then shared with building leadership for feedback and coaching. The focus of coaching must always be on supporting and encouraging teacher teams and singletons. Leaders give positive feedback centered on strengths to recognize and celebrate the work of teachers.

By creating and using a guide or expected standard tool, leaders can be absolutely clear on the expectations for the plan, the assessment, and data action. They can share the indicators for each with staff. In addition, leaders can email staff some exemplary work samples that were created in meetings not only to share the expectations with all teachers but also to celebrate the effort of the team or singleton teachers. In a school focused on learning, this is a great way to continually remind staff about the behavior they are trying to reinforce.

Does your team need to think about what celebrations could be and to build those celebrations collaboratively? Are all stakeholders part of your celebrations? The main reason reflection is included in this chapter's tools is its tendency to shed light on what should be celebrated (Zepeda, Goff, & Steele, 2019). Layered into "Tool 2.5: Celebration Revival, Part 1—Reflection" (page 80), you will find questions that drive your team to think about your current celebrations and opportunities to build in reflection, debriefing, and peer learning. It will help you move beyond passively being told what to celebrate and make plans for how you and your team can genuinely celebrate all the school's stakeholders.

Don't stop at reflection; the team will next reboot the celebrations in your building. Once you reflect on your current celebrations and identify areas for improvement, it's time to move from reflection to action. The ideas throughout this chapter and tools 2.1–2.4 prime your team so rebuilding a culture of celebration is less daunting. As for action, "Tool 2.6: Celebration Revival, Part 2—Timeline and Action Plan" (page 84) will guide you in developing a comprehensive plan for building both institutionalized and impromptu celebrations with all stakeholders. This timeline will help you translate your insights into tangible steps.

The School Culture Players

Celebrations will influence staff members with varying perspectives and have a profound impact on the dynamics of adult interactions within a school. Celebrations help school cultures move forward sustainably. Most importantly, they actually reduce adult drama.

Empowering Believers

Generally, people don't want drama in the workplace. Celebration may be a Believer's best tool for change. Even a Fundamentalist's overt opposition to celebration signifies the desire to maintain the status quo. School celebrations remind people of the purpose and priorities of their organization. Celebrating achievements reinforces the value of new knowledge and collaborative efforts, making change feel tangible and achievable (Zepeda et al., 2019).

According to Muhammad (2018), Believers are dedicated to a student-centered approach, regardless of opposition. Celebrations that highlight student learning resonate deeply with Believers, as they are committed to practices that enhance student outcomes. These celebrations create comfort and reassurance by acknowledging practices that support both learning and student success. Muhammad finds that Believers in positive school cultures frequently cite the celebratory aspects of their schools and notes how recognition of proficiency and effort fosters a sense of ease and community. This recognition energizes Believers, and when Believers' voices and energy are active, school cultures become healthier (McNeece & Sheppard, 2025; Muhammad, 2018). Recognizing even small victories can sustain momentum for change, reward hard work, and minimize resistance.

Supporting Tweeners

Celebration is also critical for the newest members of your organization and culture (Muhammad, 2018). Tweeners can include recent college graduates on their first jobs, teachers transitioning from other schools, or individuals entering the field from other professions. Initially, Tweeners often have a limited connection to the school. Celebrations play a crucial role in socializing new teachers and shaping their understanding of the school's values and norms. In the absence of celebrations, leaders should expect Fundamentalists to approach these new teachers with the intent to socialize and gain their support.

Institutionalized staff celebrations, in which colleagues celebrate one another, cultivate a positive environment where individuals actively seek out positive contributions to acknowledge. A culture of celebration boosts students' confidence in their knowledge and problem-solving abilities, which can also bolster new teachers' confidence. This sense of confidence and control is essential in overcoming initial challenges (Muhammad, 2018). Celebrations that extend into informal and social events can aid new teachers in integrating into the school community, building supportive relationships, and reducing feelings of isolation (Nohe-Dirk, 2024). When staff members participate in celebratory events, they have opportunities to learn names, recognize strengths, and expand their support networks. Furthermore, when staff members celebrate their colleagues, particularly in ways that align with the school's priorities, it reinforces the school's values and expectations. Recognition provides valuable guidance to new teachers, confirming that they are on the right track (DuFour et al., 2024).

Believers represent the future of education—potential teacher leaders, principals, and superintendents—so it's vital to model exemplary celebratory practices for them. Cultivating joy in the school combats demoralization and burnout, and it can also increase student engagement (Scoresby, 2024). Consider what Muhammad (2018) calls the moment of truth—when a Tweener finds out about a harsh reality in the profession. Fundamentalist thinking will win the day and convert a follower if there is a vacuum of celebration, joy, and connection within your school's culture. Celebration helps create a positive environment where people are more likely to ignore negative comments and focus on something positive.

Flipping Fundamentalists

Informal networks can become breeding grounds for negativity where some individuals employ tactics such as defamation and slander to undermine others. When positive celebrations, the opposite of Fundamentalist tactics, become the norm in a school, they act as a counterbalance to negative culture. Celebrations cultivate trust among staff, which can be instrumental in shifting perspectives. When excellence and positivity are regularly shared and acknowledged, conditions become more challenging for negativity to take hold. In a school where celebrations are commonplace, negative remarks about a colleague tend to lose their impact, as the prevailing positive atmosphere isolates negativity and encourages individuals to focus on the constructive aspects of their work.

In *C.R.A.F.T. Conversations for Teacher Growth*, Sally J. Zepeda, Lakesha Robinson Goff, and Stefanie W. Steele (2019) note that transforming mindsets is key: "Once teachers understand the why and the how, only one thing can hold them back from making the change: their mindsets" (p. 32). Strategically employ celebration to encourage Fundamentalists of all levels to reconsider their stance.

Level One (Need Clarity): Showing the Why With Celebrations

Celebrations help Level One Fundamentalists by communicating *why*. They provide a context for school goals and help teachers understand why needed school changes will be beneficial. It is crucial that you clearly articulate the rationale behind celebrations to Level One Fundamentalists, using research, data, and alignment with the school's core principles to build a compelling case.

Level Two (Need Trust): Promoting Credibility Among Teammates With Celebrations

Level Two Fundamentalists grow from celebrations because celebrating helps all staff build trust by focusing on *who*. Leaders must ensure that the purpose of each celebration is clear and directly linked to specific behaviors or expectations in order to establish credibility. Celebrations must be well organized and purposeful, and they must provide opportunities for staff to celebrate one another, fostering trust. Zepeda and colleagues (2019) highlight the importance of trust-based relationships between teachers and principals, noting that they are fundamental to a healthy school culture and staff empowerment. Leaders must understand teachers' mindsets, particularly the mindsets of those who struggle with change, and offer support to facilitate a shift in perspective (Zepeda et al., 2019). Celebrations can serve to strengthen these relationships, promoting a more positive and collaborative environment (Zepeda et al., 2019).

Level Three (Need Capacity or Skills): Demonstrating Possibilities With Celebrations

Level Three Fundamentalists need to build capacity by addressing *how*. They need to feel prepared for change. The plan for celebration should be clear and well defined for everyone. Celebration can demonstrate the possibility of positive outcomes, and small successes can motivate further commitment to change. DuFour and colleagues (2024) emphasize that staff members need tangible results to maintain their commitment to change initiatives, and small steps facilitate understanding.

Level Four (Resistant to the Core Mission): Countering Defamation With Celebrations

Celebration directly counters behaviors like slander and defamation, which Level Four Fundamentalists may use to resist change. Typical Level Four Fundamentalists' behavior to defame change agents (principals and teachers alike) is neutered by a culture where sharing excellence and positivity is a norm. When the majority of the team is celebrating and a Level Four Fundamentalist is not, it can create a sense of isolation.

Furthermore, a common tactic used by Level Four Fundamentalists is negative talk against the parents and community. When your team develops celebrations for these groups, you provide an alternative message to those who must listen to the Fundamentalists' negative comments or diatribes.

Does your school have an issue with defamation and slander against any layer of your school's community? As a guiding coalition, review "Tool 2.7: Celebration or Defamation" (page 86) and decide if this would be helpful to use with staff to bring this behavior to the forefront, discuss the negative impact it has on teammates, and offer a different way forward.

A well-cultivated culture of celebration is a powerful tool for mitigating adult drama and fostering a more positive and productive school environment. Leadership's act of celebrating staff models the same expectation for the classroom.

Celebration not only acknowledges those who are contributing to the goal but also reinforces the goal's importance and encourages broader participation. By strategically using celebration to empower Believers, support Tweeners, flip Fundamentalists, acknowledge positive behaviors, promote collaboration, and address resistance to change, school leaders can create a more supportive and unified community.

Chapter 2 Tools

Cultivating a genuine culture of celebration is a powerful way to reduce adult drama, empower Believers, and sustain your team's momentum. Remember, you don't need to tackle every tool in each chapter. For doing an immediate analysis of your current celebration culture, we recommend starting with tools 2.5 and 2.6. Of course, if one area of the chapter prompted you to think about growth, that is a worthwhile place to begin. No matter your choice, bringing more celebration into your school's culture is a valuable activity.

Review figure 2.2 for a summary of this chapter's tools.

Tool Number	Title of Tool	Purpose
Tool 2.1	Impromptu Celebration Ideas	Help staff brainstorm and develop concrete ideas for implementing spontaneous, unplanned (or impromptu) celebrations within the school.
Tool 2.2	Survey: Student Perceptions of Celebration	Gather student feedback on how achievements are celebrated at school, what motivates students (extrinsically and intrinsically), and their preferences for how accomplishments be recognized.
Tool 2.3	Academic Fair for Culture	Celebrate and highlight the work and leadership of teachers in their classrooms.

Figure 2.2: *Chapter 2 tools.*

continued →

Tool 2.4	Celebrating the Success of All Staff	Help the leadership team plan and document institutionalized celebrations designed to regularly recognize the contributions of all staff members throughout the school year, reinforcing school values and priorities.
Tool 2.5	Celebration Revival, Part 1: Reflection	Help teachers and support staff analyze patterns in what, how, and who they celebrate at school.
Tool 2.6	Celebration Revival, Part 2: Timeline and Action Plan	Create a master schedule to plan for conducting celebrations throughout the year.
Tool 2.7	Celebration or Defamation	Help teachers reflect on the impact of their interactions and language within the school environment.

Tool 2.1: Impromptu Celebration Ideas

Purpose

Help staff brainstorm and develop concrete ideas for implementing spontaneous, unplanned (or impromptu) celebrations within the school. The goal is to create a system where both student and staff behaviors, efforts, and achievements can consistently and meaningfully be recognized to reinforce school values and foster a positive culture.

Instructions

Complete the following process.

1. Discuss the value of impromptu celebrations.
2. Brainstorm specific actions and achievements (by students or staff) worthy of recognition (Criteria for Recognition).
3. Plan how these recognitions will occur: how they'll be noticed, initiated, and carried out (System for Recognition).
4. List needed materials or resources (Celebration Resources).
5. Share ideas and refine them for practicality.

Impromptu Celebrations		
Criteria for Recognition	**System for Recognition**	**Celebration Resources**
Example: Teachers acknowledge students for excellent teamwork, friendship, efforts, or outcomes.	*Example:* The teacher recognizes the student and hands them a positive referral that doubles as a hall pass. The student goes to the office, where an office staff member signs the referral and allows the student to pick a prize. Then the student takes the positive referral home.	*Example:* Referral slips or prizes (snacks, fidget tools, pens, and so on)

Tool 2.2: Survey—Student Perceptions of Celebration

Purpose

Gather student feedback on how achievements are celebrated at school, what motivates students (extrinsically and intrinsically), and their preferences for how accomplishments be recognized. For younger students, you will need to adjust the vocabulary in these questions. However, please review the scoring chart on page 3 of this tool to ensure any changes do not alter the questions' intended purpose.

Instructions

Anonymously administer this survey to students and collect the data for discussion. You can distribute hard copies of the survey or input these questions into your electronic survey tool of choice.

Survey

1. How often are your achievements celebrated at school?

4	3	2	1
Frequently	Sometimes	Rarely	Never

2. When your achievements are celebrated, how meaningful do you find the celebrations?

4	3	2	1
Very meaningful	Somewhat meaningful	Not very meaningful	Not meaningful at all

3. Do you agree that celebrations at school are genuine and reflect actual accomplishments?

4	3	2	1
Strongly agree	Agree	Disagree	Strongly disagree

4. What motivates you to do your best at school? (Check all that apply.)
   - ☐ Getting good grades
   - ☐ Receiving rewards or prizes
   - ☐ Making your parents or caregivers proud
   - ☐ Learning new things
   - ☐ Feeling a sense of accomplishment
   - ☐ Improving yourself
   - ☐ Other: ____ (Please specify.)

5. Rank the following from most motivating (1) to least motivating (4).
   - _____ Praise from your teachers
   - _____ Rewards (for example, stickers or treats)
   - _____ Recognition in front of the class or school
   - _____ Personal satisfaction from doing well

6. What types of celebrations or recognition do you find most motivating?

7. What are some ways the school could better celebrate student achievements, both big and small?

page 2 of 3

Scoring

Calculate your scores for each category using the following chart.

Category	Prompt	Score
Perceptions of Celebrations	Add your scores for questions 1, 2, and 3.	
Sources of Motivation	Analyze your chosen responses to question 4, and record your ranking of responses to question 5.	
Preferences for Recognition and Celebration	Identify themes in the open-ended responses to questions 6 and 7.	

Interpret your scores for each category.

Perceptions of Celebrations

- **Celebratory culture (score of 9–12):** Achievements are consistently recognized and meaningful.
- **Mixed perceptions (score of 6–8):** Some celebrations are effective, but others may lack impact.
- **Limited recognition (score of 4–5):** Students feel celebrations are infrequent or not meaningful.
- **Lack of recognition (score of 3):** Celebration practices urgently need to be improved.

Sources of Motivation

- **Question 4:** Once you tally which of these responses have the most students identifying them as motivators, you can assess your current system of intrinsic and extrinsic motivators. Pay close attention to students' write-in comments beside the Other option.
- **Question 5:** Once you have this student data, you can rank these elements based on how motivating they are for students in order to determine whether your students are more extrinsically or intrinsically motivated.

Preferences for Recognition and Celebration

- Are you surprised by any ideas that students gave in response to questions 6 and 7?

Team Reflection and Discussion

As a team, discuss the aggregated results of the anonymous survey. Analyzing patterns in scores allows for the identification of trends in student perceptions of recognition and motivation.

- What is working well?
- What areas need improvement?
- What changes can be made to better celebrate and motivate students?

Action Plan

Based on your reflection and discussion, develop an action plan.

- How should the school address the survey data?
- What specific changes need to be made to celebration practices?
- What is the first step to move in that direction?

page 3 of 3

Tool 2.3: Academic Fair for Culture

Purpose

Celebrate and highlight the work and leadership of teachers in their classrooms. During the academic fair, teachers' classrooms become learning areas for staff to visit, discuss best practices, and learn from colleagues. The purpose of the fair is not only to give all staff quality professional development but also to celebrate learning across the school.

Note: This academic fair is designed to be conducted when students are not in the building, such as during a designated professional development day. Adjustments can and should be made if you choose to do this during an instructional day by using your collaborative team planning time.

Instructions

Review the agenda and make plans so that each layer of the academic fair can be successful. Think of this process like a science fair for a teacher's academic classroom—an exhibition of practical application. Please note that schools can and should add to or adjust the specific Points of Practice (see page 3 of this tool) to align with their current initiatives.

Academic Fair Agenda

1. Leadership preparation
   - The leadership team meets to create a theme and schedule.
   - For classrooms being observed, prepare the Academic Fair Form (page 3 of this tool) with Points of Practice connected to the school's academic goals, initiatives, and improvement strategies.
   - Prepare a room with food and beverages for staff.
   - Select medals to give to all presenters.
   - Place certificates on the classroom doors to signify exemplary practices.
   - Prepare to play music over the school's intercom system (or hire a DJ) to explicitly signal to staff when it is time to rotate to the next classroom.
2. Teacher preparation
   - The teacher should not need a lot of preparation for this fair because it assesses how they structure their environment on a typical day.
   - The teacher makes sure the physical environment of the classroom is well prepared and organized.
   - The teacher completes the Academic Fair Form and posts it on the classroom door to guide visitors on what to look for and where to find it.
   - The teacher curates and displays materials from collaborative team meetings—such as lesson plans, assessments, data team minutes, and action plans—ensuring these artifacts clearly connect to the Points of Practice areas listed on their door.

- Teachers are welcome to highlight the Points of Practice in any or all ways, from just directing teammates to a space in the classroom to laying out student work to printed images or a rotating presentation on a projector.

3. Collaborative meeting (before the academic fair)
   - Review the purpose of the academic fair.
   - Build or refresh shared knowledge of the specific Points of Practice of the fair (using an article, a page from a book, research, or a team conversation). This focus will directly tie to the Academic Fair Form posted on every door.
   - Discuss the norms for visiting classrooms listed on the Academic Fair Note-Taker.
4. Academic fair visits
   - Adhere to the norms.
   - Use the teacher's posted Academic Fair Form as a map to document your findings on the Note-Taker.
   - Write down any questions to ask at our follow-up session.
5. Hallway talks (after the academic fair)
   - Discuss factual evidence of strengths observed.
   - Use the Note-Taker to reflect on instructional practices and their impact on students. Consider what new ideas you might have for your team and which team member you can celebrate based on what you saw today.
6. Leadership team celebration
   - The leadership team welcomes all staff to the celebration room.
   - Staff recognize and celebrate other staff members and teams.
   - Create a forum for follow-up questions and celebratory shoutouts.
   - Include music, food, and treats for staff.

Academic Fair Form

(To be completed by the presenting teacher and posted on the classroom door)

Teacher: ______________________________ Room: ____________

Welcome to my classroom! This guide will help you navigate the artifacts and strategies I use to drive student success. Please use the following guide to see how our collaborative work and the data we collect translate into this physical learning environment.

Points of Practice	Where to Look and What It Shows
Walkthrough focus: *(Specific improvement strategy or concept discussed in the premeeting article or research)*	Location and artifact: Connection:
Universal academic goal: *(One or two specific strategies or materials our team is using to meet the schoolwide goal)*	Location and artifact: Connection:
Collaborative growth: *(How our collaborative team meetings, curriculum planning, and this data have driven the artifacts we are looking at today)*	Location and artifact: Connection:
Other point of pride (optional): *(Is there anything else you want to share that speaks to what drives you as a classroom teacher?)*	Location and artifact: Connection:

page 3 of 4

Academic Fair Note-Taker

Date: ____________________ Rooms visited: ____

Norms for the Academic Fair

- Connect the teacher's posted processes with the outcomes you see in the classroom environment.
- Collect factual evidence.
- Look to get better—learning is required.
- Celebrate others.

Observation Notes

(Refer to the Academic Fair Form posted on each teacher's door. What specific evidence of those practices did you observe in each room?)

Reflection and Application

What connections do you see to your own practice?	What questions do I have about what I see?	What new ideas did I see that I want to share with my collaborative team?

Positive Feedback for Staff Celebration

(Jot down specific praise to share during the celebration.)

Source: Adapted from Ryan, B. (2023). The brilliance in the building: Effecting change in urban schools with the PLC at Work process. *Solution Tree Press.*

page 4 of 4

Tool 2.4: Celebrating the Success of All Staff

Purpose

Help the leadership team plan and document institutionalized celebrations designed to regularly recognize the contributions of all staff members throughout the school year, reinforcing school values and priorities.

Instructions

Complete the following process.

1. **Brainstorm celebration names:** Collaboratively decide on specific names for different awards or recognitions that will be given out (for example, Student Champion, GOAT, MVP, Learning Leader, Star Teammate, or People's Champ). Enter these in the Name of Celebration column.
2. **Define recognition criteria:** For each named celebration, clearly define the specific criteria a staff member must meet or demonstrate to be recognized. Ensure criteria align with school values and desired behaviors. Enter these details in the Criteria for Recognition column. Refer to figure 2.1 (page 64) for ideas.
3. **Describe the award:** Specify what the actual award or recognition will be (for example, a certificate, a small trophy, a mention in a staff meeting or newsletter, a designated parking spot, or a symbolic item that is passed from recipient to recipient). Enter this in the Description of Award column.
4. **Schedule celebrations:** Determine the frequency and specific timing of each celebration during the school year (for example, it will occur monthly, quarterly, or at the end of the semester). Enter these dates or time frames in the Dates to Celebrate column.
5. **Consider peer recognition:** Discuss and potentially incorporate systems where staff members can also nominate or pass on awards to their colleagues, fostering a culture where everyone participates in celebration.

Institutionalized Celebrations			
Name of Celebration	**Criteria for Recognition**	**Description of Award**	**Dates to Celebrate**

Tool 2.5: Celebration Revival, Part 1—Reflection

Purpose

Help teachers and support staff analyze patterns in what, how, and who they celebrate at school. By reflecting on different celebration types and their alignment with school values, staff can identify strengths, gaps, and imbalances to create a more inclusive, meaningful celebration culture. Part 1 will take the team of stakeholders a significant amount of time to complete. Discussing each focus area in small groups before having whole-group conversations is encouraged.

Instructions

As a team, use this tool to reflect on our school's current celebration practices across different focus areas. The goal is to analyze patterns, identify gaps, and spark discussion, leading to a more balanced and meaningful culture of celebration.

Focus Areas

1. **What we celebrate:** Understand whether we equitably celebrate academics, behavior, extracurriculars, and social-emotional growth.
2. **Academic celebrations (equity and growth):** Examine whether all students experience meaningful recognition of their progress.
3. **Who we celebrate:** Examine whether celebrations include all students and staff equitably.
4. **Motivation (extrinsic versus intrinsic):** Reflect on whether recognition fosters genuine growth.
5. **Type of celebration (institutionalized versus impromptu):** Evaluate the balance between structured and spontaneous celebrations.

1. What We Celebrate

Think about what types of student achievements our school celebrates most often. Fill in the following table based on what you observe most frequently.

Question	Academics	Behavior	Extracurriculars	Social-Emotional Growth	Other
How frequently do we see these celebrations?					

What forms do these celebrations take (awards, announcements, events, and so on)?					
Which group of students is most often recognized in each area?					

Reflection

- Do any columns have significantly more celebrations than others?
- If one area is celebrated more than others, what message does that send about what we value?
- How might we bring more balance to our celebrations?

2. Academic Celebrations (Equity and Growth)

Academic success should include recognition of both achievement and progress. How do our celebrations reflect this?

Question	How We Currently Do This	What Needs Improvement
How do we celebrate the academic growth of all students, not just high achievers?		
How do we ensure that we recognize a variety of students, rather than repeatedly recognizing the same students?		
How do we help students see the connections among effort, progress, and success?		

page 2 of 4

Reflection

- Do we regularly celebrate our students?
- How do we make sure that we celebrate different students?

3. Who We Celebrate

Consider how inclusive our school's celebrations are across different stakeholder groups.

Stakeholder Group	Type of Recognition Given	What Needs Improvement
Students		
Teachers		
Support staff		
Parents		
Community members		

Reflection

- Do some stakeholder groups receive less recognition than others? If so, which ones?
- What steps could be taken to ensure all groups feel valued in school celebrations?

4. Motivation (Extrinsic Versus Intrinsic)

Consider whether our celebrations encourage long-term motivation and growth.

Question	Extrinsic Motivators (Rewards, Prizes, or Public Praise)	Intrinsic Motivators (Personal Growth, Effort, or Work or Learning That Makes a Meaningful Difference)
What current celebrations highlight these motivations?		
Which type do students respond to the most?		

Reflection

- Do we have a balance between external validation and intrinsic motivation?
- How can celebrations foster a lasting love of learning and growth?

5. Type of Celebration (Institutionalized Versus Impromptu)

Examine how our school balances scheduled celebrations with spontaneous recognition.

Celebration Type	Institutionalized Celebration (Planned, Annual, Routine)	Impromptu Celebration (Spontaneous, Personal, Unexpected)
Student success		
Staff recognition		
Parent and community contributions		

Reflection

- Are institutionalized celebrations still meaningful? If so, why?
- How can we encourage more impromptu, personal celebrations?

Action Steps: Celebration Revival

Based on your reflections, identify one area for improvement and outline next steps.

Focus Area	What Needs to Change	First Step to Make This Happen

Tool 2.6: Celebration Revival, Part 2—Timeline and Action Plan

Purpose

Create a master schedule to plan for conducting celebrations throughout the year. A celebration must have a clear purpose, a link to a behavior or commitment, and opportunities for many winners. An example is "Tool 2.4: Celebrating the Success of All Staff" (page 79), which consists of staff recognizing and celebrating other staff based on specific criteria. After a staff member receives recognition, the staff member then selects another staff member to celebrate after a designated period of time. This is a great way to include everyone in the building in the celebration process. An easy-to-implement impromptu celebration is highlighted in "Tool 2.1: Impromptu Celebration Ideas" (page 71). Staff members recognize students, and the students go to the office for a positive referral home and a prize.

Instructions

Use this tool to translate the reflections and ideas from "Tool 2.5: Celebration Revival, Part 1—Reflection" (page 80) into a concrete, yearlong master schedule for school celebrations. This plan should ensure celebrations are purposeful, linked to desired behaviors and commitments, inclusive, and balanced between recognizing processes and recognizing outcomes.

Celebration Checklist

Use the following checklist to assess the school's use of celebrations.

- ☐ The purpose of the celebration is explicitly stated.
- ☐ All staff in the building are taking responsibility for celebrating others.
- ☐ A clear link is established between the recognition and the behavior or commitment it is attempting to reinforce.
- ☐ Celebration is process and outcome based.
- ☐ There are many opportunities for multiple winners.

Source for this tool: Adapted from DuFour, R., DuFour, R., Eaker, R., Many, T. W., Mattos, M., & Muhammad, A. (2024). Learning by doing: A handbook for Professional Learning Communities at Work *(4th ed.). Solution Tree Press; Muhammad, A. (2018).* Transforming school culture: How to overcome staff division *(2nd ed.). Solution Tree Press.*

Culture-of-Celebration Master Schedule

Month	Name of Celebration	Who This Is Celebrating	Type of Celebration: Institutionalized or Impromptu	Process or Effort Elements	Outcome Elements	Resources: Supplies, Time to Meet, or Training
August						
September						
October						
November						
December						
January						
February						
March						
April						
May						
June						

Tool 2.7: Celebration or Defamation

Purpose

Help teachers reflect on the impact of their interactions and language within the school environment. This tool encourages self-assessment of behaviors and promotes a positive, collaborative culture.

Instructions

Use the following reflection questions to individually consider the impact of your interactions and language within the school environment. This self-assessment is intended to promote awareness and encourage behaviors that contribute to a positive, collaborative culture while discouraging negativity and harmful communication.

Individual Reflection

Consider the following questions.

Identifying Fundamentalist Behaviors

- In what ways might your words or actions contribute to a negative environment like the words and actions of Fundamentalists do?
- How can you ensure you are not defaming or slandering colleagues, the community, or school initiatives?

Promoting a Culture of Celebration

- How do you currently contribute to celebrating the achievements and efforts of students, parents, colleagues, and the community?
- How can you increase your active participation in promoting a positive and celebratory atmosphere within the school?

Responding to Conflict or Disagreement

- When faced with differing opinions or challenging situations (like the one Mr. Miller and Ms. Martinez experienced at the beginning of chapter 2, page 53), how do you typically respond?
- Do you contribute to constructive dialogue, or do you participate in negativity or gossip?

Supporting New Staff Members

- How do you contribute to the socialization and support of new teachers or staff members (Tweeners)?
- How can you help Tweeners feel welcome and valued and protect them from negative influences?

CHAPTER 3

Creating Systems of Support for Tweeners

THE SQUEAK OF MS. Chambers's new sneakers echoed in the empty middle school hallway as she paused outside her grade 6 science classroom. Just months ago, she'd been the student teacher in grade 5 down the hall, nervously absorbing lessons from Mrs. Davison, whose patient guidance felt like a lifeline. Now, armed with a freshly minted alternative route certification, this room was hers. The silence of summer filled the space; the classroom was a blank slate brimming with possibility and a healthy dose of apprehension.

Her first official week wasn't just about classroom setup. It began with a districtwide orientation, a blur of faces and information. But the real support structure clicked into place when the principal handed her a hefty binder, "Time for Learning Resource," its pages already tabbed with relevant science standards and starter activities. "Don't hesitate to ask anything at all," the principal said during their initial check-in, one of the regular morning meetings he held just for new staff to help them not feel adrift.

Ms. Chambers's assigned mentor, a veteran teacher from another grade, met her for coffee, focusing less on policy than on navigation of the first few tricky weeks. Mondays meant grade 6 team meetings. The two ELA teachers, the mathematics duo, the social studies expert, and now Ms. Chambers didn't just coordinate calendars; they shared student insights, debated instructional approaches, and offered practical tips. Then came Ms. Chambers's weekly session with Ms. Evans, the instructional coach, who didn't just lecture but observed a minilesson, asking afterward, "What did you notice about student engagement when you transitioned to group work? What might you try differently tomorrow?" Ms. Chambers's grade-level leader, Mr. Henderson, popped in later that week, not with a clipboard for evaluation but with an invitation. "Let's walk around during third period," he suggested, leading her on informal instructional rounds, pointing out different classroom management techniques and engagement strategies in action. He made a point of asking, "What supply orders are still outstanding? Do you have the log-ins you need?," ensuring the practical hurdles were cleared. The science curriculum leader dropped by too to co-plan an upcoming lab with Ms. Chambers, sharing resources from the professional learning platform the school subscribed to. Even the staff lounge felt welcoming; the biweekly Friday "wins" celebration wasn't mandatory, but the shared laughter and snacks chipped away at any feelings of isolation she had.

Ms. Chambers still had moments of doubt, challenging interactions that tested her resolve, and the inevitable moment of truth every new teacher faces. But when that moment came, she wasn't alone. She had Mr. Henderson's observations to draw on, Ms. Evans's coaching questions echoing in her mind, her mentor's reassurances, and the shared experiences of her grade-level team. This web of support held firm. It showed in her increasingly confident classroom presence, in the innovative projects her students undertook, and ultimately, in the surprise announcement at the end-of-year assembly: Ms. Chambers was the district's Expect Excellence Award recipient. In years to come, she would often be seen leading discussions during the learning block meetings and sharing the strategies that were once shared with her.

This chapter may be the most pressing one in the book. *Transforming School Culture* (Muhammad, 2018) affirms that some of the most potent leadership strategies involve the intentional development of new teachers—Tweeners. They are not just the new members of the culture. Tweeners also represent the future leaders within your school and possess the potential to shift a toxic school culture into a healthy, thriving one. Neglecting their development is a missed opportunity; nurturing them is paramount.

Teacher isolation has become more acute since the return from COVID-19 shutdowns; this has contributed to burnout because it has increased feelings of emotional disconnection among staff (Freelander, 2024). Therefore, this chapter provides contemporary best practices and practical tools designed to help you systematically and intentionally cultivate the next generation of Believers within your staff. We'll begin with why it's so important to support Tweeners, provide a deep dive into the moment of truth, and explain the impact that support systems have on all the school culture players.

The Critical Importance of Supporting Tweeners

As a profession, education typically does not support new teachers well. Unfortunately, the prevailing macroculture in education often initiates new members by metaphorically throwing them into the deep end of the pool, alone, while they are still learning to swim. Muhammad (2018) notes, "No other professional faces this unique isolation. For most of their professional lives, teachers will be the only adult in their immediate area of practice" (p. 130). This isolation is compounded by an education system that frequently lacks a robust, organized commitment to genuine teacher development and acclimation (Cone, 2024). Consider some generally accepted, yet fundamentally counterproductive, norms that our profession often imposes on Tweeners.

- From day one, they bear immediate and full responsibility for classroom planning, instruction, and behavior management, typically without consistent in-person support from seasoned colleagues or administrators readily available to them in *their* classroom (Cone, 2024).

- Mentoring programs, while well intentioned, often devolve into reactive "ask for help if you need it" or buddy system scenarios. They lack proactive structure and quality professional learning processes that define effective mentoring (Radford, 2017; Rhode Island Department of Education, 2025; Thornton, 2024).
- Structured, collaborative planning time with experienced peers remains a rarity in many school schedules, limiting opportunities for shared learning and strategy development (Boogren, 2022).

Beyond these systemic shortcomings, Tweeners grapple with a complex social landscape that contributes to their isolation, some of which is self-imposed. New teachers often arrive with the preconceived notion that admitting struggles equates to incompetence, leading them to keep difficulties private (Barnes & Gonzalez, 2015; Wilcoxen, Newman, & Wulff, 2025). This internal pressure is exacerbated by the subtle (and sometimes not-so-subtle) adult drama that permeates toxic school cultures. A new teacher might get caught in the cross fire of conflicting advice from veteran teachers with differing philosophies and feel pressured to align with one faction or another. They might observe cliques forming in the staff lounge and feel excluded from informal conversations where crucial school information and relational capital are exchanged. Or perhaps they witness gossip about colleagues or administrators and feel unsure whether to participate, stay silent, or push back, fearing social or professional repercussions either way.

Understanding the hurdles your Tweeners face, including systemic isolation, the pressure of navigating complex social dynamics, and the level of support (or lack of support) they feel, is the critical first step. Do you want to know if your new teachers struggle with any of these elements? You can use "Tool 3.1: New Teacher Survey" (page 107) to generate data for the guiding coalition and principal to understand the views of your new teachers. The survey results will be helpful for the other tools in this chapter as well.

However, awareness alone won't cultivate the positive, efficacious educators your school needs. Leaders must make sure new teachers are prepared for an event that all Tweeners will experience. Muhammad (2018) uses the term *moment of truth*, while other researchers describe it as a *tipping point* (Perryman, Bradbury, Calvert, & Kilian, 2025). The moment of truth is something all educators can look back on as the first crossroads they experienced in their profession.

The Moment of Truth

As alluded to in the introduction, the moment of truth is an inevitable experience and a critical juncture during Tweeners' initial experiences within a school organization (Muhammad, 2018). A Tweener's future hangs in the balance: disillusionment and rigidity or growth and commitment. Essentially, the moment of truth can be triggered by various events that challenge a new teacher's ideals. These experiences might include encountering student apathy or defiance, facing challenging or aggressive parent interactions, navigating unsupportive colleagues or administrative practices, or grappling with policies that seem misaligned with their pedagogical beliefs (Baatz & Wirzberger, 2025; Middleton-Cox, 2025;

Muhammad, 2018; Pelletier, 2024; Perryman et al., 2025; Tan, 2015). Such discrepancies between expectations and reality can lead to a period of questioning and reassessment for the new educator.

Alex's moment of truth was shared in the introduction: He was told, without explanation, to remove the animals from his classroom. During his first year of teaching, the classroom pets were instrumental in developing students' love of learning and building a community. Alex's students were wonderful caretakers. Sadly, in his second year, he had a new principal who was determined to have people fear her; she walked in and introduced herself by telling him to "get all these animals out." This crushed Alex because he knew the experience that his students would be missing. Shortly after that, he left the school.

Bo's moment of truth came in his first year when some class sizes were as high as fifty students, he received no instructional support or materials, and the district mentor was nonexistent. He realized that what the school needed to be for students was not the reality. Bo's love for the school, the neighborhood, the city, and the students, who were just like him growing up, helped him push through, but there was no organizational support. He made it *despite* the system.

Our stories are about administrative failures. Many situations like the following can develop into Tweeners' moments of truth.

- A new teacher spends all weekend designing a highly creative, inquiry-based lesson, convinced it will finally engage their most apathetic students. When they deliver it, the class meets the lesson with disinterest.
- During a new teacher's first parent-teacher conference, a parent dismisses all the data the teacher has collected and aggressively accuses them of being "too young" and "incompetent" and "picking on" their child.
- In the staff lounge, a new teacher excitedly shares a small success story about a struggling student only to have a veteran teacher (a Fundamentalist) roll their eyes and say, "Oh, just wait until they regress next week. That stuff never sticks with *these* kids."

While challenging moments like these can't always be avoided, the quality of the school's social fabric plays a pivotal role in shaping a new teacher's response to such moments (Muhammad, 2018). The social fabric of school connection could potentially be introduced as early as the interview process and include supports before the school year even begins. While you are reflecting on your moment of truth, think about how you help your Tweeners as they inevitably experience theirs. How can you let them know that moment is coming while also showing them the school is proactively ready to support them? You can use "Tool 3.2: Tweeners—Preparing for the Moment of Truth" (page 111) to help center this priority. Meanwhile, keep in mind the majority of the research points in two major directions: (1) developing belonging and (2) revamping mentoring systems.

Developing Belonging

As we have established, intentionally developing Tweeners into Believers requires targeted strategies. Schools must move beyond superficial welcomes to actively cultivate a deep sense of belonging. Researcher Brené Brown (2012) powerfully captures the core issue here, highlighting the crucial difference between asking newcomers to merely fit in and creating an environment where they truly belong:

> *Belonging is not fitting in. In fact, fitting in is the greatest barrier to belonging. Fitting in, I've discovered during the past decade of research, is assessing situations and groups of people, then twisting yourself into a human pretzel in order to get them to let you hang out with them. Belonging is something else entirely—it's showing up and letting yourself be seen and known as you really are.*

This distinction is not just semantic; it's fundamental. While most schools intend to be welcoming, the pressure to conform often overshadows efforts to foster authentic connections, leaving many new teachers (even experienced ones new to the building) grappling with significant obstacles on their path to belonging (Charner-Laird, Szczesiul, Kirkpatrick, Watson, & Gordon, 2016; Middleton-Cox, 2025). To build belonging, schools must recognize and actively dismantle these common hurdles.

- **Pressure to conform versus authenticity:** Newcomers often feel compelled to navigate implicit expectations and unwritten school rules by suppressing their unique ideas or teaching styles—the very definition of Brown's (2012) *human pretzel.* Imagine a passionate new science teacher who is eager to implement inquiry-based labs but feels pressured by veteran colleagues to stick to textbook chapters and worksheets simply because "that's how we've always done it here." Research tells us this is very common in mentoring relationships, where the mentor just prescribes the tried-and-true practices (Kwok & Macfarlane, 2025; Thornton, 2024). True belonging allows that new teacher to share, reflect on, and potentially pilot their approach.
- **Transactional interactions versus meaningful relationships:** Belonging requires moving past superficial exchanges, like handing over a curriculum binder or offering quick advice in the hallway. Tweeners need spaces to form reciprocal relationships where they feel safe to be honest and share both successes and struggles, knowing they have genuine allies (Charner-Laird et al., 2016; Thornton, 2024). Without these, they receive resources but lack relational anchors.
- **Fear of vulnerability versus the experience of being seen:** The pervasive fear of appearing incompetent or burdensome often prevents Tweeners from asking for help or admitting difficulties (Barnes & Gonzalez, 2015; Boogren, 2018). A new teacher might sit silently through a team meeting because they are afraid to ask clarifying questions about a data protocol they are confused by, but this will hinder their growth and reinforce their sense of being an outsider. Effective mentoring must balance constructive feedback with recognition of a teacher's strengths (Kwok & Macfarlane, 2025). Belonging means creating a culture where questions are welcomed and vulnerability is seen as strength.

- **Lack of voice versus valued contribution:** Too often, school cultures default to established solutions driven by senior staff, leaving Tweeners feeling like recipients rather than contributors (Charner-Laird et al., 2016; Kwok & Macfarlane, 2025; Thornton, 2024). Perhaps a Tweener observes inefficiencies during student arrival but finds no clear avenue to suggest improvements, or their idea is politely dismissed without real consideration. Belonging requires structures where new perspectives are actively sought and valued in collaborative problem solving. New teachers both need and should have two-way input on school processes (Thornton, 2024).
- **Social exclusion versus community fabric:** New teachers have to be part of a school's network of teachers (Kwok & Macfarlane, 2025). Feeling excluded from informal social interactions, such as lunch groups, inside jokes, and sidebar conversations, significantly impacts one's sense of belonging, as these interactions often are where relational trust and a sense of community are built (Boogren, 2018; Charner-Laird et al., 2016). Consistently seeing established groups head out for coffee while you pack up alone sends a powerful message.
- **Overwhelm versus capacity for connection:** The sheer weight of workload and stress, particularly in the initial phases of teaching, leaves many Tweeners with little time or emotional energy to build the strong relationships required for belonging (Charner-Laird et al., 2016; Middleton-Cox, 2025; Wilcoxen et al., 2025). The exhaustion after a sixty-hour week makes attending that optional Friday staff social feel impossible to some newcomers, further limiting their opportunities to connect.
- **Central focus versus life component:** Differing generational paradigms regarding the nature of work and communication can make Tweeners feel isolated. For instance, baby boomers may traditionally define their work as their central focus, whereas Gen Z often views work as just one important component of their life (Elmore, 2022). This divergence extends to communication, where younger generations often have an entrepreneurial "hacker" mindset or social media savvy that makes them prefer new platforms (Elmore, 2022). When these generational mindsets impact the communication and socialization of new staff (such as in induction programs that partner experienced staff with new staff from a different generation), problems can result. Without knowledge about such differences, people are extremely biased toward their own generations' thought patterns (Elmore, 2022).

These challenges aren't static; they ebb and flow throughout the demanding first year. New teacher support expert Ellen Moir's (1999) work on the phases of first-year teaching offers a valuable lens to better understand this trajectory and provide timely support. Moir identifies a predictable cycle of attitudes and concerns: anticipation (experiencing initial excitement and idealism), survival (dealing with the daily onslaught), disillusionment (questioning one's competence and commitment), rejuvenation (regaining energy and perspective, often after breaks), and reflection (looking back and planning forward). Interestingly, many veteran teachers recognize echoes of these phases in their own annual cycles, suggesting that supports designed for Tweeners can benefit the entire staff's resilience (Boogren, 2021).

Brilliant Voice From the Field

ANN ALFONSO

Principal, Bethke Elementary, Timnath, Colorado

Teachers new to a school need clear expectations. Whether they have taught before or they are first-year teachers, educators need to know how to hit the target, and that starts in the interview. While interviewing for new staff members, we make our expectations very clear on what the role entails and what is expected from a new candidate. My teachers talk eloquently about what it means to work at Bethke and what they are looking for in a teammate. Before the year starts, I as well as my staff reach out to welcome the new staff members so they know the culture they are walking into. From the very first days on the job, the new teachers are shown resources to guide their work: curriculum maps, scopes and sequences, red word lists, common agreements from our K–5 instruction, collective commitments of our school, teachers' manuals, maps of the school, safety protocols, and more. (A. Alfonso, personal communication, September–October 2025)

Charting New Teachers' Month-by-Month Struggles

Let's keep it real: Navigating the first year isn't just about pedagogy. It involves deciphering school politics, handling difficult parent communications, managing unexpected student behaviors, and constantly battling one's workload. When leaders can predict the needs of and support for Tweeners, it frees up their abilities to dive into teaching and learning. Understanding how Moir's phases intersect with these monthly realities (as shown in figure 3.1, page 96) can help leaders anticipate needs and offer targeted support.

The cumulative weight of trying to belong while navigating this intense emotional and professional roller coaster is the catalyst or backdrop for the Tweener's moment of truth. Again, this is a critical juncture, a point where challenges feel overwhelming and the teacher must make a fundamental choice about how they will proceed in the profession. Any combination of the hurdles to belonging and the monthly struggles can trigger this pivotal event.

If you're looking for a tool to help Tweeners proactively map out and prepare for these highs and lows, consider "Tool 3.3: Tweeners—The Year Ahead" (page 114). This tool builds belonging when completed collaboratively, but it extends much further into anticipating the flow of important skills a Tweener needs over the course of a school year.

Preventing Survivors Before They Happen

Until now, we haven't focused much on the school culture player group called the Survivors. While we will talk more about them later, it is essential to acknowledge that all Survivors begin their careers as hopeful Tweeners. Facing relentless challenges without adequate support or a sense of belonging causes a critical shift: Their motivation moves from

Months	Dominant Phases	Typical Tasks and Focus Areas	Common Challenges	Emotional Landscape
August–September	Anticipation to Survival	• Establishing routines and procedures (daily flow, transitions, and materials) • Doing initial lesson planning and curriculum development (often from scratch) • Establishing management systems and authority • Learning about school policies and culture • Meeting students and colleagues • Making initial parent communications	• Being overwhelmed (constantly running) • Facing reality shock (idealism versus complexity) • Having an intense workload (way more than forty hours per week) • Having poor work-life balance • Lacking time for reflection • Having students test boundaries • Feeling isolated • Navigating school culture, politics, and personalities • Addressing initial challenging student behaviors and outbursts	• **Highs:** These include initial excitement, elation, energy, commitment, and idealism. • **Lows:** These include anxiety, terror, and feelings of overwhelm, stress, and tiredness. • **Stress:** High stress is driven by the newness and volume of tasks. • **Self-efficacy:** High efficacy and idealism are quickly challenged by reality.
October–November	Survival to Disillusionment	• Doing ongoing planning and grading • Managing persistent behavior issues • Preparing for and executing parent-teacher conferences • Preparing for and executing formal observations and evaluations • Preparing for and executing school events (such as back-to-school night) • Doing initial student data analysis	• Feeling accumulated exhaustion and being at risk of burnout • Feeling increased stress and low morale • Questioning your own competence and commitment • Getting sick • Experiencing major distress about classroom management • Facing difficult parent interactions and criticism • Experiencing evaluation anxiety • Having your family and friends complain about your time management • Feeling isolated and lacking support • Deciphering parent communications and making difficult calls home • Handling persistent student outbursts • Navigating school politics during evaluations and conferences	• **Highs:** These include occasional small wins (if celebrated). • **Lows:** These include disenchantment, frustration, self-doubt, low self-esteem, vulnerability, and inadequacy. • **Stress:** Stress peaks due to accumulated demands and new pressures. • **Self-efficacy:** Often, efficacy is at its lowest point; you question your ability.

December–January	Disillusionment to Rejuvenation	• Managing preholiday excitement and behavior • Resting, recharging, and reconnecting during winter break • Using winter break for organization and planning • Implementing new strategies after winter break • Focusing on long-term planning • Making student adjustments after the break	• Encountering preholiday student fatigue and behavior • Restarting routines during a postholiday slump • Facing curriculum-pacing pressures • Maintaining postbreak momentum	• **Highs:** These include postbreak relief, renewed hope and energy, fresh perspective, increased confidence, and a sense of accomplishment. • **Lows:** These include lingering prebreak disillusionment and potential postbreak anxiety. • **Stress:** Stress decreases significantly after the break. • **Self-efficacy:** Efficacy begins to rise; belief in your ability to cope or succeed grows.
February–April	Rejuvenation (with potential dips)	• Preparing for standardized testing • Implementing and refining teaching strategies • Monitoring and documenting student progress • Refining classroom management • Continuing to deliver and pace curriculum • Facing potential midyear observations and evaluations	• Facing teacher and student testing pressures and anxiety • Handling student outbursts and restlessness related to spring fever • Feeling spring fatigue and being at risk of burnout • Maintaining student engagement • Experiencing a resurgence of management issues • Facing pressures due to the approaching year-end	• **Highs:** These include increased confidence and competence. • **Lows:** These include susceptibility to stress, fatigue, and overwhelm (especially around testing and over long stretches). • **Stress:** Stress can increase due to testing and fatigue. • **Self-efficacy:** Efficacy is generally higher but can dip with fatigue and pressure.
May–June	Reflection to Anticipation	• Doing final assessments and grading • Preparing report cards • Experiencing final teacher evaluations and conferences • Preparing for the end-of-year classroom closedown (cleaning and inventory) • Making final parent communications • Reflecting on the year (successes and challenges) • Planning and thinking about next year • Celebrating accomplishments	• Experiencing end-of-year exhaustion and burnout • Feeling overwhelmed by closedown tasks and deadlines • Having anxiety about final evaluations or your contract • Finding time and energy for reflection • Managing end-of-year student behavior and disengagement	• **Highs:** These include relief; a sense of accomplishment, pride, fulfillment, or invigoration from reflection and planning; and renewed anticipation for next year. • **Lows:** These include exhaustion, anxiety about evaluations, and sadness about having students leave. • **Stress:** Stress is high due to wrap-up tasks and evaluations, but it is offset by relief. • **Self-efficacy:** Efficacy is often high from reflecting on survival and growth; it is solidified by planning.

Source: Adapted from Baatz & Wirzberger, 2025; Boogren, 2018, 2021, 2022; Cone, 2024; Holloway & Brass, 2018; McClure, 2024; Middleton-Cox, 2025; Pelletier, 2024; Perryman et al., 2025; Radford, 2017; Tan, 2015.

Figure 3.1: *Tweener realities by month.*

implementation of best practices for students to basic professional survival (Muhammad, 2018). When the school culture fails to provide the necessary support systems, relational anchors, and sense of psychological safety, this critical juncture can become a turning point not just in a new teacher's career but in their life. Instead of striving for student growth and embracing best practices, their energy becomes consumed by applying coping mechanisms, managing stress, and simply getting through the day or week. It's this unresolved struggle, this pivot toward self-preservation within an unsupportive environment, that represents the slide toward becoming a Survivor, and it all starts with the absence of belonging when the moment of truth hits.

Brilliant Voice From the Field

SONIA A. MATTHEW

Assistant Principal, Mary B. Neal Elementary School, Waldorf, Maryland

At a middle school where I served as an assistant principal and the mascot was a bulldog [NBCTSchool], I supported our new teachers through the Bulldog Academy. Our vision was "Leverage over labor." We focused on one high-impact change at a time through the BULLDOG framework.

The framework began with building understanding (B), where we diagnosed the root cause, and then uncovering the one thing to focus on (U). We then leveraged the structure (L) by implementing a small change and locked in the implementation (L) through daily accountability checks (D). This process differentiated the outcome (O). Finally, we ensured the teacher owned the success with specific praise for their growth (G). (S. A. Matthew, personal communication, September–October 2025)

Actively and intentionally working to ensure that your school culture doesn't create Survivors is critical, and fostering genuine belonging, as we've discussed, is the essential first step in supporting Tweeners through their inevitable challenges. Feeling accepted and valued provides the crucial foundation. However, another critical ingredient is required to fully equip them for success and firmly guide them toward the path of becoming Believers. While belonging opens the door to growth, how do new teachers systematically build the complex pedagogical skills needed for today's classroom realities? Moreover, how do they learn to recognize and internalize the resilient, self-efficacious mindsets demonstrated by the Believers on your staff? This crucial development, bridging the gap between feeling included and becoming highly effective, happens through powerful, structured mentorship.

Revamping Mentoring Systems

Supporting Tweeners requires more than just making them feel welcome; leaders must also equip them with the skills and resilience needed to thrive. All educators know how those initial years can feel like trying to build an airplane midflight. Don't let that happen.

The positive impact of new teacher support systems on student learning is not just speculative. A rigorous randomized controlled trial showed a direct link: New fourth- to eighth-grade teachers in a two-year comprehensive induction program achieved student learning gains in mathematics and reading equivalent to two to four additional months of learning compared with teachers without such support (Kwok & Macfarlane, 2025). Without robust support structures, particularly effective mentoring, schools risk having new teachers feel overwhelmed and underprepared and then potentially leave the profession or settle into survival mode. The good news is that research provides clear guidance on what makes mentoring programs impactful in developing new teachers' competence and confidence (Cone, 2024). Let's go over some key elements of effective mentoring, how effective mentoring works, and how you can build your ideal mentoring system.

Key Elements of Effective Mentoring

Building a system that genuinely supports Tweeners requires moving beyond informal pairings and embracing intentional design. Several key elements are crucial.

- **Proactive structure and planning:** Simply pairing a novice with a veteran and hoping for the best is insufficient (Cone, 2024; Kwok & Macfarlane, 2025; Muhammad, 2018). Effective mentoring programs require a clear, proactive plan that outlines roles, responsibilities, and key focus areas throughout the year (Boogren, 2022; Cone, 2024; Kwok & Macfarlane, 2025). Without structure, mentoring often becomes reactive firefighting rather than proactive development (Boogren, 2022). Leveraging a developmental guide, like the month-by-month phases illustrated in figure 3.1 (page 96), allows mentors to anticipate needs and provide timely support. For instance, knowing that parent-teacher conferences loom in October helps a mentor ensure guidance on preparation and communication *before* the Tweener feels overwhelmed by the task. A strong mentoring team, actively backed by school leadership, is essential for implementing this structure (Cone, 2024). Research shows that the most successful induction programs provide new teachers with ninety minutes of instructional coaching at least every two weeks (Kwok & Macfarlane, 2025).
- **Focus on instructional growth and professional relationships:** Mentoring extends far beyond orienting someone to the building layout or basic procedures (Boogren, 2022). At its core, it's about fostering a trusting professional relationship focused on enhancing teaching practice (Boogren, 2022; Cone, 2024). While new teachers need to understand school policies, targeted instructional support significantly boosts their confidence and effectiveness (Boogren, 2022; Cone, 2024). The goal, as educational leadership expert Ellyce Cone (2024) describes it, is helping Tweeners transition from being *students of teaching* to *teachers of students*. This involves collaborative analysis of practice, moving beyond stating, "That lesson bombed," to exploring *why* and identifying alternative strategies. Utilizing a shared language about instruction can facilitate these focused, growth-oriented conversations (Boogren, 2022).

- **Bridging of theory to practice through specific actions:** New teachers arrive with theoretical knowledge, and mentoring helps them connect that theory to the complex reality of their own classrooms. Effective mentors actively facilitate this growth with the following actions.
    - *Prompting self-reflection and goal setting*—Mentors act as guides, prompting mentees to analyze their own practice and identify areas for growth rather than simply prescribing solutions (Boogren, 2022; Cone, 2024; Wilcoxen et al., 2025). Research highlights the value of using a structured tool, like a shared digital guide, to anchor reflective conversations (Wilcoxen et al., 2025). Asking questions like "What did you notice about student engagement during that transition?" or "How might you adjust that approach for learners needing more support?" fosters self-awareness and ownership (Cone, 2024). This reflective practice, coupled with collaboratively set clear and achievable goals, provides direction and builds an internal compass for continuous improvement (Boogren, 2022; Cone, 2024).
    - *Creating opportunities for observation and discussion*—Seeing effective teaching in action is invaluable (Boogren, 2022; Radford, 2017). Mentors should facilitate observations of skilled colleagues (including themselves) demonstrating specific strategies (Boogren, 2022; Cone, 2024). A new teacher struggling with classroom management, for example, could observe a veteran who is known for strong routines. However, the crucial element is the structured debrief afterward, in which the mentor guides the mentee to analyze what they saw and connect it to their own practice (Boogren, 2022; Kwok & Macfarlane, 2025; Radford, 2017; Thornton, 2024).
    - *Connecting mentees with resources and learning*—Mentors serve as vital conduits to necessary resources, both within the school (such as curriculum materials, tech support, and special education contacts) and beyond (such as professional development, relevant articles, and online communities; Barnes & Gonzalez, 2015; Boogren, 2021, 2022; Radford, 2017). They can direct Tweeners to targeted support, ensuring they know where to turn for specific challenges.
    - *Providing specific and actionable feedback*—Feedback must move beyond generic comments. Effective mentors offer concrete, behavior-based feedback tied to observations or discussions, coupled with actionable suggestions for improvement (Boogren, 2022; Cone, 2024; Kwok & Macfarlane, 2025). Instead of "Your pacing was off," try "I noticed during the guided practice that several students finished early while others were still working. What might be a strategy to differentiate the task next time?" This feedback should be frequent, and growth should be acknowledged to build momentum (Cone, 2024; Maready, Cheng, & Bunch, 2021).
    - *Helping mentees navigate school culture and the hidden curriculum*—Every school has unspoken expectations, communication preferences, and power dynamics (Boogren, 2022; Kwok & Macfarlane, 2025). Mentors,

as experienced insiders, can help Tweeners understand and navigate this *hidden curriculum*, like "If you want to do *X*, make sure you speak with *Y* for the extra support." That also applies to school micropolitics, like how to navigate the school culture players and what to expect in locations within the informal networks where norms may be much more negative. This understanding can help Tweeners negotiate the informal culture of a school.

Do you need to review the focuses of your current mentoring system? Consider using "Tool 3.4: Self-Reflection Guide for Our Current Mentoring System" (page 116).

The How of Effective Mentoring

Building a system that genuinely supports Tweeners must be intentionally done. Consider the following elements.

- **Formal and ongoing mentor training and development:** Being an excellent teacher doesn't automatically equate to being an excellent mentor (Kwok & Macfarlane, 2025; Weisling & Gardiner, 2018). Mentors need specific training on using coaching techniques, providing effective feedback, facilitating reflection, and understanding the developmental needs of new teachers (Boogren, 2022; Cone, 2024). This training shouldn't be a one-off event; ongoing support and learning opportunities are crucial, as mentors' needs evolve alongside their mentees' development (Cone, 2024). Investing in mentors directly improves the quality of support that Tweeners receive, and without specific training, even well-intentioned mentor teachers are likely to revert to the less effective "I'm the expert" model where they just tell the newer teachers what to do (Kwok & Macfarlane, 2025).
- **Active leadership support and cultural integration:** School leaders, particularly principals, must champion the mentoring program and embed it in the school's culture (Boogren, 2022; Cone, 2024; Middleton-Cox, 2025). Strong principal engagement is directly linked to new teacher success and retention (Cone, 2024; Kwok & Macfarlane, 2025; Middleton-Cox, 2025; Thornton, 2024). When leaders visibly value mentoring, allocate time and resources for it, regularly check in with mentors, and celebrate the program's successes, they signal that supporting new teachers is a collective priority.
- **Mentorship with many different supporters:** Consider incorporating key noninstructional staff, like counselors or administrative assistants who frequently interact with new staff, into the mentoring team or committee. This was successfully done by Alex's school-improvement team at Douglas Elementary in Douglas, Michigan. Shortly after the team members read the Tweeners chapter of the first edition of *Transforming School Culture* (Muhammad, 2009), they developed the new teacher committee approach shown in figure 3.2 (page 102).This multifaceted committee approach to mentoring aligns with the most innovative models in new teacher support, which are moving away from a single mentoring system. Team mentoring structures like Next Education Workforce™ show that supporting new teachers with collaborative teams that have distributed expertise reduces burnout and turnover (Audrain, Ingersoll, & Laski, 2025; McCormick, 2025).

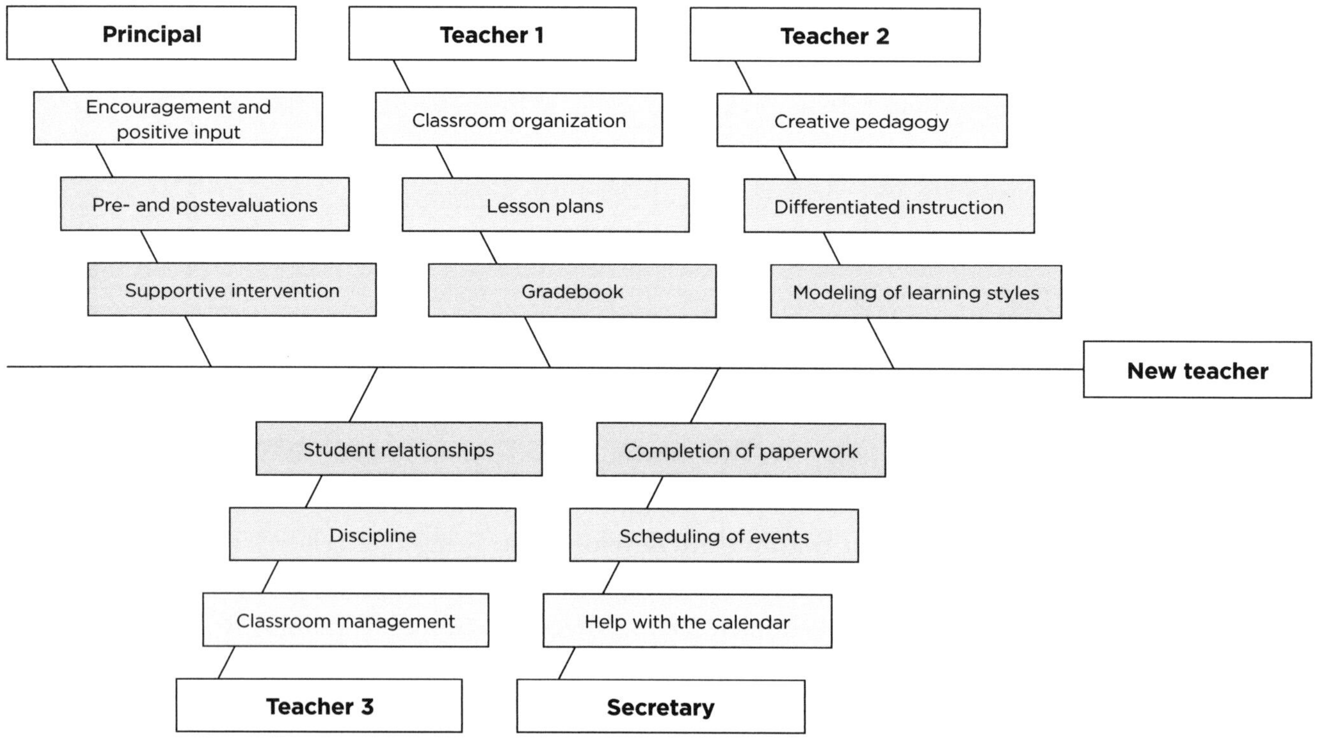

Source: © 2008 by Douglas Elementary. Used with permission.

Figure 3.2: *New teacher committee.*

Your Ideal Mentoring System

Ultimately, the true power of a revamped, intentional mentoring system becomes most evident during a Tweener's inevitable moment of truth. When a Tweener is faced with overwhelming challenges that test their resolve and commitment, a trusted, skilled mentor provides more than just strategies; this mentor offers perspective, encouragement, and a vital human connection.

More importantly, consider the Tweener's thoughts immediately after they face such a critical challenge. The crucial difference lies in where they instinctively turn when they are shaken and perhaps questioning their own abilities. Because an authentic, supportive mentoring relationship has been cultivated, their immediate thought isn't necessarily despair or validation from the nearest cynic confirming the job's impossibility. Instead, we predict the Tweener will actively choose constructive dialogue and problem solving with someone they trust, rather than retreating into isolation or gravitating toward those Fundamentalists who might readily encourage abandoning their initial ideals.

This proactive, supportive relationship can be the critical factor that helps the new teacher navigate feelings of disillusionment or inadequacy. It can reinforce their capacity to overcome obstacles and choose the path of growth toward becoming a Believer, rather than succumbing to the pressures that lead to Fundamentalist behavior or even survival mode. A strong mentoring system may be the most unused and potentially powerful lever a school can pull to develop a healthy school culture.

We suggest that translating these research-based principles into a practical, effective mentoring program tailored to your school's specific context requires careful planning and collaborative effort. This is precisely where "Tool 3.4: Self-Reflection Guide for Our Current Mentoring System" (page 116) becomes invaluable. Once you complete that, consider using "Tool 3.5: Building Our Ideal Mentoring System" (page 120). Gather your guiding coalition or leadership team to utilize this tool to critically examine your current mentoring system and plan a reboot.

The School Culture Players

Intentionally cultivating Tweeners through robust belonging initiatives and revamped mentoring systems, as detailed in this chapter, yields benefits extending far beyond the individual new teacher. These strategies act as powerful levers for positively influencing the entire adult ecosystem within the school. By strengthening the school's newest members, leaders create ripple effects that influence the dynamics among all key players in the school's culture—the Believers, the Fundamentalists, and even other Tweeners. Ultimately, this fosters a healthier, more collaborative environment and reduces the adult drama that can impede progress.

Empowering Believers

Supporting Tweeners directly benefits the Believers within the school culture. When new teachers feel integrated and supported, they become contributing members more quickly, lessening the burden often shouldered by Believers who traditionally step in to assist struggling colleagues and counteract negativity. Well-supported Tweeners become allies in the mission for student success and a positive school environment. Furthermore, the visible success of these new teachers serves as tangible proof that positive practices and support systems are effective; this reinforces existing Believers' commitment and validates their efforts.

Supporting Tweeners

The positive effects ripple out to other Tweeners as well. When new teachers observe their peers successfully navigating the challenges of the initial years through structured support systems like mentoring and belonging initiatives, it normalizes vulnerability and the growth process. Seeing others ask for help that leads to positive outcomes makes it easier for all Tweeners to integrate, build confidence, and resist the isolating narrative that the job is solely about individual survival. This shared experience fosters a collective sense of efficacy and mutual support among the newest members of the staff.

It is crucial to remember that these cultural roles are not immutable character traits. Ideally, contributors to a healthy school culture (Believers) make the best mentors; however, this does not mean Fundamentalists lack valuable classroom skills. People can, and often do, grow and change—especially when the surrounding culture becomes healthier and more supportive. As belonging initiatives take root and mentoring systems strengthen, the conditions that may have pushed an individual toward fundamentalism or survival mode can diminish.

Consider the model in figure 3.2 (page 102) where multiple mentors support a Tweener; in some cases, a highly skilled Fundamentalist can make an excellent mentor for specific areas.

Also consider the potential impact when individuals entrenched in negativity are given mentoring roles—and properly trained for them. That activity can foster connection and contribution. Bo experienced this in his school. Although initially resistant to the new collaborative process, Fundamentalists who were given leadership roles on teams to guide new teachers participated fully and even embraced the recognition that came with it. Sometimes, when Fundamentalists take on the responsibility of mentoring, they not only guide a Tweener but also experience a renewed sense of purpose and belonging themselves. Feeling valued for their expertise, contributing positively to a colleague's development, and being part of a constructive support system can be transformative. This sense of belonging, fostered through the act of mentoring within a supportive structure, can challenge previous cynicism and open the door to more positive engagement.

Ultimately, fostering a culture of belonging and implementing robust, intentional mentoring are not just strategies for onboarding new teachers; they are investments in the potential for positive change within every member of the school community. Good mentoring programs help teachers stay in the profession, and just as important, they help keep them at your school (Boogren, 2022). They create environments where growth is possible, collaboration is valued, and the collective focus remains steadfastly on students' success and well-being.

Do you need a tool that will drive conversation between the new teachers and their mentors? You can use "Tool 3.6: Tweeners—Four Key Areas" (page 123) as a conversation starter about the classrooms, collaboration, and instruction that new teachers and mentors need to reflect on.

Flipping Fundamentalists

Strategically supporting Tweeners can also positively influence the Fundamentalists within the staff. Tweeners who experience a strong sense of belonging and receive guidance from effective mentors are significantly less likely to be swayed or recruited by Fundamentalists seeking to maintain a negative status quo or resist change initiatives. As more Tweeners thrive and contribute positively, the overall cultural balance shifts, isolating negativity and resistance. The success stories of these supported new teachers directly challenge cynical narratives and demonstrate the viability of new approaches, potentially weakening the influence of those resistant to growth and making it harder for defamation or slander to gain traction. This positive influence can manifest differently across the various levels of fundamentalism.

Level One (Need Clarity): Answering the Why

For Level One Fundamentalists, who need the why, seeing Tweeners successfully integrated through explicit belonging and mentoring initiatives provides tangible evidence of the school's values in action. It demonstrates why investing in people and fostering a positive culture matter. Leadership's visible commitment to maintaining these support systems reinforces the rationale behind school-improvement efforts. Sharing Tweener success stories openly, perhaps during staff meetings, can further solidify this understanding.

Level Two (Need Trust): Building Credibility

For Level Two Fundamentalists, who need trust and focus on the who, witnessing respected mentors successfully guide Tweeners builds both the mentors' and the support systems' credibility. Positive, trust-based relationships modeled through mentoring can make these individuals more receptive. Additionally, belonging initiatives often foster interactions across existing cliques. As Tweeners build positive relationships throughout the staff via structured opportunities, mistrust erodes, and Fundamentalists see the trustworthiness of colleagues they previously viewed with suspicion.

Level Three (Need Capacity or Skills): Demonstrating the How

For Level Three Fundamentalists, who need to see how and believe change is possible, mentoring provides concrete examples. Seeing Tweeners learn and successfully implement new strategies or navigate challenges with mentor guidance demonstrates that growth is achievable, countering the belief that initiatives are unmanageable or that staff lack capacity. The existence of structured support systems shows how the school intends to build capacity, proving it has a dedicated plan and resources and not just an expectation to change without help. The success of Tweeners can therefore challenge and potentially shift the perspective of Level Three Fundamentalists.

Level Four (Resistant to the Core Mission): Isolating the Negativity

For Level Four Fundamentalists, who tend toward active resistance, a growing cohort of positive, engaged, and well-supported Tweeners shrinks the potential audience for their negativity and defamation. These Tweeners' positive experiences serve as a direct counternarrative within the school's social network. Direct administrative support of new teachers, as highlighted by Brian Middleton-Cox's (2025) research, insulates both Tweeners and their mentors from personal attacks. As belonging and mentoring strengthen the positive core of the school culture, Level Four Fundamentalists who persist in active resistance become increasingly isolated. The prevailing positive dynamics make their stance less tenable, potentially leading them to detach as their negativity finds less traction.

Chapter 3 Tools

Providing a robust support system and mentoring for your Tweeners is a crucial investment in the future of your school and its culture. Again, you don't need to use this chapter's tools in a linear fashion, but we suggest starting with tool 3.1 (page 107) to gather data about your new teachers' experiences. Use the other tools as the leadership team members have a chance to review this data and share their perspectives.

Figure 3.3 (page 106) contains a summary of chapter 3's tools.

Tool Number	Title of Tool	Purpose
Tool 3.1	New Teacher Survey	Gather feedback from new teachers about their experiences, challenges, and support systems at the school.
Tool 3.2	Tweeners: Preparing for the Moment of Truth	Help Tweeners prepare for and reflect on the inevitable moment of truth by focusing on self-care, reflection, and ways to seek support within the social fabric of the school.
Tool 3.3	Tweeners: The Year Ahead	Help Tweeners proactively map out and prepare for the predictable highs and lows of their first year, aligning potential challenges with planned support.
Tool 3.4	Self-Reflection Guide for Our Current Mentoring System	Evaluate and enhance current new teacher mentoring practices by reflecting on key elements and comparing them to best practices.
Tool 3.5	Building Our Ideal Mentoring System	Collaboratively design a comprehensive, proactive, and supportive mentoring system tailored to the school's context, translating reflections from tool 3.4 into a concrete, yearlong plan.
Tool 3.6	Tweeners: Four Key Areas	Provide new staff and mentors with a self-assessment and reflection tool focused on four key areas of teaching (classroom layout, instruction preparation, classroom culture, and team expectations) with clear success criteria.

Figure 3.3: *Chapter 3 tools.*

Tool 3.1: New Teacher Survey

Purpose

Gather feedback from new teachers about their experiences, challenges, and support systems at the school.

Instructions

Anonymously administer this survey to new staff members (those who have been at the school for three years or less) and collect the data for discussion. You can distribute hard copies of the survey or input these questions into your electronic survey tool of choice.

Tips for Success

- **Ensure anonymity:** Clearly communicate how anonymity will be maintained to encourage honest responses.
- **Communicate the purpose:** Explain why the survey is being conducted and how the results will be used to improve support.
- **Act on feedback:** Schedule time for the guiding coalition or leadership team to review results promptly and develop concrete action steps. Share a summary of findings and planned actions with the staff.

page 1 of 4

Survey

1. How often do you feel supported in your role as a new teacher?

4	3	2	1
Frequently	Sometimes	Rarely	Never

2. How would you rate the effectiveness of the mentoring programs or support provided by the school?

4	3	2	1
Very effective	Somewhat effective	Minimally effective	Not effective

3. Do you agree that the school administration and your colleagues acknowledge your contributions and struggles?

4	3	2	1
Strongly agree	Agree	Disagree	Strongly disagree

4. Beyond just receiving suggestions and resources, do you agree that you are building meaningful and supportive professional relationships?

4	3	2	1
Strongly agree	Agree	Disagree	Strongly disagree

5. What challenges have you experienced as a new teacher? (Check all that apply.)
   - ☐ Classroom planning and preparation difficulties
   - ☐ Difficulty with instructional strategies
   - ☐ Behavior management issues
   - ☐ Lack of support from colleagues
   - ☐ Lack of support from administration
   - ☐ Feelings of isolation
   - ☐ Difficulty navigating school culture
   - ☐ Other: ____ (Please specify.)

6. Rank the following support elements from most helpful (1) to least helpful (4).
   - _____ Mentoring programs
   - _____ Collaborative planning time
   - _____ Administrative support
   - _____ Professional development opportunities

page 2 of 4

7. What types of support or recognition do you find most helpful or motivating?

8. What are some ways the school could better support new teachers, both professionally and personally?

Scoring

Calculate your scores for each category using the following chart.

Category	Questions	Score
Perceptions of Support: Mentoring	Add your scores for questions 1 and 2.	
Perceptions of Support: Belonging	Add your scores for questions 3 and 4.	
Sources of Challenges and Support	Analyze your chosen responses to question 5, and record your ranking of responses to question 6.	
Preferences for Support and Recognition	Identify themes in the open-ended responses to questions 7 and 8.	

Interpret your scores for each category.

Perceptions of Support Categories

- **Strong support systems (score of 7–8):** New teachers feel consistently supported and valued.
- **Mixed perceptions (score of 5–6):** Some support elements are effective, but others may be lacking.
- **Limited support (score of 3–4):** New teachers feel that support is infrequent or not very helpful.
- **Lack of support (score of 2):** There is an urgent need to improve support practices for new teachers.

Sources of Challenges and Support

- Analyze the highest frequency challenges and the most supportive resources.

Preferences for Support and Recognition

- Analyze the open-ended responses to identify specific suggestions and preferences.

page 3 of 4

Team Reflection and Discussion

As a team, discuss the aggregated results of the anonymous survey. Analyzing patterns in scores allows for the identification of trends in new teacher perceptions of support and challenges.

- What is working well?
- What areas need improvement?
- What changes can be made to better support and recognize new teachers?

Action Plan

Based on your reflection and discussion, develop an action plan.

- How should the school address the survey data?
- What specific changes need to be made to support new teachers?
- What is the first step to move in that direction?

Tool 3.2: Tweeners—Preparing for the Moment of Truth

Purpose

Help Tweeners prepare for and reflect on the inevitable moment of truth by focusing on self-care, reflection, and ways to seek support within the social fabric of the school.

Instructions

Have new staff come together as a small group. Either before the meeting or at the beginning of the meeting, they should independently complete part 1 to build their foundation of resilience. Have the group members share their answers to build a toolbox of personal strategies. Then, in the small group, use part 2 to talk through and plan how they *want* to respond when they are facing a critical challenge. Consider ideal actions for relaxing, pausing, confronting reality, and seeking support.

Tips for Success

- **Normalize the experience:** Openly discuss the moment-of-truth concept during orientation and mentoring sessions so Tweeners expect it and feel less isolated when it happens.
- **Integrate this tool with mentoring:** Encourage Tweeners to share reflections from this tool with their mentor to identify patterns or areas needing support.
- **Focus on proactive preparation:** Emphasize the following preparation section as a way to build resilience before the moment of truth hits.

Part 1: Proactive Preparation and Resilience Building

Regularly reflect on these areas to build your foundation.

- **Sleep and rest:** How are you prioritizing sufficient sleep? What routines help you wind down?

  Notes and strategies—

- **Hydration and nutrition:** Are you drinking enough water and eating regularly throughout the school day?

  Notes and strategies—

- **Reflection time:** Do you have dedicated time (even if it's brief) to reflect on your teaching day's highlights and challenges? When and how does this occur?

  Notes and strategies—

- **Boundaries:** How are you managing your workload and time? Are you setting realistic boundaries for leaving the building or checking your email?

  Notes and strategies—

- **Proactive seeking of support:** Do you regularly connect with your mentor or trusted colleagues, even when things are going well?

  Notes and strategies—

- **Professional learning:** Are you engaging with resources or learning opportunities that build your confidence and skills?

  Notes and strategies—

- **Mindfulness and stress management:** What practices do you use (or could you try) to manage stress (for example, deep breathing, short walks, or a mindfulness app)?

  Notes and strategies—

Part 2: Navigation of the Moment

When you feel overwhelmed or face a critical challenge, pause and consider these steps.

- **Relax and recognize:** What physical signs tell you you're stressed or overwhelmed? What immediate calming technique can you use (for example, take three deep breaths or briefly step away if possible)?

  In-the-moment action and thoughts—

- **Pause:** Can you create a brief pause before reacting? What's one clarifying question you can ask yourself or someone else?

  In-the-moment action and thoughts—

- **Confront the reality:** What is the actual situation, separate from your emotional reaction? What is within your control right now?

  In-the-moment action and thoughts—

- **Seek support:** Who is your go-to person (mentor, colleague, or leader) for this type of challenge? When and how can you reach out to them?

  In-the-moment action and thoughts—

Tool 3.3: Tweeners—The Year Ahead

Purpose

Help Tweeners proactively map out and prepare for the predictable highs and lows of their first year, aligning potential challenges with planned support.

Instructions

Collaboratively use this template with Tweeners and their mentors to anticipate needs throughout the year based on Ellen Moir's (1999) phases (anticipation, survival, disillusionment, rejuvenation, and reflection). Review pages 96–97. Identify their immediate needs and then brainstorm specific belonging and mentoring ideas for different phases or dates.

Tips for Success

- **Make it collaborative:** This tool is most effective when completed and periodically reviewed by the Tweener with their mentor.
- **Be specific:** Instead of general ideas, list concrete actions, resources, or check-in points for both belonging and mentoring support.
- **Revisit it regularly:** Treat this as a living document that does not need to be completed all at once. Review and adjust the plan every two months or as new needs arise.

page 1 of 2

Yearlong Plan for Support

Months	**Potential Tweener Focus and Needs** *Knowledge and skills needed*	**Key Mentor Actions and Support**	**Evidence of Competence and Growth** *How we will know*	**Additional Supports Needed**	**Celebrations and Recognition**
August–September					
October–November					
December–January					
February–April					
May–June					

page 2 of 2

Tool 3.4: Self-Reflection Guide for Our Current Mentoring System

Purpose

Evaluate and enhance current new teacher mentoring practices by reflecting on key elements and comparing them to best practices.

Instructions

In each part (proactive structure and planning, focus on instructional growth and professional relationships, and bridging of theory to practice through specific actions, like reflection, observation, feedback, and culture navigation), reflect on the current approach using the provided prompts. Compare current practices to the provided best practice summaries, and note ideas for improvement.

Tips for Success

- **Involve multiple perspectives:** Complete this reflection with input from administrators, mentors, and recent Tweeners for a more comprehensive view.
- **Be honest:** Encourage candid reflection on weaknesses as well as strengths.
- **Bridge reflection to action:** Use your ideas for improvement as direct input for planning with tool 3.5 (page 120). Don't let the reflections sit idle.

Part 1: Proactive Structure and Planning

<table>
<tr><td rowspan="3">Specific Actions:
How are structure and planning currently addressed in our new teacher mentoring?</td><td>Best Practice Summary:
Effective mentoring has a clear, proactive plan with defined roles, responsibilities, and focus areas throughout the year, often using a developmental guide. Strong leadership support for the mentoring team is crucial.</td></tr>
<tr><td>Current Practice:</td></tr>
<tr><td>Ideas for Improvement:
What steps can we take to move toward a more proactive and structured approach?</td></tr>
</table>

Part 2: Focus on Instructional Growth and Professional Relationships

Specific Actions: How are instructional growth and professional relationships emphasized in our mentoring?	**Best Practice Summary:** Mentoring prioritizes professional relationships that build trust and enhance teaching practice through collaborative analysis and a shared instructional language.
	Current Practice:
	Ideas for Improvement: How can we better prioritize instructional growth and strengthen professional relationships within our mentoring program?

Part 3: Bridging of Theory to Practice Through Specific Actions

Specific Actions: How are the following actions currently implemented in our mentoring?	**Best Practice Summary:** Effective mentoring bridges theory to practice by guiding self-reflection and goal setting, facilitating observation and discussion of effective teaching, connecting mentees with resources, providing specific and actionable feedback, and helping mentees navigate school culture.
Self-Reflection and Goal Setting	Mentors guide mentees to analyze their practice and collaboratively set goals.
	Current Practice:
	Ideas for Improvement: How can we strengthen implementation of these specific actions to better support new teachers?

page 2 of 4

<table>
<tr><td rowspan="3">Observation and Discussion</td><td>Mentors facilitate observations and structured debriefs.</td></tr>
<tr><td>Current Practice:</td></tr>
<tr><td>Ideas for Improvement:
How can we strengthen implementation of these specific actions to better support new teachers?</td></tr>
<tr><td rowspan="3">Resource Connection</td><td>Mentors link mentees to internal and external supports.</td></tr>
<tr><td>Current Practice:</td></tr>
<tr><td>Ideas for Improvement:
How can we strengthen implementation of these specific actions to better support new teachers?</td></tr>
</table>

page 3 of 4

Specific and Actionable Feedback	Feedback is concrete and behavior based, and it offers clear improvement strategies.
	Current Practice:
	Ideas for Improvement: How can we strengthen implementation of these specific actions to better support new teachers?
School Culture Navigation	Mentors help new teachers understand school norms and dynamics.
	Current Practice:
	Ideas for Improvement: How can we strengthen implementation of these specific actions to better support new teachers?

page 4 of 4

Tool 3.5: Building Our Ideal Mentoring System

Purpose

Collaboratively design a comprehensive, proactive, and supportive mentoring system tailored to the school's context, translating reflections from tool 3.4 (page 116) into a concrete, yearlong plan.

Instructions

Use the guiding questions (for Tweeners, mentors, and leadership) and the month-by-month plan to map out the ideal system. This should be accomplished with the guiding coalition and all mentors.

Tips for Success

- **Dedicate time:** Effective planning requires focused time. Schedule dedicated sessions for the guiding coalition or leadership team to work through this tool. Ideally, this is done before the school year begins, but if mentors need guidance, there is no better time than the present.
- **Review and refine:** Treat the resulting plan as a dynamic document. Schedule periodic reviews (for example, quarterly) to assess progress and make adjustments. This will make next year even better.
- **Do mentor training:** Because mentors bring different skills to the talk, making sure they get additional support is important. This extra training could be as intensive as outside professional development, or mentors could receive training from a master teacher in the building or simply read a suggested professional article or chapter.

Guiding Questions

Discuss and take notes on the team's answers to these questions. Use those answers to fill in the yearlong mentoring needs and training plan.

For Tweeners

- **Knowledge and skills:** What essential knowledge and skills (instruction, management, culture navigation, procedures, and so on) will our Tweeners need to acquire or refine each month?
- **Evidence of competence:** How will we (and our Tweeners) know if they are achieving competence in these skills? What will successful application look like?
- **Targeted support:** What specific supports (mentor actions, resources, or interventions) will we provide when our Tweeners need extra help or face predictable challenges?
- **Celebration and recognition:** How will we celebrate progress and acknowledge the hard work and success of our Tweeners throughout the year?

For Mentors and Leadership

- **Mentor selection and training:** What criteria will guide mentor selection? What initial and ongoing training will prepare mentors for effective coaching, feedback, and relationship building?
- **Mentor support and development:** How and when will we provide continuous support, resources, and development opportunities for mentors?
- **Leadership actions and culture:** What concrete actions will school leadership take to actively promote, provide resources for, monitor, and embed mentoring as a valued component of our school culture?

Yearlong Mentoring Needs and Training Plan

Months	Tweener Support Needed This Month	Mentor Development and Training Needed
August–September		
October–November		
December–January		
February–April		
May–June		

Tool 3.6: Tweeners—Four Key Areas

Purpose

Provide new staff and mentors with a self-assessment and reflection tool focused on four key areas of teaching (classroom layout, instruction preparation, classroom culture, and team expectations) with clear success criteria.

Instructions

New staff use this tool to reflect on their current practice in four key areas against the success criteria, rating themselves on a scale of 1 to 4 (1 = not yet implemented, 4 = exemplary). Mentors and Tweeners discuss the outcomes. This tool can be used multiple times over the span of a school year. It can be used for self-awareness, goal setting, and celebrations of growth.

Tips for Success

- **Set goals:** Encourage Tweeners to use this tool with their mentor to identify one or two specific areas of focus and set actionable goals.
- **Focus on growth, not judgment:** Frame this as a developmental tool, emphasizing making progress over achieving a perfect score. In fact, having a Tweener use this tool while visiting their mentor's room is a great way to spark important conversations.
- **Don't use all four key areas at once:** This is a big tool that covers multiple areas. The success criteria highlight that conversations about best practices and their level of implementation are key to this tool. Doing one section at a time allows mentors and Tweeners to have important conversations.

Classroom Layout				
Success Criteria	**1**	**2**	**3**	**4**
The classroom is arranged for success; it is neat, safe, well organized, inviting, and welcoming.				
Learning targets and goals are clear to students.				
Behavior standards are posted in the room.				
The teacher is constantly swapping what words are on the classroom walls: academic vocabulary, high-frequency words, words that are commonly misspelled in students' work, and so on.				
Student work that aligns with grade-level expectations is posted on the classroom walls as a teaching tool.				
Anchor charts, hint walls, student resources, and reminders in the room guide students during independent practice.				

page 1 of 3

Instruction Preparation				
Success Criteria	**1**	**2**	**3**	**4**
Lesson plans allow all students access to the grade-level priority standards and focus on getting all students to mastery of the priority standards.				
All staff understand the four Depth of Knowledge (DOK) levels: (1) recall, (2) skills and concepts, (3) strategic thinking, and (4) extended thinking.				
Assignments and tasks align with the DOK level of the grade-level priority standards.				
The teacher builds into all lessons an assessment process that consists of checks for understanding, classroom formative assessments, and team-created common formative assessments.				
Flex time is planned after every common formative assessment to give all students more time and support on the priority standards.				

Classroom Culture				
Positive Climate Success Criteria	**1**	**2**	**3**	**4**
The teacher creates a positive learning climate in the room as evidenced by interactions between the teacher and students.				
The teacher verbally and nonverbally encourages, supports, and motivates students.				
The teacher's tone of voice, nonverbal body language and gestures, and other behaviors reflect genuine care and respect for students.				
The teacher uses intentional strategies to establish strong relationships with students.				
The teacher uses nonverbal corrections, positive group corrections, and private conferences to demonstrate respect for students and provide the least invasive forms of intervention.				
The teacher never loses their cool, never demeans students, and doesn't use sarcasm.				
The teacher acknowledges and recognizes students' efforts.				
Norms and Procedures Success Criteria				
The teacher establishes class norms, routines, and procedures and provides precise directions to students.				
The teacher has a system to recognize students for following class norms.				

Teacher Passion Success Criteria				
Positive energy is evident in the classroom.				
There is clear evidence of teacher credibility.				
Commitment to High Expectations Success Criteria				
The teacher expects all students to participate and work hard and challenges all students to think critically.				
The teacher uses grade-level assignments and challenges so that all students can be successful.				

Team Expectations				
Success Criteria	**1**	**2**	**3**	**4**
The teacher participates in their collaborative team and shares collective responsibility for the learning of all students.				
During collaborative time, the teacher shares ideas with their colleagues and focuses on the issues that are most significant to improving student learning.				

Source: Adapted from Ryan, B. (2023). The brilliance in the building: Effecting change in urban schools with the PLC at Work process. *Solution Tree Press.*

CHAPTER 4

Removing the Walls of Isolation

THE CHAOTIC SYMPHONY OF Teal Elementary struck Mr. Terry the moment he walked through its doors. Students darted through hallways like errant musical notes following different rhythms, a stark contrast to the empty display boards that should have celebrated their work. Those blank spaces were missed opportunities for the kinds of celebrations that were needed in the building. Near the office, a small boy sat alone in a room, the stark label of "In-School Suspension" his only company. With each hushed, hurried conversation Mr. Terry had with a teacher, the picture solidified: This school was a ship without a rudder, adrift in a sea of academic neglect and disciplinary turmoil. The previous principal's legacy was one of disconnected staff passively listening to random professional development topics, never truly engaging with each other or the pressing needs of their students. There was no real school-improvement team or guiding coalition structure in the school.

A team, Mr. Terry thought. The word seemed to echo in the hallways. *That's what this place needs.*

His summer letter, outlining a new era of teacher collaboration and a guiding coalition to support needed changes, ignited a firestorm of back-channel text messages. These were veteran educators, many of whom had walked Teal's halls as students themselves. This was their school, and his proposed changes felt like an invasion. Once the school staff returned in late summer, whispers sharp and personal—classic defaming tactics—were hurled at Mr. Terry from many corners of the school. No one responded that they wanted to be part of this new guiding coalition.

At the first August staff meeting, Mr. Terry's vision for collaborative teams was met with a collective groan; a visible wave of eye rolls rippled across the library. "We already tried PLCs five years ago," someone grumbled from the back of the room. The Fundamentalists were making their presence known. This was a tactic they had successfully used before. Mr. Terry pressed on, explaining the system and assuring the staff that they would grow together.

The next day, a delegation marched into the central office. "Our prep time is personal!" they declared. A summons landed on Mr. Terry's new desk—first month, first major battle lost. The central office sided with the teachers; prep time remained sacrosanct.

Undeterred, Mr. Terry got creative. If prep time was off-limits, he'd find other minutes. University students were soon supervising recess, freeing up teachers. Schoolwide assemblies, minus the staff, carved out more precious collaborative slots. Problem solved? Not quite.

"Plan units together? Study curriculum? We've been teaching this way for twenty years!" A delegation trod the familiar path to the central office once more, another disrupting tactic. But this time, Mr. Terry changed tack. He didn't just present a mandate; he painted a picture of student success and shared ownership, connecting it with teachers' potential to achieve universal academic goals. He brought easy-to-use protocols to team meetings, sat with the teams, listened to them, and gently guided them. "This is about our students," he'd emphasize, "and you are the experts who will lead this."

Slowly, the frost began to thaw: a hesitant question about a shared student, a spark of an idea for a joint project. Then, conversations truly focused on student learning began to fill the meeting rooms. It wasn't instantaneous, but something magical began to bubble up. Test scores, once a source of dismay, began to climb. In just two years, Teal Elementary went from languishing at the bottom of district rankings in mathematics, writing, and reading to proudly standing among the top three. The hallways, once discordant, now buzzed with purposeful energy; student work was proudly displayed on every wall as a testament to collective efforts and a reason for authentic celebration. Teachers started coming to Mr. Terry and wanting to be part of the guiding coalition.

Mr. Terry's experience at Teal Elementary, where initial resistance to teacher collaboration nearly derailed his efforts, underscores a profound truth: Fostering a culture of collaboration is not just beneficial for schools; it is the most critical form of professional development. Both of us (Alex and Bo) have witnessed this firsthand. Initial pushback is rarely widespread but rather originates from a vocal few who fear the change to collaboration. It's tempting to view this resistance as a roadblock, but in reality, it is often a sign that vital changes are stirring.

The key lies in embracing the journey. Learning by doing is paramount, and the approach of getting started and refining practices along the way is far more effective than waiting for a perfect plan. Principals and guiding coalitions have an indispensable role in setting collaborative teams up for success; their guidance and support can transform initial hesitation into powerful momentum. In Mr. Terry's case, he had to implement collaborative teams on his own. Sadly, that is sometimes how you have to start to change a toxic school culture.

The challenge to implement collaborative teams should not be underestimated. Establishing and maintaining effective collaborative teams requires dedicated work and resilience. There will be hurdles, resistance, and moments when the effort feels daunting. However, the rewards are immense and make the struggles worthwhile. This chapter delves into why starting this process can be so challenging, illuminates the compelling reasons why abandoning the pursuit of collaborative teacher teams is not an option, and explores the common problems that arise and how to correct them.

Challenges of Collaboration

As we explored in chapter 1, a basic tenet of a thriving education ecosystem is a systematic and schoolwide focus on learning. However, achieving this collective focus requires dismantling the artificial walls of teacher isolation that often characterize traditional school structures. The persistent *egg crate model* attributed to Dan Lortie (1975), in which educators operate largely in silos and are disconnected from the collective wisdom and shared experiences of their colleagues, represents a significant structural impediment to sustained growth and meaningful improvement (Schleifer, Rinehart, & Yanisch, 2017). This isolation hinders the shared pursuit of universal academic goals, and it can also leave educators, particularly the Tweeners we discussed in chapter 3 (who are navigating their moment of truth), feeling unsupported and vulnerable during their critical early years. Without collaborative structures, the apprenticeship of observation often reigns, perpetuating outdated or ineffective practices simply because "that's how it's always been done."

The challenge of staffing schools with qualified educators, compounded by teacher resignations and a shrinking pipeline of new teachers, further underscores the need for supportive, collaborative environments. In the United States, one in eight K–12 teaching positions is staffed by a substitute or an adult who is not fully certified, and this number continues to rise (Learning Policy Institute, 2025). In such a climate, fostering a culture where teachers feel connected, valued, and empowered is not just beneficial but essential for the longevity and improvement of the public school system.

Researchers in the area of organizational psychology have long recognized the profound impact of structure on productivity and culture and highlighted the necessity of moving beyond models that inherently limit professional interaction and can inadvertently foster Fundamentalist perspectives (Archbald, 2016; DuFour et al., 2024; Johnson, 2016; Schleifer et al., 2017). As a teacher in a fully functional PLC at Levey Middle School, Alex felt the profound impact of an effective collaborative team on his teaching and success with students. We would opine that any teacher who has worked as part of such a team would greatly prefer the strengthening support and bonds that a collaborative team provides. You're not alone anymore!

It stands to reason, then, that teacher, school, and district leadership must deliberately cultivate environments where collaborative team meetings are not a peripheral activity but a non-negotiable priority of professional practice, directly supporting the mission, vision, and collective commitments established by the school community (Archbald, 2016; Savage, 2023; Schleifer et al., 2017; Wiley, 2024). Such intentional structuring signals a commitment to a culture of shared responsibility and continuous learning and recognizes that the complexities of contemporary education demand collective intellect and coordinated action to truly live the belief that all students can learn (Archbald, 2016; DuFour et al., 2024; Hierck, 2017; Kiral, 2025).

Because you're reading a book published by the company whose purpose has been developing the concept of the PLC process, you are probably no stranger to what that process expects of a collaborative team. What follows is an expedited explanation of the basic functions of a collaborative team.

The Essential Functions of Collaborative Teams

Within a high-functioning PLC, collaborative teams are the engine that drives improvement, relentlessly focusing on student learning through structured, ongoing work (DuFour et al., 2024). DuFour and colleagues (2024) define *collaborative teams* as teams that work "interdependently to achieve common goals for which members are mutually accountable" (pp. 18–19). They also state, "The best team structure for improving student achievement is simple: a team of teachers who teach the same course or grade level" (p. 69). If it seems we are heavy on travel metaphors when talking about collaborative teams, that is because they are all about movement: Collaborative teams are what move student achievement. Let's look at what these teams do within a school and how they benefit students, teachers, and the culture itself.

What Collaborative Teams Do

Collaborative teams must meet regularly to dig into student data, scrutinize instructional practices, and collectively tackle learning obstacles (DuFour et al., 2024). This isn't casual shoptalk; it's a disciplined cycle centered on clarifying learning targets that align with the school's universal academic goals, using common assessments to track student progress toward those targets, and collaboratively adjusting teaching based on the evidence gathered (DuFour et al., 2024). The core principle is to share ownership of the learning of every student the team serves (DuFour et al., 2024). More specifically, these teams typically undertake several key responsibilities.

- They maintain an unwavering focus on student learning as their fundamental purpose, ensuring every discussion and action directly aims to improve outcomes for all students (DuFour et al., 2024; Kramer, 2021).
- They operate collaboratively and interdependently, working together to reach common learning objectives and accepting collective accountability for the results their students achieve (DuFour et al., 2024; Kramer, 2021; McBride & Duncan-Davis, 2021).
- They commit to a continuous cycle of collective inquiry regarding their teaching methods, honestly assessing which strategies are effective and which need refinement based on student performance (DuFour et al., 2024). This provides a vital space for reflection that is especially important for supporting the growth of Tweeners.
- They develop and administer common formative and summative assessments to gain accurate insights into student understanding, which then inform timely instructional shifts (Bailey & Jakicic, 2017; DuFour et al., 2024).
- They analyze student data frequently, identifying learning trends and students requiring intervention or enrichment, gauging the impact of their instruction, and creating opportunities to celebrate growth (DuFour et al., 2024).
- They plan and implement instructional strategies as a team, share effective practices and resources, and often develop common lessons or units to provide coherent, high-quality learning experiences (DuFour et al., 2024).
- They establish and adhere to clear team norms and protocols for their meetings and collaborative work, ensuring efficiency, focus, and productive conversation (DuFour et al., 2024; York-Barr, Sommers, Ghere, & Montie, 2016).

- They consistently reflect on their collective impact on student achievement, making ongoing adjustments to their practice grounded in the evidence they collect (DeJesus, 2021; DuFour et al., 2024; Mertler & Charles, 2011).

To ensure that collaborative teams embody these essential functions and maximize their impact, it's crucial to periodically pause and reflect on current practices. Honing these collaborative processes is vital for both teacher growth and student success. "Tool 4.1: Survey—Analysis of Our Collaborative Practices" (page 146) provides a structured way to do just that. This tool features a survey and targeted reflection questions, which directly align with the preceding team responsibilities, to help your team gather perception data, identify strengths, pinpoint areas for improvement, and decide how to enhance your collective work the next time you meet.

Beneficial Outcomes of Collaborative Teams

The benefits accrued from well-devised teacher collaboration are multifaceted and deeply impactful, extending across individual practice, team effectiveness, and ultimately, student achievement. When educators engage in purposeful collaboration, moving beyond isolation toward collective efficacy, several positive outcomes usually materialize.

- The link between structured collaboration and student success isn't just theoretical; a rigorous evaluation of teachers' collaboration as part of the PLC process implemented in Arkansas schools found that within nineteen months, the program had a statistically significant positive impact on mathematics achievement test scores, equivalent to an effect size of 0.083 standard deviations ($p = 0.014$; Hanson et al., 2021). If we use John Hattie's (2023) widely recognized benchmark where 0.40 equals a standard year of growth, this translates to students gaining roughly two additional months of learning because their teachers collaborated properly as part of the PLC process. This study provides a direct link between a specific, structured model of collaboration and improved student outcomes (Hanson et al., 2021).
- Collaboration fosters shared expertise and innovation through the exchange of diverse ideas, strategies, and techniques, which allows teachers to tap into a richer pool of knowledge than individual practice affords (Archbald, 2016; DuFour et al., 2024; Hierck, 2017; Johnson, 2016; Wiley, 2024). This collective brainstorming can lead to more innovative and effective approaches to curriculum design, lesson planning, and assessment, directly supporting the school's universal academic goals (Archbald, 2016; DuFour et al., 2024).
- Instructional practice improves through dialogue, analysis of student work, and shared reflection, which allow teachers to gain valuable insights into their own practice and the impact of their instructional decisions (DuFour et al., 2024). This iterative process of inquiry and refinement, which is often missing in isolated settings, is a powerful driver of the continuous professional growth needed to support all learners (Archbald, 2016; Johnson, 2016; Schleifer et al., 2017; York-Barr et al., 2016).
- Understanding of student learning patterns, areas of need, and effective intervention strategies is enhanced as collaborative teams analyze student data

from multiple perspectives (Archbald, 2016; Kramer, 2021; Talbert, 2009). This shared analysis can inform targeted support and ensure that students' needs are not overlooked (Esqueda, 2024; Savage, 2023; Talbert, 2009).

- Through regular interaction and a shared purpose, a stronger professional community emerges, isolation is reduced, and stronger social ties among teachers are built, fostering the sense of belonging crucial for retaining Tweeners and empowering Believers (Archbald, 2016; Schleifer et al., 2017). This combats the pervasive issue of teacher isolation, which can lead to burnout, increase teachers' risk of becoming Survivors, and hinder the innovation and positive culture that we discussed building through celebration in chapter 2 (Archbald, 2016; DeJesus, 2021).
- Teachers' efficacy and empowerment increase when they feel supported by their colleagues and are actively involved in decision making related to curriculum and instruction. This empowerment and professional agency to impact student learning can translate into greater motivation and a stronger commitment to schoolwide goals, reflecting the positive energy of Believers (Archbald, 2016; Flanagan, Grift, Lipscombe, Sloper, & Wills, 2021; Gallagher & Thordarson, 2018; Johnson, 2016; Wiley, 2024).

These are outcomes that every school wants and needs, yet it is challenging for organizations to implement collaboration effectively. Why do so many well-intentioned efforts to establish and sustain effective PLCs and collaborative teams fall short of their potential? This is a question that resonates with educators across diverse contexts. If you've grappled with the frustrations of unproductive meetings, felt the resistance from Fundamentalists derail progress, or sensed that collaborative initiatives were merely performative rather than transformative, know that you are far from alone (Archbald, 2016; Johnson, 2016; Talbert, 2009; Wiley, 2024).

The Building or Rebuilding of Supportive Collaborative Teams

Our goal is to equip you with the insights necessary to build, rebuild, or refine supportive collaborative teams because the journey toward a truly collaborative school environment is rarely seamless. In the sections that follow, we delve into the complexities of building and maintaining thriving collaborative teams amid school culture dynamics. Specifically, we explore two overarching categories of challenges that frequently derail PLC and collaborative team initiatives: (1) systemic flaws and, yes, (2) adult drama.

Systemic Flaws and How to Correct Them

While the outlined responsibilities of a collaborative team within a PLC appear logical and indeed represent the ideal, the gap between theory and practice can be significant. All too often, collaborative teams break down due to systemic flaws embedded within the culture, structure, and leadership of schools. Understanding these breakdowns and, more importantly, identifying pathways to address them are paramount for schools to move beyond teacher isolation and cultivate genuine improvements in teaching and learning. If you are starting from scratch, these elements should frame what a collaborative team does: the right work and collaborative team goals.

 **Brilliant Voice From the Field** 

SARAH MARQUEZ

ELA Teacher, Ana Grace Academy of the Arts Middle School, Bloomfield, Connecticut

For the past few years, I have collaborated with a small team of ELA teachers to develop and refine the districtwide ELA curriculum for middle school. This has been one of the most impactful and important professional experiences of my career. The process allowed me to collaborate with colleagues across the district to ensure that our curriculum was rigorous, equitable, and aligned with standards, while also reflecting the needs of our students. Through editing, I was able to advocate for the inclusion of culturally responsive texts and intentional scaffolds to support diverse learners, ensuring that all students could access and engage with complex ideas. This work also deepened my understanding of vertical alignment, helping me see how skills build from one grade level to the next. Contributing to a districtwide curriculum was not only about creating materials but about shaping meaningful learning experiences that support both teachers and students. It reinforced my belief in the power of collaboration and my commitment to fostering equity and excellence in literacy instruction. (S. Marquez, personal communication, September–October 2025)

The Right Work

Collaborative teams need to be doing the *right work*, which means they contribute to the school's functioning as a PLC. DuFour and colleagues (2024) define a *PLC* as "an ongoing process in which educators work collaboratively in recurring cycles of collective inquiry and action research to achieve better results for the students they serve" (p. 14). The reason why staff move from isolation to collaboration is to do the work that improves student learning: planning, assessment, instruction, and data analysis. This creates more time and support for the goal of high-quality instruction in every classroom. The focus on the right work directly connects with your school's mission and vision by ensuring that collaborative time is purposefully spent on activities that bring those guiding statements to life.

Both of us suggest building the right work for collaborative teams on three main actions.

1. **Collaboratively plan the curriculum:** Staff members discuss and collaboratively select priority standards, unwrap the priority standards into learning targets, create learning scales, discuss and create success criteria, create and administer common formative assessments, analyze the data, and take action. They are continually assessing, collaborating, and taking action to support students. They ensure all students have access to a guaranteed and viable curriculum.
2. **Collaboratively improve instruction:** Teams relentlessly focus on ensuring all students receive high-quality instruction. The staff understand that the reason

for the collaboration is to improve instructional practices. The priority standards discussed in collaborative team meetings are broken down into proficiency scales. Teams meet to create instructional plans before each cycle of learning and visit other classrooms to further their own learning.

3. **Collaboratively create a plan to give all students more time and support:** Schools guarantee a block of time during the day to give students foundational support, enrichment, extension, behavioral support, and time for special education and other services. The teachers, in collaborative teams, create individual plans for all students based on their data, the kind of solid data that "Tool 1.6: Preparing the Presentation for Staff—Solid Data, Empirical Evidence" (page 45) covers. In an equitable environment, all students must have access to Tier 1 instruction focused on the priority standards. Schools must find ways to help students access grade-level priority standards without removing them from core instruction. They must also find ways to enrich and extend the learning for students who have mastered grade-level priority standards.

Brilliant Voice From the Field

PAUL GOLDBERG

Superintendent, East Prairie School District #73, Skokie, Illinois

In 2020, I brought the leadership team [at East Prairie School] together to commit to the right work, and student and staff outcomes changed. Teacher teams identified essential standards by course and grade level. Teachers were assigned to logical teams and provided with daily common planning time. Teams began creating common formative assessments aligned to each essential standard, and the master schedule was modified to ensure that every student received timely, targeted, and systematic intervention and extension each day. This commitment to teacher learning, which has enabled students to learn more, has resulted in twenty-point gains in student literacy proficiency on the state assessment, placing East Prairie among the top ten schools in Illinois. (P. Goldberg, personal communication, September–October 2025)

Many times, schools start with one cycle that includes one standard, assessment of that standard, collaboration, intervention, and reassessment. This cycle of collective inquiry grows when teams see the logical system developed to assist them. Bo's school frames this as the cycles of learning process. These cycles involve planning, teaching, assessing, and using the results to take action with a collaborative data team. Teachers collaborate to create common formative assessments that not only measure learning but also gauge whether teachers are teaching a guaranteed and viable curriculum. Teachers use the data from the assessments to reflect on their instructional practices and to create action plans for the students who didn't learn and for those who did. If your team needs to reflect on these practices, use "Tool 4.2: Cycles of Learning" (page 152) as a model to identify whether the team is focusing on the right work.

In an interesting parallel, both of us started as principals in districts without these elements in place. We learned about PLCs on our own by reading everything we could and attending PLC at Work® Institutes. The benefit of having staff do the right work was that students learned more, and at higher levels, than ever before.

 **Brilliant Voice From the Field** 

AMY MOORE

PLC Manager, Deer Valley Unified School District, Phoenix, Arizona

Deer Valley Unified School District in Phoenix, Arizona, is a large district serving forty-two schools. To provide fifth- to eighth-grade teachers who departmentalize with opportunities to collaborate by content area, the district established a unified, districtwide system of multi-school collaborative teams (MSCTs). These teams extend the principles of PLCs across campuses, addressing challenges that arise from teacher isolation and variations in standards implementation. By connecting educators who teach the same standards, MSCTs leverage the collaborative structure of PLCs to create a cohesive network focused on deepening understanding of what students must know and be able to do.

Additionally, MSCTs include administrators who form an administrator cohort—a collaborative team that works together to build on the successes demonstrated at each school and to collectively monitor progress across MSCTs.

This system at Deer Valley Unified School District unites leaders and singleton teachers around shared standards to foster collaboration across schools, reduce instructional variability, and improve student achievement. By creating a structure of unprecedented support, Deer Valley Unified School District not only strengthens professional practice but also enhances its ability to attract and retain high-quality educators committed to continuous improvement. (A. Moore, personal communication, September–October 2025)

Collaborative Team Goals

PLCs aim to improve teaching and learning through teacher collaboration. As you think about your collaborative teams, these are the three key goals.

1. **Plan:** Ensure a guaranteed and viable curriculum.
2. **Measure learning:** Create common formative assessments.
3. **Be results driven:** Take action with the data team process.

Once teams are engaged in the right work of collaboratively planning a guaranteed and viable curriculum and assessing the learning, they must ensure those plans translate into actual student learning. Our experience with collaborative teams has shown us that common planning and sharing of teaching content make sense to teachers, as does collaboratively building assessments. However, acting on that data seems to be the most challenging step to take.

The true magic happens when teams take collective action on that data. This is the goal of a collaborative team. They must grow each other to help be better for today and tomorrow. They have to plan intervention. Mike Mattos and colleagues (2025) state:

> *In a multitiered system of supports, all students have access to rigorous curriculum and effective initial teaching as part of their core instruction, and students are provided additional time and support to fill academic and behavior gaps based on each student's needs. (p. 3)*

Teams must expect to pause new instruction after every common formative assessment to reteach, review, and provide targeted enrichment. To do this effectively, teams need a clear, actionable protocol. Here are the steps teams can use in a data team process, adapted from *The Brilliance in the Building: Effecting Change in Urban Schools With the PLC at Work Process* (Ryan, 2023):

1. Greet team members and review outcomes and norms.
2. Review priority standards.
3. Chart the overall data.
4. Chart the learning target data (the percentage of students who reached mastery).
5. Indicate learning target strengths and needs; discuss learning targets the students mastered and the learning targets to review.
6. Create a plan of action for the students who did not learn and a plan for the students who learned, based on the assessment.

To ensure that these actions are robust and that collaborative teams are indeed documenting and acting on the right work, a guiding coalition or leadership team needs a way to evaluate their output and the overall health of each team. "Tool 4.3: The Right Work Artifact Review" (page 156) is designed for this purpose, assessing the documentation and artifacts that teams produce to ensure they are aligned with effective collaborative practices. It allows a team to identify systemic missteps and provides the best practice steps to fix those flaws.

Adult Drama and How to Prevent It

Building effective collaborative teams is not merely a matter of scheduling meetings or assigning roles; it requires navigating the complex terrain of adult interaction. Beyond the foundational structural impediments to effective collaboration, the function of collaborative teams is profoundly influenced by interpersonal dynamics, which, when negative, we call *adult drama.* Education literature champions collaboration as a cornerstone of professional growth and improved student outcomes, but the reality on the ground is often complicated by dynamics that, while perhaps not always intentionally malicious, certainly impede progress (DeJesus, 2021; Kramer, 2021; Talbert, 2009). The interpersonal friction and unproductive behaviors that emerge in group settings can be significant barriers to productive teamwork. Addressing these human dynamics is not an afterthought to the work of collaboration; it is central to transforming collaboration from a mandate to a genuinely effective engine for professional learning and improved student outcomes (Coder, 2024; DeJesus, 2021; Kanold, 2021; Savage, 2023).

Navigating these interpersonal complexities is as critical as managing the systems of collaboration because they will impede authentic collaborative practice. Failure to address these elements may lead to frustration or superficial engagement rather than genuine professional learning. Also, many of these behaviors can be hallmarks of Fundamentalist resistance. Figure 4.1 (page 138) presents common adult drama elements and the school culture players who are most likely to exhibit or be affected by the behaviors.

Recognize when you or a teammate is exhibiting these types of feelings. Effectively addressing these interpersonal barriers requires intentional facilitation, the building of relational capacity alongside technical process knowledge, and leadership that models trust, vulnerability, and constructive communication. Structures like clear agendas, established norms, and designated roles can support positive interactions, but they cannot replace the fundamental need to cultivate a space where these adult drama elements are acknowledged and navigated with professionalism and a shared commitment to the collective work (York-Barr et al., 2016; Young et al., 2023). Ignoring them ensures that a PLC remains an imposed program rather than a vibrant, effective learning culture. To address them, we recommend trust building and targeted protocols to promote collegiality.

Trust Building

A foundational challenge lies in the level of trust and psychological safety within the team (Ford, 2023). Without a climate in which individuals feel safe to be vulnerable, admit errors, or express disagreement, collaboration remains superficial (Talbert, 2009; York-Barr et al., 2016). Even experienced teachers may hesitate to ask for help or share struggles if they fear negative feedback, which can stem from a lack of trust among colleagues (DeJesus, 2021). When starting collaborative teams at your school—or, just as important, when beginning a school year—make sure you intentionally build trust within your school's collaborative teams (akin to how we suggested using soul stories in the introduction).

As you think about your school's teams, ponder some of the barriers to trust. Make sure honest feedback is welcome without fear of repercussions (DeJesus, 2021). Conversely, a team (like the kumbaya team mentioned in figure 4.1) can be hindered by pervasively avoiding necessary conflict or critical feedback in favor of maintaining superficial harmony (Van Soelen, 2021; York-Barr et al., 2016). While positive relationships are valuable, a team that is too "comfortable" and avoids difficult conversations about differing perspectives or practices may not be engaging in the rigorous dialogue essential for growth. Productive collaboration often requires navigating healthy friction and disagreement, pushing each other's thinking (York-Barr et al., 2016).

Common Element of Adult Drama	Description of the Issue	What Might Be Heard or Observed in a Meeting Context	Potential School Culture Player Connection
Walking on Eggshells (Lack of Trust)	• In this climate, educators do not feel safe sharing their vulnerabilities, struggles, or requests for help. They fear judgment, perceived incompetence, or retribution. • Trust and mutual respect are underdeveloped or fragile.	• Silence or hesitation when challenges are asked about • Statements like "I'm not sure how to approach this student's reading deficit, but I'll figure it out." • Avoidance of sharing actual difficulties • Superficial agreement without genuine vulnerability • Questions like "Are we sure this is a safe place to discuss sensitive student issues?"	It primarily affects Tweeners, who may fear judgment while developing their confidence, and Survivors, who may be hesitant to contribute for fear of judgment. A lack of trust can also frustrate Believers if it hinders productive collaboration.
The Minefield (Poorly Navigated Conflict)	• There are unavoidable disagreements and differing perspectives during substantive collaboration. • Conflict is not handled constructively, leading to tension, avoidance of difficult conversations, or unproductive personal clashes.	• Overt tension or awkward silence following a difference of opinion • Statements like "Well, I've never seen that approach work in my classroom." • Avoidance of challenging ideas or practices to maintain surface-level congeniality • Discussions that become circular or devolve into personal beliefs rather than progressing to problem solving	This is often instigated by Fundamentalists, who are resistant to change. It can make Tweeners hesitant to share ideas and cause Believers frustration if progress is stalled. Survivors may withdraw further.
The Silent Sabotage (Relational Aggression or Negativity) or the Steamroller (Dominating Personality)	• Behaviors of negativity, abrasiveness, manipulation, or bullying undermine colleagues or the collaborative process. • This can include individuals dominating conversations, dismissing others' contributions, or engaging in passive-aggressive behavior.	• Mumbled statements like "This is just another fad . . . a waste of time." • One person who consistently does most of the talking or drives the agenda despite team input • Team members who disengage or show frustration through their body language when one person dominates • Side conversations or a proper debriefing that occurs outside the meeting, excluding certain members	Steamroller behavior is often exhibited by Fundamentalists trying to maintain control or resist new initiatives. Silent sabotage can also be a tactic of Fundamentalists. These behaviors can disengage Tweeners, frustrate Believers, and further isolate Survivors.
My Classroom, My Castle (Resistance to Collaboration)	• This is rooted in a tradition of teacher autonomy and professional privacy. • It manifests as a preference for isolation, a reluctance to share practice, or a belief that independent work is more effective than collaborative efforts.	• Teachers who are physically present but disengaged (for example, glancing at their phones or looking away) • Statements like "I'm already doing this on my own," or "I have more important things to do than sit in meetings." • Teachers who make minimal contributions during discussions, hoping the initiative will go away • Resistance to sharing resources or opening classroom practice to colleagues	This is strongly characteristic of Fundamentalists using distraction tactics (the three Ds—defame, disrupt, and distract). It can also be seen in Survivors, who are overwhelmed and prefer to focus on their individual tasks. This mindset is contrary to the collaborative nature of Believers.

Lost in Translation (Unclear Purpose or Expectations)	• There is ambiguity regarding the specific goals, expected outcomes, or processes of collaborative work. • Meetings lack clear agendas or specific objectives for each item. • Confusion hinders productive effort and can lead to frustration.	• Questions like "What exactly are we supposed to accomplish by discussing this data?," "Are we making a decision on this today or just talking about it?," or "Who is responsible for following up on this?" • Teachers who leave feeling confused and lost about next steps • Discussion that jumps between unrelated topics without a clear thread or purpose	This can affect all players, but Tweeners may be particularly vulnerable due to their developing understanding of processes. Believers can become frustrated if the lack of clarity impedes meaningful work. Fundamentalists might use ambiguity to stall progress or discredit initiatives (disrupt).
Uneven Pull (Engagement and Accountability Gaps)	• There are disparities in commitment and participation levels among team members. • This includes a lack of accountability for attendance, punctuality, preparation, or contribution, leading to resentment among more engaged members. • Some members consistently contribute little, while others carry the weight.	• One or more team members who consistently arrive late or are absent • Lack of preparation, such as not bringing required materials or data • Statements like "I finished the common assessment myself since no one else had time." • Complaints made privately about colleagues' lack of contribution	Fundamentalists may disengage as a form of resistance, letting others do all the work only to complain about the product. This can frustrate Believers, who are committed to the work. This may negatively influence Tweeners by modeling poor collaborative habits.
The Kumbaya Trap (Avoidance of Difficult Issues)	• There is a focus on superficial congeniality, positive affirmations, or low-hanging fruit that prevents the team from engaging in the more challenging, messy work required to do deep professional learning and address critical student needs. • This can involve avoiding productive conflict.	• Meetings that start with good things but never progress to addressing significant student struggles or instructional challenges • Statements like "Let's just focus on the positive today." • Team members who quickly agree on easy topics and avoid anything that might require deeper analysis, data scrutiny, or potential disagreement • Superficial dialogue that doesn't push collective thinking	While seemingly positive, this can be a comfortable space for Survivors to avoid extra stress or a tactic by Fundamentalists to avoid substantive change. It can frustrate Believers who want to tackle real issues and prevent Tweeners from experiencing the rigorous dialogue needed for growth.

Source: Adapted from Archbald, 2016; DuFour et al., 2024; Flanagan et al., 2021; Ford, 2023; Kiral, 2025; McBride & Duncan-Davis, 2021; Muhammad, 2018; Savage, 2023; Schleifer et al., 2017; Toll, 2023; York-Barr et al., 2016; Young, Julien, & Osborne, 2023.

Figure 4.1: *Elements of adult drama.*

To develop trust, teams can use "Tool 4.4: Team Trust" (page 158) to independently decide how they want to grow. Team members will fill out the form and discuss how they are going to build trust; suggestions involve a team-based activity and reflection questions.

Alex's experience with his collaborative team at Levey Middle School made him a Believer and significantly contributed to his growth as a middle school teacher. It empowered him to support others and ultimately played a major role in student success. However, not all meetings and interactions were easy; in fact, most involved collegial arguments about what was best for students. That is what we want for your school. It is very important that collaborative teams effectively address these interpersonal barriers. Ignoring adult drama will ensure that collaborative teams remain an imposed program rather than a vibrant, effective learning culture for your school's teachers.

Protocols

What we call *tools* in this book can also be referred to as *protocols*. Protocols are tools that guide meetings. They aren't bureaucratic hurdles designed to make your life harder; fundamentally, they are processes for managing the inherently messy complexity of humans' interactions as they try to achieve something significant together (Flanagan et al., 2021). When team conversations risk devolving into unproductive patterns, whether through dominance, avoidance, or simply a lack of focus, structured protocols provide a necessary scaffolding (Flanagan et al., 2021).

Dialogue protocols also ensure equitable participation, especially for quiet individuals, by providing structured steps that discourage judgment and disrespect and fostering safe spaces for sharing challenging ideas, which are crucial for sensitive topics (Flanagan et al., 2021). Fidelity to these facilitated processes is vital because unmanaged dialogue can lead to problems like those identified in figure 4.1, which protocols aim to avoid. Beyond managing conversation flow, protocols elevate dialogue from superficial sharing to deeper professional inquiry and compelling evidence-based discussions for examining practice and solving problems (Flanagan et al., 2021).

Within the team structure itself, dysfunctional dynamics can take various forms. There can be unequal participation, with some individuals dominating discussions while others remain silent (Flanagan et al., 2021). Educators need to recognize that previous negative interactions and a downward spiral of interaction complicate how they get along as adults. It is almost like they force themselves to relive their past challenges. Teams that have had adult drama in the past need an extra layer of support.

Issues of accountability are also critical. When team members consistently miss meetings, fail to fulfill commitments, stay on their phones, or even distract conversations from the stated topics, they make effective teamwork impossible. Think of *distract* from the three Ds (see Barriers to a Focus on Learning in chapter 1, page 19). That is really about collective teacher efficacy. If a team says they are going to collaborate in a certain way, and a member breaks that norm, how do team members respond? That response is the most important step to avoid falling into a cycle of adult drama that will hinder the team's success.

Brilliant Voice From the Field

PATSY GRAY

Elementary Reading and Language Arts Facilitator, Campbell County School District #1, Gillette, Wyoming

When our school [Hillcrest Elementary School] made the commitment to create a culture where teachers felt valued, empowered, and focused on learning, we knew the work had to start with systems teachers helped create and could genuinely stand behind. To start, the leadership team built a unit-planning document around the four PLC questions, refined through teacher feedback to reflect real classroom work.

Once that foundation was in place, we turned our attention to how teams met and collaborated. Traditional principal- or coach-driven agendas weren't giving teachers ownership of their work, and we noticed the meetings falling flat, so again, we leveraged the leadership team and feedback from all staff to create the Data Reflection Protocol. This new structure gave teams a place to analyze student data, study effective teacher moves, plan interventions and enrichments together, and determine next steps in instruction.

Over time, the Data Reflection Protocol became more than a document. It became the powerhouse of our collaborative culture. Teachers left meetings with clarity, direction, and a sense of shared purpose. The most rewarding shift was the feeling of empowerment. They left knowing the work was theirs and not driven by others. (P. Gray, personal communication, September–October 2025)

Do your school's collaborative teams currently employ protocols? How do you take data on what team members discuss at your collaborative meetings? A guiding coalition needs a protocol for collaborative team meetings, so if you don't have one, build it. Use "Tool 4.5: Guiding Coalition's Collaborative Team Protocol Development" (page 160) to help your team blend best practices and avoid adult drama in your team meetings.

Building and maintaining trust is essential for a collaborative team. This is where protocols earn their keep. While they might initially feel rigid or unnatural, their power lies in providing a deliberate structure for dialogue (Flanagan et al., 2021). They ensure every voice has a defined space, counteracting dominance and creating equitable participation (Flanagan et al., 2021). They establish boundaries against disrespect and judgment, fostering the psychologically safe environment necessary for people to actually share their struggles and ask for help (Johnson, 2016). By providing this predictable, safe framework for interaction, protocols actively contribute to the trust needed for genuine vulnerability and deep collaborative inquiry to thrive.

Leaders, including the guiding coalition, play a crucial role in modeling this authenticity and addressing what is happening (and not happening) within the collaborative space. Pretending that collaboration is effective in all spaces when it is not is a recipe for failure; it will mean that the culture (including all the people within it) is willing to overlook what it has deemed essential. When what a school deems essential is not really essential, cynicism forms, and teachers often end up believing that reforming the system of isolation is a waste of time. Addressing these human dynamics is not peripheral to teamwork; it's key to making collaboration actually work for teacher learning and better student results.

Our friend and colleague Tom Hierck (2017) is 100 percent correct when he says that proper collaboration isn't just about carving out time. Positive relationship building and norms are equally important (Coder, 2024). The research is clear: If you want to develop a healthy school culture, you have to pay close attention to both the systems and group dynamics. And looking at group dynamics, let's revisit how collaborative teams impact the school culture players.

The School Culture Players

The journey from isolation to collaboration requires patience, persistence, and a clear understanding of the human dynamics at play. The presence of collaborative teams significantly impacts and is impacted by the various roles that individuals play within a school's culture. Understanding these interactions is key to fostering truly effective collaboration.

Empowering Believers

Believers are the natural collaborators, and collaboration among teachers can amplify their impact. When teacher conversations clearly and logically address students' learning, Believers thrive in team settings, readily share their expertise, and are eager to learn from colleagues. For Believers, collaborative teams provide a platform to spread their positive influence and model effective practices. These teachers are the ones who often initiate discussions, volunteer for roles, and push for student-focused outcomes. However, they can become frustrated if collaboration is unproductive or if other members are not equally committed. To keep Believers engaged, collaborative time must be structured, meaningful, and centered on improving student learning. They need to see that their contributions are valued and lead to tangible results.

Muhammad's (2018) original study found that in a team with significant adult drama, Believers shy away from changing Fundamentalists' minds and only speak out directly against the status quo, maintaining behavior in extreme circumstances. Every Believer reading this book needs to know how important their voice is to their collaborative team. Every leader and guiding coalition must push to make sure the Believers' voices are part of the conversation. Alex and his coauthor Charles Sheppard state, "Cultures become healthier when Believers' voices balance Fundamentalists' voices" (McNeece & Sheppard, 2025, p. 25). Ensure that your system of collaborative teams makes that happen.

Supporting Tweeners

As stated in chapter 3, a collaborative team can be a lifeline for Tweeners. These are the newer or more cautious educators who are still developing their professional identity and confidence. A well-functioning team provides a safe space for them to ask questions, observe experienced colleagues, and receive constructive feedback. The formal or informal mentorship that can blossom within a strong team is invaluable for Tweeners. However, if the team dynamic is dominated by negativity or a lack of clear focus, Tweeners will become hesitant to share ideas or admit they need support. They may even abandon the push to adopt strategies to increase success in the classroom.

Furthermore, a routine of poor collaboration will establish that prototype in Tweeners' minds. They are especially in danger of developing negative concepts of collaboration. Because teacher collaborative work is rarely witnessed by students (Lortie, 1975), Tweeners, whose firsthand experiences of the classroom consist mainly of their own time as students, are likely to enter the organization without that expectation for their job. Clear protocols, shared leadership opportunities, and a welcoming atmosphere are crucial to engage and nurture Tweeners within collaborative settings and to make sure your school's culture prevents cynicism about the collaborative work that is essential to all teachers' growth.

Flipping Fundamentalists

Fundamentalists' behavior can pose the most significant challenge to effective collaboration. Their resistance, stemming from a desire to maintain the status quo and a belief in their own isolated expertise, can manifest in various ways. In toxic cultures, Fundamentalist-driven collaborative team time can include all three Ds being used against the administration, students, parents, the community, the guiding coalition, or other teacher leaders. Fundamentalists might dominate conversations with negativity, subtly undermine new initiatives, or simply disengage. They might resist sharing data or strategies, viewing it as an intrusion or a challenge to their autonomy. For Fundamentalists, the shift to collaborative work often feels like a loss of control.

You can't let three D behaviors go unchecked. For example, a collaborative team meeting should never be used for defamation, such as a staff member talking about the principal's or a colleague's experience level and discrediting their accomplishments and knowledge. Using disruption, Fundamentalist members of the collaborative team can delay the implementation of policies or strategies that will force them to change, such as by trying to shift the work of the team to an eleventh-hour idea that will inevitably delay progress. Finally, don't allow collaborative team time to get bogged down in distraction or passive-aggressive behavior that Fundamentalists exhibit when they do not agree with or like the ideas, the initiative, or even the structure of the meeting. Sometimes, Fundamentalists will even defame the process of collaboration while collaborating, citing they should be allowed to work alone in their rooms. With that said, excellent collaborative structures can and will flip Fundamentalist thinking.

Level One (Need Clarity): Communicating the Research

For Level One Fundamentalists, leaders, including the guiding coalition, must be prepared to address resistance directly and also strategically. This involves clearly communicating the why behind collaboration, linking it directly to student outcomes, and providing evidence of its effectiveness. Have the research and rationale, much of which you will find in this chapter, ready to share. Consider the extra learning that principals and guiding coalitions will need to make this point; leaders must build their expertise so they can directly answer questions about the process.

Level Two (Need Trust): Supercharging Trust

Level Two Fundamentalists can sometimes be swayed by witnessing the positive impact that collaboration has on student learning or by seeing their peers genuinely benefit. This "supercharges" their trust in the process. Make sure to point out the successful outcomes from the work that collaborative teams accomplish. Full-staff meetings are an excellent time to highlight these successes. Share how one of the teams used the elements in this chapter to make a data-based difference in students' learning.

Level Three (Need Capacity or Skills): Supercharging Capacity Building

Level Three Fundamentalists benefit the most from structured collaboration and protocols, especially when the conversation covers the skills that educators need to add to their tool belts. Furthermore, protocols make expectations less abstract. Once team members see the goals of collaboration, the path to get there becomes much clearer, and resistance and worries about the how of collaboration ease. Again, consider staff meeting or professional learning time for some of the tools in this chapter to make sure that team members process how collaboration is different from just talking.

Level Four (Resistant to the Core Mission): Neutralizing Resistance

Level Four Fundamentalists who persistently and deliberately obstruct team collaboration, as discussed in the Adult Drama and How to Prevent It section (page 136), may require more direct intervention. How do leaders approach a Level Four Fundamentalist in the most ethical, supportive, and direct way? For those who steadfastly oppose collaboration, leadership must be firm, clearly stating expectations and the potential for close monitoring if these expectations are not met. Leaders may need to directly facilitate team meetings, always prioritizing what is best for students, which unequivocally is teacher collaboration.

If resistance still exists, consider the RESIST procedure, which can be found in chapter 5 of *Time for Change: Four Essential Skills for Transformational School and District Leaders* (Muhammad & Cruz, 2019). This is a helpful process for giving a Fundamentalist the last opportunity to evaluate their actions and see a different path. Your students and community need educators to collaborate properly, and by avoiding tough conversations and not acting, you will let them down.

Saving Survivors

These educators, who are often overwhelmed and focused on just getting through the day, may initially view collaboration as an additional burden. They might hesitate to contribute, fearing judgment or simply lacking the energy to engage deeply. Being so overwhelmed, they may even dismiss the entire collaborative process and remain silent during collaborative team meetings. However, effective collaboration can actually be a powerful support system for Survivors. By sharing the load, providing practical strategies, and fostering a sense of collective responsibility, teams can reduce the feelings of isolation and overwhelm that often define the Survivor experience. For collaboration to be effective with Survivors, it needs to be highly practical and emotionally supportive, and it must offer concrete solutions and resources that they can immediately implement in their classrooms. Celebrating small wins and acknowledging their efforts can also shift their perspective from merely surviving to actively participating and growing. This might be their only lifeline.

Chapter 4 Tools

Ultimately, a school culture that genuinely values and practices collaboration offers the best environment for all school culture players to thrive and contribute positively. It creates a space where Believers can lead and inspire, Tweeners can grow and develop, Fundamentalists can be challenged and potentially transformed, and Survivors can find support and hope for renewed purpose.

The journey of removing the walls of isolation is not a one-time event but rather an ongoing, committed process. It requires continuous effort to foster trust, establish effective collaborative practices, and address the inevitable challenges that arise from both systemic flaws and adult drama that can hinder progress. However, the transformative power of this journey, the shift from isolation to a culture of collaboration, is what is best for both the teachers and the students.

Figure 4.2 provides a breakdown of chapter 4's tools.

Tool Number	Title of Tool	Purpose
Tool 4.1	Survey: Analysis of Our Collaborative Practices	Provide a structured way for collaborative teams to gather perception data on their current practices, identify strengths, pinpoint areas for improvement, and collaboratively decide how to enhance their collective work.
Tool 4.2	Cycles of Learning	Have staff members participate in creating a guaranteed and viable curriculum, which will ensure that all students have access to the curriculum and the time to learn it.
Tool 4.3	The Right Work Artifact Review	Rate the current system as either meeting the standard or not meeting it yet.
Tool 4.4	Team Trust	Support collaborative teams in identifying factors that contribute to effective teamwork and addressing common challenges that can hinder trust and productivity.
Tool 4.5	Guiding Coalition's Collaborative Team Protocol Development	Support the guiding coalition in creating a collaborative team protocol that aligns teamwork with the school's vision and collective commitments. Emphasize effective collaboration to improve student learning.

Figure 4.2: *Chapter 4 tools.*

Tool 4.1: Survey—Analysis of Our Collaborative Practices

Purpose

Provide a structured way for collaborative teams to gather perception data on their current practices, identify strengths, pinpoint areas for improvement, and collaboratively decide how to enhance their collective work. This tool's survey and targeted reflection questions directly align with the key responsibilities of effective collaborative teams and encourage both celebration of successes and a focus on growth.

Instructions

Have all members of the collaborative team complete this survey anonymously. You can distribute hard copies of the survey or input these questions into your electronic survey tool of choice. Collect the data for discussion during a team meeting.

Survey

Rate your level of agreement with the following statements about your collaborative team's practices.

Focus on Student Learning

1. Our team maintains an unwavering focus on student learning as our fundamental purpose in all discussions and actions.

4	3	2	1
Strongly agree	Agree	Disagree	Strongly disagree

2. Every discussion and action our team undertakes directly aims to improve learning outcomes for all students we serve.

4	3	2	1
Strongly agree	Agree	Disagree	Strongly disagree

Collaboration and Interdependence

3. Our team operates collaboratively and interdependently, working together to reach common student learning objectives.

4	3	2	1
Strongly agree	Agree	Disagree	Strongly disagree

4. Our team accepts collective accountability for the learning results our students achieve.

4	3	2	1
Strongly agree	Agree	Disagree	Strongly disagree

Collective Inquiry and Reflection on Teaching

5. Our team commits to a continuous loop of collective inquiry regarding our teaching methods.

4	3	2	1
Strongly agree	Agree	Disagree	Strongly disagree

6. We honestly assess which instructional strategies are effective and which need refinement based on student performance, creating a vital space for reflection and growth.

4	3	2	1
Strongly agree	Agree	Disagree	Strongly disagree

Assessment Practices

7. Our team collaboratively develops and administers common formative assessments to gain accurate insights into student understanding, which then inform timely instructional shifts.

(4)	(3)	(2)	(1)
Strongly agree	Agree	Disagree	Strongly disagree

8. Our team collaboratively develops and administers common summative assessments to measure student learning and inform our practices.

(4)	(3)	(2)	(1)
Strongly agree	Agree	Disagree	Strongly disagree

Data Analysis and Celebration of Growth

9. Our team analyzes student data frequently and systematically, identifying learning trends and students requiring intervention or enrichment.

(4)	(3)	(2)	(1)
Strongly agree	Agree	Disagree	Strongly disagree

10. We use data analysis to gauge the impact of our instruction and to create opportunities to celebrate student growth.

(4)	(3)	(2)	(1)
Strongly agree	Agree	Disagree	Strongly disagree

Instructional Planning and Implementation

11. We plan and implement instructional strategies as a team, sharing effective practices and resources.

(4)	(3)	(2)	(1)
Strongly agree	Agree	Disagree	Strongly disagree

12. We often develop common lessons or units to provide a coherent, high-quality learning experience for all students.

(4)	(3)	(2)	(1)
Strongly agree	Agree	Disagree	Strongly disagree

Norms and Protocols

13. Our team has established and adheres to clear team norms and protocols for our meetings and collaborative work.

(4) Strongly agree (3) Agree (2) Disagree (1) Strongly disagree

14. These norms and protocols ensure our conversations are efficient, focused, and productive.

(4) Strongly agree (3) Agree (2) Disagree (1) Strongly disagree

Reflection on Impact and Continuous Adjustment

15. Our team consistently reflects on our collective impact on student achievement.

(4) Strongly agree (3) Agree (2) Disagree (1) Strongly disagree

16. We make ongoing adjustments to our practice grounded in the evidence of student learning that we collect.

(4) Strongly agree (3) Agree (2) Disagree (1) Strongly disagree

Scoring

Calculate your scores for each category using the following chart.

Category	Statements	Score
Focus on Student Learning	Add your scores for statements 1 and 2.	
Collaboration and Interdependence	Add your scores for statements 3 and 4.	
Collective Inquiry and Reflection on Teaching	Add your scores for statements 5 and 6.	
Assessment Practices	Add your scores for statements 7 and 8.	
Data Analysis and Celebration of Growth	Add your scores for statements 9 and 10.	
Instructional Planning and Implementation	Add your scores for statements 11 and 12.	
Norms and Protocols	Add your scores for statements 13 and 14.	
Reflection on Impact and Continuous Adjustment	Add your scores for statements 15 and 16.	

Interpret your scores for each category.

- **Strength (score of 7–8):** Your team demonstrates strong alignment and consistent implementation in this area. This is an area to celebrate and build on!
- **Developing area (score of 5–6):** Your team has a foundational understanding, but there are opportunities for growth and more consistent application. Identify what's working well and where targeted improvements can be made.
- **Area of focus (score of 3–4):** There are significant gaps in this area requiring focused attention and improvement efforts. Discuss them openly and plan for growth.
- **Critical need (score of 2):** This area requires urgent intervention and a dedicated plan for improvement. It's important to address this collaboratively and supportively.

Team Reflection and Discussion

As a team, discuss the aggregated results of the anonymous survey. Ensure the discussion is balanced, celebrating successes and constructively addressing areas for growth.

- Celebrate successes.
    - Which areas emerge as clear strengths for our team based on the data?
    - What specific practices or behaviors contribute to these strengths? Let's acknowledge and appreciate these.
    - How can we ensure we sustain and even build on these successful practices?
- Identify areas for improvement.
    - Which areas indicate a need for improvement or further development?
    - What are the potential reasons or challenges contributing to these gaps (for example, time, resources, clarity, and skills)?
    - Are there any surprising results or any areas where perceptions within the team differ significantly? Why might this be?
- Connect successes and areas for improvement to impact.
    - How do our identified strengths positively impact student learning and our team's effectiveness?
    - How might our areas for improvement be hindering student learning or our collective efficacy?

Action Plan

Based on your reflection and discussion, collaboratively develop a plan that both reinforces strengths and addresses areas for growth.

- Reinforce and celebrate.
    - What is one specific action we can take to celebrate or share a key strength identified by the team?

- Focus on growth.
    - On what one or two key areas will the team focus its improvement efforts?
    - For each focus area, what strategic and specific, measurable, attainable, results-oriented, and time-bound (SMART) goals and actionable steps can the team take?
    - Who will champion or take the lead on these actions?
    - What resources, training, or support (internal or external) might be needed to achieve these goals?
- Monitor and adjust.
    - What timeline will the team establish for implementing these actions?
    - How and when will the team revisit its progress on these goals?
    - How will we measure the impact of these changes on our team's collaborative practices and, most importantly, on student learning and growth?

Tool 4.2: Cycles of Learning

Purpose

Have staff members participate in creating a guaranteed and viable curriculum, which will ensure that all students have access to the curriculum and the time to learn it. The learning plan is for all certified teachers of all grade levels in the school: grade-level teams, subject-specific teams, and singleton teachers.

Instructions

Have staff members use the allotted time during the day to study and take notes on the curriculum, review priority standards, create proficiency scales, build mastery models of expected student work, develop a pacing guide, and design an instructional plan. Coaches can also use this tool to guide teachers and offer support.

Accountability Log		
Meeting Dates	**Location**	**Staff Present**

Curriculum Resources to Study

Priority Standards for the Cycle of Learning and Key Vocabulary Post the list of priority standards in the room and highlight the key vocabulary words.

page 1 of 4

Use this process for creating proficiency scales.

1. Write the learning target.
2. Include success criteria for mastery; include exemplars or mastery models of what good work looks like.
3. Determine vocabulary; teach vocabulary and prerequisite content.
4. Discuss thinking beyond mastery with examples of work that exceeds mastery.
5. Discuss scaffolds for each target and teaching tips.

<table>
<tr><th>Learning Target</th><th>Success Criteria</th><th>Approaching the Standard
Prerequisite skills and vocabulary of the standard</th><th>Exceeding the Standard
Thinking beyond mastery</th><th>Scaffolds for the Learning Target and Teaching Tips</th></tr>
<tr><td>1</td><td></td><td></td><td></td><td></td></tr>
<tr><td colspan="5">Mastery Model of the Learning Target</td></tr>
<tr><td>2</td><td></td><td></td><td></td><td></td></tr>
<tr><td colspan="5">Mastery Model of the Learning Target</td></tr>
<tr><td>3</td><td></td><td></td><td></td><td></td></tr>
<tr><td colspan="5">Mastery Model of the Learning Target</td></tr>
</table>

page 2 of 4

4				
Mastery Model of the Learning Target				

Pacing of the Cycle

Map out days or a period of time for teaching the standards, administering common formative assessments, and monitoring and reflecting on the data.

1. Study the curriculum, the district assessment calendar, and the overall district calendar.
2. Map out days for teaching specific standards and plan for measuring learning with common formative assessments.
3. List expected team meeting times during the day when you will align professional learning to plans. Review and create a learning cycle plan, create and administer common formative assessments, review and reflect on data, and create a data-driven action plan.
4. List when you are administering common formative assessments.

Focus:			Number of Days:	
Pacing of the cycle from ________________ to ________________				
Monday	**Tuesday**	**Wednesday**	**Thursday**	**Friday**

Instructional Plan
1. How will you ensure *all* students have access to grade-level assignments? 2. How will you plan the daily lessons in mathematics, arts, and literacy? 3. What specific strategies are you using to support student learning and engagement? 4. How will you plan small-group instruction and conferences for students who have not reached mastery?

Source: Adapted from Ryan, B. (2023). The brilliance in the building: Effecting change in urban schools with the PLC at Work process. *Solution Tree Press.*

Tool 4.3: The Right Work Artifact Review

Purpose

Rate the current system as either meeting the standard or not meeting it yet.

Instructions

Have staff members circle either *meeting the standard* or *not yet meeting the standard*. If they circle *meeting the standard*, then list some evidence from team meetings in the row labeled Evidence.

The Right Work: The Standard	Staff Rating	
Collaborative teams: Teachers work in collaborative teams and take collective responsibility for student learning, rather than working in isolation. Teams must work interdependently to achieve common goals for which all members are mutually accountable.	Meeting the standard	Not yet meeting the standard
Evidence:		
Planning of the guaranteed and viable curriculum: Teams establish and implement a guaranteed and viable curriculum, unit by unit, that ensures all students have access to the grade-level priority standards, regardless of their assigned teacher.	Meeting the standard	Not yet meeting the standard
Evidence:		
Instruction: Teams understand the purpose of collaboration is to help teachers become better by discussing, reflecting, sharing, accepting coaching, and creating products as a team to support classroom instruction.	Meeting the standard	Not yet meeting the standard
Evidence:		

page 1 of 2

Monitoring of learning: Teams monitor student learning through an assessment process that includes daily checks for understanding, formative assessments aligned to learning targets, and team-created common formative assessments.	Meeting the standard	Not yet meeting the standard
Evidence:		
Results-driven data system: Teams meet to analyze the results of team-created common formative assessments, reflect on and improve teacher practice, build collective efficacy, intervene, and enrich or extend student learning.	Meeting the standard	Not yet meeting the standard
Evidence:		
More time and support: Teams provide a systematic process to identify students who need intervention, more time and support, extension, and enrichment.	Meeting the standard	Not yet meeting the standard
Evidence:		

page 2 of 2

Tool 4.4: Team Trust

Purpose

Support collaborative teams in identifying factors that contribute to effective teamwork and addressing common challenges that can hinder trust and productivity.

Instructions

Use this tool during a dedicated team meeting or retreat. The team will work through a cycle of reflection and discussion culminating in the identification of specific actions to strengthen their collaboration.

Materials

- A copy of this tool for each team member
- Chart paper or a whiteboard
- Markers

Each team member should individually reflect on the following questions, jotting down their thoughts.

Part 1: Reflecting on Effective Teams (Fifteen Minutes)

Each team member should individually reflect on the following questions, jotting down their thoughts.

- **Ideal team:** Think of the most effective team you have ever been part of (it could be in any context, not just professional). What were the key characteristics and dynamics that made that team so effective? What made you trust that team?
- **Essential elements:** Based on that experience, what do you believe are the three to five most essential elements for a team to function at a high level of trust and effectiveness?
- **Current team strengths:** What are one or two strengths you currently observe in our team's dynamics? What helps you trust your teammates?
- **Current team challenges:** What is one challenge or area for improvement you currently perceive in our team's dynamics? What hinders trust?

Part 2: Analyzing Team Dynamics (Thirty Minutes)

Reflect as a team on the following prompts.

- Review the following common adult drama elements that can hinder team effectiveness.
    - Walking on eggshells (lack of trust)
    - The minefield (poorly navigated conflict)
    - The silent sabotage (relational aggression or negativity) or the steamroller (dominating personality)

- My classroom, my castle (resistance to collaboration)
- Lost in translation (unclear purpose or expectations)
- Uneven pull (engagement and accountability gaps)
- The kumbaya trap (avoidance of difficult issues)

- Allow team members to share any observations or experiences they have related to these elements within the team or in previous team settings. They can share these anonymously using a technology tool such as Google Forms if they prefer that.
- Focus on identifying any patterns and their impact on communication, trust, and productivity.
- Determine what the team can commit to doing to avoid these adult drama pitfalls.

Part 3: Defining Trust Norms (Thirty Minutes)

Work as a team on the following prompts.

- **Develop a collective definition:** On your chart paper or whiteboard, record how you define trust in a professional team setting. What behaviors foster trust, and what behaviors erode it?
- **Identify key actions:** Based on the discussion, collaboratively identify two or three specific, actionable steps the team will take to support the following.
    - Reinforce positive team dynamics.
    - Address the identified challenges.
    - Strengthen trust and effectiveness.

page 2 of 2

Tool 4.5: Guiding Coalition's Collaborative Team Protocol Development

Purpose

Support the guiding coalition in creating a collaborative team protocol that aligns teamwork with the school's vision and collective commitments. Emphasize effective collaboration to improve student learning.

Instructions

Have the guiding coalition use this tool to develop a collaborative team protocol outlining the essential functions of collaborative teams focused on impactful work for student outcomes. Develop that protocol in a separate document as you discuss the following parts.

Part 1: Foundation—Vision Statement and Collective Commitments

- How does the team's work directly support and advance our vision and commitments?
- Should our mission statement, vision statement, or collective commitments be on any part of this document?

Part 2: Roles of the Team Member and Organization

Organizational Considerations

- Frequency and duration of meetings
- Roles and responsibilities (for example, facilitator, notetaker, and timekeeper)
- Agenda format and process
- Team interaction norms (for example, active listening, respect, and participation)

Discussion

Will our protocol have areas for teams to input this information?

Part 3: Essential Functions of a Collaborative Team

Plan: Ensuring a Guaranteed and Viable Curriculum

- Collaboratively study the curriculum.
- Select priority standards.
- Develop learning targets and scales.
- Develop common assessments.
- Plan pacing.
- Use student data.
- Discuss grade-level assignments.
- Create instructional plans.

page 1 of 2

Discussion

- How do we help teams reflect on our expected collaboration norms as they begin a team meeting?
- How will we know that teams are effectively developing and using common formative assessments?
- How will we know that teams collaboratively study data and create plans to reflect on instruction and support student learning?
- How will we know that all voices are heard in team meetings? What question can we add to the end of discussions to prompt teammates who have not yet shared so that we consider their input?

Part 4: Review and Refinement

- Take your new tool to a group of teachers or to a staff meeting. Allow for feedback.
- Make sure your team protocol is not too cumbersome. Know that items can be added later in the process. Listen to the team's feedback.
- It is not ethical to ask for data without using that data. Determine how the guiding coalition will use the data to support teams.

CHAPTER 5

Providing Intensive Professional Development

AS THE TEACHERS ENTERED the school on the first day back from summer, the high school band, a little off-key but full of spirit, blasted a fight song that echoed off the lockers. The air in the main hall was thick with the scents of fresh coffee and pastries, a welcome-back gesture that never failed to soften the edges of summer's end. A teacher named Mrs. Farid nudged her colleague, Ms. Nichols, and smiled. "Smells like hope," she whispered. Ms. Nichols smiled back, clutching the glossy folder, crisp notebook, and new pen they'd each been handed at the door. Everything looked so well organized this year. Maybe this was the year it would all click.

In the auditorium, their principal, Mr. Hartel, stood at the podium, a silhouette against the bright glare of the projector screen. After a warm welcome and introductions of the new staff, he dived into the day's agenda. The first slide was titled Building Operations. He clicked through procedures: the new rotating lunch duty schedule, the updated protocol for signing in, and more. He even had Mrs. Gable, the office secretary, come to the front to demonstrate the new digital sign-in process, which felt too simple compared to the unnecessarily complex presentation.

Ms. Nichols glanced down at her folder. In bold, elegant script, the day's theme was declared: "Learning for All." A flicker of that hope Mrs. Farid had mentioned sparked in her chest.

Then came the keys.

"All right, folks, we're going to get your building fobs and room keys sorted," Mr. Hartel announced. What followed was a slow, methodical roll call. One by one, teachers shuffled down the aisles. Ten minutes passed. Then twenty. Ahead of Ms. Nichols, the familiar blue-and-white glow of a social media page shone from a colleague's laptop. Two rows up, another teacher scrolled through Amazon. A few others made quiet exits for the fourth or fifth time, phones pressed to their ears. By the time Ms. Nichols's name was called, nearly an hour had evaporated. Mr. Hartel, sensing the restlessness, finally dismissed them. "Take the next hour to work in your rooms before lunch."

The afternoon session started with a new set of faces at the front of the library. Mr. Hartel gestured vaguely toward them. "The district literacy team is here to share some thoughts on how to improve student engagement," he said before retreating to a seat in the back row, his attention quickly absorbed by his phone.

The lead presenter launched into a dense monologue on instructional practices, her voice a steady drone against the hum of the projector. Slides filled with impenetrable jargon clicked by, one after another. No questions were asked. No table discussions were prompted. No resources or tools were offered. Ms. Nichols's new notebook remained open on her lap, its pages still starkly, disappointingly blank.

She glanced back at Mr. Hartel. He wasn't on his phone anymore. He was just watching the presentation, his eyes glassy. It was the same look of weary compliance visible on the faces of her colleagues all morning. It reminded Ms. Nichols of some students' faces when she popped her head into a few of her colleagues' hour-long lectures. In that moment, Ms. Nichols felt there was something deeply and sadly ironic about the glaring disconnect between message and method.

Excellent professional development is widely recognized as a cornerstone of education improvement. We firmly share this perspective; however, we both agree that our field has not lived up to its promise, like in the preceding vignette. We believe effective professional development should yield significant positive impacts for students. Indeed, research indicates that when teachers engage in at least forty-nine hours of high-quality professional development annually, their students can demonstrate achievement gains of up to 21 percentile points (Guskey & Yoon, 2009; Rock, 2019). Despite this potential, the education field must confront some challenging realities regarding the functional impact of many professional development practices. Alarmingly, studies suggest the following.

- Only a small fraction of teachers, as low as 10 percent in one analysis, effectively transfer skills learned during training to their classroom practices (Cobbin, 2025; Gulamhussein, 2013).
- Traditional professional development programs of shorter durations (five to fourteen hours) have shown no statistically significant effect on student achievement (Joyce & Showers, 2002; Roche, 2021).
- Even when participants report finding training beneficial, observation data often reveals a lack of frequent implementation of the learned techniques (Partin-Dunn, 2020).

Early in his teaching career, before his time at Levey Middle School, Alex experienced a mind-numbing sit-and-get presentation; ironically, this presentation was also on student engagement, like in the story that opens this chapter. The delivery method starkly contrasted with the guidance offered, a common juxtaposition that leaves educators frustrated rather than inspired. To be clear, the critical question this chapter addresses is not whether professional development occurs but whether it grows teachers' practice, helps students learn at higher levels, and supports the growth of a healthy school culture. Professional development is not something to engage in merely for its own sake; instead, schools must treat those minutes like they are the most important of a school year.

Bo started his career as a graduate assistant football coach at Syracuse University. The number-one lesson he took from his experience was the relentless focus on teaching and learning that the coaches displayed on a daily basis. Coaches always shared and presented their learning with each other. Even after they won the Big East championship in 1996, the coaches were relentless in their learning in order to be the best they could possibly be. In our leadership roles, we both focused on ensuring professional development was both engaging and collaborative.

If the core purpose of professional development is to improve teaching and learning, and we firmly believe it is, then transformation is imperative. How, then, can you ensure professional learning experiences genuinely empower teachers, refine their practice, and ultimately enhance student outcomes? This chapter touches on the familiar disconnect that educators tend to experience with traditional professional development before exploring the two big ideas that research highlights as critical to change professional development culture: (1) understanding and development of teacher agency, which articulates why teachers' active roles and intrinsic motivation are paramount for meaningful growth, and (2) the architecture of transformative professional learning, which explores the how—the specific structures and design principles that bring agency-driven, effective professional development to life. Throughout, we will consider the multifaceted payoffs of professional development: positive effects on teacher well-being, student outcomes, and overall school culture, including its impact on all the school culture players. Our aim is to help you rebuild or reframe professional development within your school culture from a mere requirement to a vital, continuous investment in your most crucial educational asset: your teachers.

The Familiar Disconnect of Traditional Professional Development

Many educators and administrators have come to expect professional development to be largely irrelevant, disjointed, and planned in isolation (Cabeen, 2018; Sanfelippo & Sinanis, 2016). One-shot and decontextualized sit-and-get sessions rarely lead to lasting impact (Clark & Duggins, 2016; Sanfelippo & Sinanis, 2016). It's clear there is a profound disconnect inherent in the traditional system of professional development. Research consistently highlights a significant mismatch between common professional development practices and the actual pressing needs of teachers (Cabeen, 2018; Hose, 2022; Partin-Dunn, 2020; Rodman, 2019). Mandatory, one-size-fits-all sessions are frequently perceived as too broad, failing to address specific classroom challenges or rehashing familiar content (Barber, 2019; Hose, 2022). Staff absentee rates on designated professional development days can serve as indicators of this perception.

Even worse for school culture, Fundamentalists will use ineffective professional development to, unfortunately, strengthen their arguments against change. Conversely, well-designed professional development, as detailed in this chapter, can be instrumental in shifting

Fundamentalists' perspectives. Even Believers can become disenfranchised by professional development they perceive as disconnected from student needs, potentially leading them to prioritize other commitments (like doctor appointments) because they would prefer to miss the professional development day over a day when students are present. If you fail to commit to best practices, you risk a cycle of demotivation where educators increasingly question the value of such critical teacher learning activities (Cobbin, 2025; Hooper, 2025; Hose, 2022; McClusky, Goddard, & Yoon, 2021; Rock, 2019; Sanfelippo & Sinanis, 2016).

As you think about your school culture and professional development, consider using "Tool 5.1: Survey—Dissonance of Traditional Professional Development" (page 181). The feedback from this staff survey will help you see your teachers' perceptions and develop future learning experiences.

As we explore the shift toward more impactful professional development, it's important to recognize that the principles fostering true teacher empowerment are deeply interwoven with the design of effective learning experiences. You will notice significant shared ideas and some overlapping applications of concepts, as the why and how are not separate endeavors but rather two sides of the same coin in creating professional development that truly resonates and transforms practice.

With many educators dreading professional development days, now is the time to act. This chapter offers an essential mental model and tools to help you and your team experience fast wins as you work to develop a healthy school culture. To move beyond this failing paradigm, we turn to the foundational principle of teacher agency.

Development of Teacher Agency

Teacher agency refers to the active involvement and ownership that teachers take in their professional growth. Without this genuine investment, attempts to change practice are unlikely to be sustained (Hooper, 2025; Omare, 2021). We further define teacher agency as the capacity of teachers to act purposefully and constructively to direct their professional growth and contribute to that of their colleagues (Mieliwocki & Fatheree, 2019; Nicklas, 2025; Partin-Dunn, 2020). What does this mean for schools? There has to be an immediate shift from top-down mandates to a more bottom-up, teacher-centered approach, recognizing educators as active agents in their learning journey (Cabeen, 2018; Clark & Duggins, 2016; Hooper, 2025; Rodman, 2019; Sanfelippo & Sinanis, 2016). Their needs, existing knowledge, attitudes, and beliefs must be at the forefront of professional development planning (Cabeen, 2018; Clark & Duggins, 2016; Omare, 2021; Sanfelippo & Sinanis, 2016).

Teachers expect professional development to provide relevant knowledge for professional growth, an expectation that frequently is unmet. This inefficiency breeds dissatisfaction. It's possible to invest significantly in research-backed materials and still fail to see student gains if the accompanying professional development and implementation support are lacking (Hall, 2018). And, again, this cycle of ineffectual professional development leads educators to question its value (Hooper, 2025).

Effective professional development requires leaders to attend critically to the quality of the experience (Hose, 2022; McClusky et al., 2021; Partin-Dunn, 2020). Teachers are professionals who are capable of guiding their own growth, especially to meet the goals we discussed in chapter 1 (Clark & Duggins, 2016; Nicklas, 2025; Omare, 2021). Allowing them an authentic voice in planning and executing their professional learning is key to its success (Cabeen, 2018; Clark & Duggins, 2016; Rodman, 2019; Sanfelippo & Sinanis, 2016). A stronger professional identity, their sense of "Who am I?" and "Who do I want to be?" as an educator, makes them more likely to engage purposefully in their own development (Pi, Ma, Hu, & Wang, 2024). The following sections discuss a nuts-and-bolts approach to agency, how to create the conditions for agency, and the professional impact of agency.

A Nuts-and-Bolts Approach to Agency

How do principals, guiding coalition members, and other teacher leaders foster agency in practice? Consider the following concrete actions: Operationalize voice, choice, and personalization; systematize empowerment through goal setting and reflection; and build robust collaborative structures for shared inquiry.

Operationalize Voice, Choice, and Personalization

Teachers overwhelmingly prefer having more say in selecting professional development activities (Hose, 2022; Nicklas, 2025; Partin-Dunn, 2020; Sanfelippo & Sinanis, 2016). Actionable steps for leaders include the following.

- **Conduct needs assessments:** Regularly survey teachers and analyze student data with them to identify perceived needs and interests for professional growth; use this data to inform professional development offerings (Cabeen, 2018; Clark & Duggins, 2016; Sanfelippo & Sinanis, 2016). Tools like Google Forms can be effective for this (Clark & Duggins, 2016).
- **Offer a menu of professional development options:** Provide a variety of learning opportunities (such as workshops, book studies, action research, peer observations, online courses, education camps, make-and-take sessions, flipped meetings, and concurrent sessions) from which teachers can choose (Cabeen, 2018; Clark & Duggins, 2016; Hall, 2018; Rodman, 2019; Sanfelippo & Sinanis, 2016).
- **Support teacher-proposed professional development:** Create pathways for teachers or teams to propose and lead professional development based on their expertise and identified needs, providing resources and support (Cabeen, 2018; Clark & Duggins, 2016).
- **Provide flexible formats and pacing:** Offer professional development in various formats (in person, blended, and online asynchronous) and allow for flexible pacing, recognizing different adult learner schedules and preferences (Hall, 2018; Nicklas, 2025). For example, offer make-up sessions for scheduling conflicts (Clark & Duggins, 2016). That is a very important point; if a teacher misses a professional development training, why is there rarely another opportunity to learn the content?

Autonomy leads to perceptions of greater relevance and timeliness (Hose, 2022). As Shawn Clark and Abbey Duggins (2016) observe in their book *Using Quality Feedback to Guide Professional Learning*, surveying teachers demonstrates that their feedback is valued and used to adjust professional development plans. This intrinsic motivation makes professional development less likely to be seen as one more thing (Hose, 2022).

Systematize Empowerment Through Goal Setting and Reflection

Agency is fueled when teachers set their own developmental goals and reflect deeply on their practice (Clark & Duggins, 2016; Mieliwocki & Fatheree, 2019). Actionable steps for leaders include the following.

- **Facilitate individual goal setting:** Implement a structured yet flexible process for teachers to set meaningful, student-focused professional growth goals that are aligned with schoolwide priorities but personalized.
- **Embed reflective practices:** Integrate regular opportunities for individual and collaborative reflection. Have teachers use tools like Socrative (www.socrative.com) to reflect on professional development (Clark & Duggins, 2016). Even better, respond in the moment to real-world activities using AI tools. For example, have teachers write reflective exit tickets on sticky notes during a break in a professional development training; they can post these exit tickets on the door as they leave. Then take a photo of those reflections, upload it to an AI chatbot (such as Gemini, ChatGPT, or Claude), and instruct the chatbot to compose a short summary or letter that communicates the staff zeitgeist at that moment and staff's needs moving forward. Share that feedback with the teachers when they return from the break, or take the feedback to a later meeting where you're planning the next step of professional development.
- **Coach peers for goal attainment:** Train teacher leaders or establish peer-coaching partnerships focused on supporting colleagues in achieving goals and reflecting on progress.

These measures move professional development from passive reception to active knowledge construction, allowing teachers to connect learning to their practice and colleagues' growth (Mieliwocki & Fatheree, 2019). Teachers often find such reflective engagements very rewarding (Clark & Duggins, 2016).

Build Robust Collaborative Structures for Shared Inquiry

Collaboration is a key component of agency building and effective professional learning (Clark & Duggins, 2016; Hooper, 2025; Mieliwocki & Fatheree, 2019; Partin-Dunn, 2020; Roche, 2021; Sanfelippo & Sinanis, 2016). Networks of relationships are where learning takes place (Hall, 2018). Actionable steps for leaders include the following.

- **Establish effective collaborative teams:** As detailed in chapter 4, the PLC process provides the best professional development and ensures the continued impact of other professional development activities.

- **Support teacher-led action research:** Provide frameworks, resources, and time for teacher teams to engage in collaborative action research on problems they identify (Hooper, 2025). For example, a group of mathematics teachers who are concerned about student performance on problem-solving tasks can initiate their own action research; they collectively identify the problem, research approaches, implement and test strategies, and share findings.
- **Facilitate cross-grade and department collaboration:** Create opportunities for teachers from different areas to collaborate on shared challenges or initiatives (Cabeen, 2018; Clark & Duggins, 2016).

Working together deepens understanding, supports risk taking, enables shared problem solving, and allows learning from diverse perspectives (Hooper, 2025; Hose, 2022). When teachers learn from each other, their research and experiences can effect systemwide change (Sanfelippo & Sinanis, 2016). Make-and-take sessions, in which teachers create something they can immediately use in their classrooms, are successful because they offer collaboration opportunities (Cabeen, 2018).

Conditions for Agency

For teacher agency to flourish, certain conditions are necessary.

- **Leadership and support:** Principals and guiding coalition members must foster trust (Clark & Duggins, 2016; Hall, 2018), distribute leadership (for example, empowering teacher leaders to facilitate professional development; Briese, Dirkx, Mueting, & Wiemers, 2016; Cabeen, 2018; Clark & Duggins, 2016; Roche, 2021), and provide necessary time, resources, and structures for teacher-led learning (Hooper, 2025; Hose, 2022; Mieliwocki & Fatheree, 2019; Nicklas, 2025). This includes championing a supportive culture that encourages risk taking and views occasional failure as part of learning (Cabeen, 2018; Hose, 2022; Nicklas, 2025). Perceived social support also plays a role (Pi et al., 2024).
- **Quality and coherence:** Chosen professional development experiences must be high quality and research based, and they must involve opportunities for practical application, observation, assessment, and reflection (McClusky et al., 2021; Partin-Dunn, 2020). Professional development must be coherent and align with existing practices, professional beliefs, and schoolwide goals (like those discussed in chapter 1), rather than introducing fragmented initiatives (Clark & Duggins, 2016; Hose, 2022; Omare, 2021; Partin-Dunn, 2020). Systemwide change, such as for a multitiered system of supports, cannot be pieced together haphazardly (Hall, 2018). Teachers need clear and articulated learning paths for large implementations. Those plans for research-based reforms require attention to subtle details, not just superficial understanding (Partin-Dunn, 2020).
- **Sustained and embedded learning:** Agency is nurtured through sustained, ongoing, and intensive professional development, not isolated workshops (Hose, 2022; Partin-Dunn, 2020; Rodman, 2019). Job-embedded professional learning,

with ongoing opportunities to try new strategies with consistent support and feedback, is particularly effective (Darling-Hammond, Hyler, & Gardner, 2017; Hooper, 2025). This includes one-on-one postobservation conferences, feedback on assessments (Clark & Duggins, 2016), or collaborative scoring (Briese et al., 2016). Professional development in the presence of students, such as through model classrooms, is highly contextualized and impactful (Roche, 2021).

Are you interested in having your guiding coalition reflect on these different elements that build teacher agency? "Tool 5.2: Guiding Coalition Teacher Agency Reflection" (page 186) can assist you.

Agency's Professional Impact

Leaders must ensure that the organizational culture focuses on agency in the experiences and activities they develop to meet the school's goals. With that said, professional development is not just about what the principal or guiding coalition puts together. Teachers' personal motivation, developed in the ways that they see are needed, is critical.

As discussed in chapter 3, the high attrition rates for Tweeners reflect the urgency of providing meaningful, agency-driven support from the outset. New and preservice teachers may need more intense, scaffolded professional development to build efficacy and agency (Partin-Dunn, 2020). Effective professional development that fosters agency is key to retaining, supporting, and growing all teachers (Clark & Duggins, 2016; Hooper, 2025; Pi et al., 2024).

Experienced teachers also need their agency reinforced. Even Believers who are *positive focusers* (that is, they have a positive disposition for new programs to support students) need support to become *continuing renewal professionals* (that is, they constantly seek new information to help them achieve their positive focus; Muhammad, 2025; Snyder, 2017). This means it is paramount to put systems in place to consistently identify and meet teachers' needs (McClusky et al., 2021). By listening to teachers' perceptions of professional development, administrators and guiding coalitions can adjust practices to improve classroom impact and student outcomes (Hose, 2022; Partin-Dunn, 2020).

Consider Ms. Jensen, a fictional third-year teacher (a Tweener) who often felt overwhelmed by managing her classroom and differentiating instruction for her diverse learners. Her self-efficacy was wavering. However, her district began offering professional development with more teacher agency. Ms. Jensen chose a cohort focused on project-based learning that included active workshops, peer observations, and collaborative planning time. She was able to design a unit relevant to her students' interests, try new grouping strategies with support from a coach, and reflect on her practice with colleagues. This mastery experience significantly boosted her confidence. She saw her students become more engaged and started to identify as an educator who could successfully implement innovative practices. Her newfound self-efficacy made her more resilient when facing challenges and eager to participate in further professional development, illustrating a positive feedback loop.

Consider the different experience a Tweener would have in the professional development session from this chapter's opening vignette. Which would you want for your school or district?

Embracing their professional identity strengthens a teacher's self-efficacy, or their belief in their ability to positively impact student learning (Marcolini, 2022; Mavi, Tuti, & Ozdemir, 2025; Pi et al., 2024). High-quality, teacher-driven professional development with active learning provides mastery experiences that boost self-efficacy (Marcolini, 2022; McClusky et al., 2021), and high self-efficacy drives further professional development (Pi et al., 2024). Teachers with agency and self-efficacy become more open to new ideas, more willing to attempt innovative techniques, and more resilient (Marcolini, 2022; Omare, 2021; Pi et al., 2024). This enhanced self-efficacy, coupled with academic optimism (Mavi et al., 2025), creates a positive feedback loop. Excellent teachers are not born; they are developed. While some experienced teachers may initially resist new methods that leaders tell them to use, providing tailored, relevant, coherent support that respects their professionalism and empowers their agency remains crucial for every educator (Cabeen, 2018).

Consider the kind of professional growth you want for all your colleagues, new and experienced. You may use "Tool 5.3: My Professional Growth and Efficacy Plan" (page 193) for this purpose. This tool is multidimensional. First, it grounds professional growth in the individual teacher's professional identity, asking them to reflect on personal successes and aspirations before choosing a goal. This ensures the process is driven by them, for them. Second, it is intentionally designed to create a mastery experience by having them plan a specific, achievable learning cycle. This process of trying something new with support and seeing its impact is proven to build self-efficacy (Muhammad, 2025). Third, when the teacher comes back to part 3 of the tool at a later time, it helps establish a positive feedback loop for continuous improvement. By reflecting on the impact of their actions, they not only see the tangible results but also build the resilience necessary to tackle future challenges, making professional development an energizing and sustainable part of their career. In addition to growing teachers' professional self-concept, this tool provides principals, guiding coalitions, coaches, and collaborative teams with data on what they can do to help their fellow educators grow.

Andragogy and the Architecture of Transformative Professional Learning

How can you build professional development experiences that develop teachers' agency and make a difference in your school? To truly transform professional development into a powerful engine for school improvement, schools must adopt a coherent architecture for learning. This architecture is built on a simple, research-backed foundation: treating teachers as the adult learners they are.

The art and science of adult learning, or *andragogy*, provides the blueprint. When you are designing a professional development experience, six principles are key for your adult learners (Hooper, 2025; Knowles, 1980; Nicklas, 2025).

1. **The need to know:** Professional development must clearly articulate the why. Active learning tasks that solve real problems naturally address this.
2. **The learner's self-concept:** Teachers require self-direction. Differentiated and personalized approaches, which offer voice and choice, respect this.

3. **The role of the learner's experience:** Teachers bring with them vast experience. Active learning and collaborative structures should leverage this rich resource.
4. **Readiness to learn:** Adults are most ready to learn what is immediately relevant. Professional development focused on practical applications to current classroom challenges meets this need.
5. **Orientation to learning:** Adults are generally problem centered. Professional development should focus on solving authentic classroom problems and improving practice.
6. **Motivation:** Intrinsic motivators like the desire to improve and achieve mastery are powerful. Active and relevant professional development that allows for success can tap into these motivators.

As leaders and designers of professional learning, we must constantly ask, "How does this approach honor our teachers as adult learners?" (Clark & Duggins, 2016; Hooper, 2025; Nicklas, 2025; Roche, 2021). As you read about the six principles in this section, hopefully you will see that we have framed many of our chapters with the same principles. Let's build the architecture of transformative professional learning, one principle at a time.

Principle 1: The Need to Know (the Why)

Adult learners are pragmatic. Before they invest their time and energy, they must understand the purpose of the learning and see a direct line between the content and their professional responsibilities. The most common failing of traditional professional development is its inability to answer the simple question "Why should I do this?" Effective professional development architecture begins by making the why clear, compelling, and connected to the realities of the classroom. Here are some points to consider when designing professional development for the why.

- **Frame learning around authentic problems:** The most effective way to establish the why is to ground professional development in the real pressing challenges teachers face. Instead of starting with a new initiative, start with a problem of practice identified by the staff. This could be anything from improving reading fluency in third grade to increasing engagement in high school physics. When professional development is positioned as a collaborative effort to solve a shared problem, the need to know is self-evident (Hooper, 2025; Partin-Dunn, 2020). This is why we open each chapter with a short vignette that highlights a school culture issue; we know if our readers have experienced a similar event, they are far more likely to open their minds to the content of the chapter.
- **Use data to tell the story:** Move beyond anecdotes by engaging teachers in analysis of student work samples or schoolwide data. Every survey in this book was developed to help you do this. When teachers themselves identify trends and learning gaps, they build shared understanding of the problems and become intrinsically motivated to find solutions. This active data analysis makes the why both personal and undeniable (Hooper, 2025).

- **Model the impact:** Don't just tell teachers a new strategy is effective; show them. Use video case studies, live demonstrations with students, or master teachers' modeling of lessons. Seeing a strategy in action provides concrete proof of its value and creates a powerful, tangible reason for learning (Marcolini, 2022; Rodman, 2019).

Principle 2: The Learner's Self-Concept (the Who)

Adults see themselves as self-directed individuals. They enter a learning environment with a sense of ownership over their choices and a desire to be seen as capable professionals. When professional development ignores this, imposing a one-size-fits-all agenda, it creates resistance and disengagement. Transformative professional development architecture respects the teacher's self-concept by building in autonomy, voice, and choice. Consider these points for designing professional development for self-direction.

- **Operationalize voice and choice:** The most direct way to honor teacher autonomy is to offer choices. These can range from "un-conference"-style professional development days, where teachers set the agenda, to a menu of concurrent sessions based on interest or need (Cabeen, 2018; Rodman, 2019). Using preassessment surveys to gauge needs and interests is a critical first step in designing relevant options (Clark & Duggins, 2016; Hooper, 2025).
- **Create personalized pathways:** Just as teachers differentiate for students, leaders must do so for teachers. Acknowledge that educators have different starting points, skill levels, and goals. Structure professional development with tiered activities or different pathways—one for beginners exploring a concept and another for advanced practitioners seeking to refine their techniques. This practice respects existing expertise and ensures everyone is appropriately challenged (Briese et al., 2016; Nicklas, 2025). In this book, we asked that you first go to the chapter on the element of greatest need for you. This might actually be the first chapter you are reading!
- **Empower teacher leadership:** True respect for teachers' self-concept involves seeing them not just as learners but as leaders. Create genuine opportunities for teachers to propose, design, and facilitate professional development for their colleagues. These tap into the immense talent within your school walls and foster a culture where expertise is shared and valued (Cabeen, 2018; Sanfelippo & Sinanis, 2016).

Principle 3: The Role of Experience (the What)

Adults do not arrive as blank slates. Teachers bring all their successes, failures, and deep contextual knowledge to every professional development. This rich reservoir of experience serves as a critical resource for learning. Ignoring this experience is a colossal waste of intellectual capital. Effective professional development architecture is designed to deliberately tap into and leverage the collective wisdom of the staff. The following points explore designing professional development for experience.

- **Make peer-to-peer learning the norm:** The most valuable expertise in a school often resides in its classrooms. Build structures that allow teachers to learn from each other. Instructional rounds, nonevaluative peer observations, and lesson study protocols provide a framework for teachers to see different practices in action and discuss instruction with colleagues (Roche, 2021). Just as this book has tools that create opportunities for peer discussion, every professional development you design must have collaboration.

Brilliant Voice From the Field

SARAH MARQUEZ

ELA Teacher, Ana Grace Academy of the Arts Middle School, Bloomfield, Connecticut

Instructional rounds allowed me and new staff members to observe classroom instruction through a reflective, nonevaluative lens, which helped identify patterns of strength as well as opportunities for growth. New staff members gained insight into how teachers structure their classes, implement instruction, and manage the classroom environment.

Interdisciplinary meetings provide the team with extra time to meet and discuss the priority standards that we focus on each week in our classes. During our interdisciplinary meetings, we discussed how the team could incorporate more fluency instruction during our classes. I fostered a space where teachers could share strategies, address common challenges, and build cross-curricular connections that ultimately benefit students. Through this work, I have supported a culture of continuous improvement, collaboration, and student-centered instruction. (S. Marquez, personal communication, September–October 2025)

- **Harness the power of shared inquiry:** When teachers collaboratively tackle common problems, they engage in a powerful process of co-constructing knowledge (Mieliwocki & Fatheree, 2019). Encourage collaborative inquiry or action research teams in which educators can systematically investigate challenges, test new strategies, and analyze the results together. This process honors their professional judgment and positions them as agents of change (Hooper, 2025).
- **Structure professional development for cross-pollination:** Intentionally break down silos. Create opportunities for teachers across different grade levels, departments, or even schools to connect. Vertical team meetings focused on curriculum articulation or staff meetings structured as book studies with small-group discussions can spark new insights and build a stronger, more unified professional community (Cabeen, 2018; Sanfelippo & Sinanis, 2016).

Principle 4: Readiness to Learn (the When)

Adults are most ready to learn when the learning is immediately applicable to their real-world context. The further removed professional development is from the daily realities of the classroom, the less likely it is to be retained or implemented. Transformative professional development architecture closes the gap between learning and doing, ensuring that new knowledge is timely and relevant and that it can be put into practice right away. Consider these points for designing professional development for readiness.

- **Embed learning in the workday:** The most powerful professional development isn't an event; it's a process integrated into the fabric of the school day (Briese et al., 2016; Roche, 2021). This includes instructional coaching cycles, co-teaching partnerships, and dedicated collaborative planning time where new ideas can be immediately discussed, adapted, and prepared for the classroom.
- **Provide just-in-time support:** Learning shouldn't cease when a workshop ends. The most critical moments often occur when a teacher first tries a new strategy with students. Ensure there is ongoing support through coaching, peer mentoring, or collaborative discussions. This allows for refinement, troubleshooting, and sustained growth, turning a one-time event into a continuous learning cycle (Hall, 2018; Hooper, 2025).

 **Brilliant Voice From the Field** 

ADRIAN GOODMAN

Consultant of Special Services, Richland County School District One, Columbia, South Carolina

As a special education consultant, I believe the most powerful professional development happens when we work as one team. I do not come into schools as the expert to fix things. I come in as a teammate ready to roll up my sleeves. Together, we study real IEPs, share student data, practice accommodations, and role-play tough scenarios. Every voice matters. General educators, special educators, paraprofessionals, and administrators all sit at the same table, learning together and building each other up.

The intensity comes from our collective commitment. We push one another, celebrate one another, and remind ourselves constantly that every student belongs to all of us. When a teacher masters a new strategy, we cheer. When a para finds a way to connect with a student, we spotlight it. When an administrator clears barriers, we honor it.

This is not just professional development. It is a culture shift rooted in teamwork. We transform from isolated classrooms into a united force. And when the team grows stronger, students thrive. That is the brilliance: professional development that does not divide by roles but unites by purpose. (A. Goodman, personal communication, September–October 2025)

- **Conclude with concrete action planning:** Never end a professional development session without answering the question "What will I do with this on Monday?" Guide teachers in creating a concrete action plan outlining their implementation steps, anticipated challenges, and needed resources. Collaboratively develop timelines to make sure teachers get what they need. This simple step dramatically increases the likelihood of transfer from the initial workshop to the classroom. Many of the tools in this book culminate in creating a concrete action plan or timeline, reinforcing this principle by structuring the transition from learning to immediate implementation.

Principle 5: Orientation to Learning (the How)

Adults are generally problem centered, not content centered. The need to solve problems motivates them to learn. Therefore, the process of learning should mirror this orientation. Instead of passively receiving information about a topic, teachers should be actively engaged in doing the work and solving problems with the new content. Here are points to consider when designing professional development for problem solving.

- **Shift from sit-and-get to learn-and-do:** Deep learning occurs when individuals are actively engaged (Knowles, 1980; Nicklas, 2025). Structure professional development with less lecturing and more dynamic, interactive work. Use simulations and role plays to practice challenging conversations, engage teams in problem-based learning scenarios, or have teachers practice a new instructional strategy by micro-teaching to their peers (Partin-Dunn, 2020). Consider many of the tools in this book, but especially "Tool 2.3: Academic Fair for Culture" (page 75), where we help your team create an experience by visiting colleagues' classrooms.
- **Focus on creating usable products:** A powerful way to ensure active, problem-centered learning is to have teachers create something they can use immediately. Dedicate professional development time for teachers to adapt curriculum materials for their students, design new classroom activities, or build a shared bank of formative assessments. The make-and-take session is popular for a reason: It is inherently practical and productive (Cabeen, 2018).

Principle 6: Motivation (the Drive)

While external factors play a role, the most powerful motivators for adult learners are internal: the desire for mastery, increased self-efficacy, and professional pride. Professional development that is designed to be a series of compliance hoops to jump through kills intrinsic motivation. Transformative professional development architecture is designed to fuel teachers' internal drive by helping them become more effective in their work. Consider these points for designing professional development for motivation.

- **Make efficacy the goal:** The ultimate aim of all professional development should be to enhance both individual and collective teacher efficacy, or the belief in their power to make a difference for students. The mastery experience of trying a new strategy and seeing it work is the most powerful driver of teacher self-efficacy and motivation (Marcolini, 2022; McClusky et al., 2021).

- **Celebrate and share success:** Create systems and platforms where teachers can share their successes. When a team's action research leads to a breakthrough, or a teacher's new approach sparks incredible student engagement, that story needs to be told. This reinforces a positive culture and inspires others to take risks. We have an entire chapter about celebration; if you started with this chapter, make chapter 2 the next one you read!
- **Build a supportive professional community:** By designing professional development through the lens of these principles, you do more than build skills; you build a culture. You foster networks of relationships where learning, trust, and professional support can flourish (Hall, 2018). This sense of belonging and mutual respect is a profound intrinsic motivator that transforms a workplace into a true PLC. That is why so many of the tools in this book are built around reflection. Reflecting on their practice directly nurtures teachers' intrinsic motivation, which fuels sustained professional growth and excellence.

By intentionally designing professional learning through the lens of andragogy, leaders create experiences that are naturally active, tailored, and relevant. This is not just about having better workshops; it is about respecting your educators as the dedicated professionals they are and building a culture of continuous improvement where both teachers and students thrive.

Are you planning a professional development experience? You can use "Tool 5.4: The High-Impact Professional Development Design Rubric—From Compliance to Transformation" (page 196) to make sure you are hitting all the principles of andragogy and designing professional development experiences that make a difference. Use the tool before, during, or after development of the professional development, but use it before you implement the learning experience.

The School Culture Players

Professional development is a powerful lever that can either fortify Fundamentalist resistance or catalyze profound cultural growth. When teachers experience poorly designed, irrelevant professional development, a school essentially guarantees the strengthening of Fundamentalist behaviors and thinking. Conversely, when professional learning is intentionally designed to respect teachers as professionals, it becomes a potent force for positive change across all school culture players. In even the most challenging school cultures, a single powerful learning experience framed with the principles of agency and andragogy can open the minds of resisters and represent a monumental step forward.

Empowering Believers

Believers thrive in environments that are serious about improvement. Professional development that is active, relevant, and clearly connected to student success confirms their core convictions and leads to the following benefits.

- **Getting validated and energized:** When professional development honors teachers' agency and is built on sound adult learning principles, it validates

Believers' passion. It signals that the system is genuinely committed to the growth they champion, which energizes their efforts.

- **Sharpening the saw:** Believers crave professional growth. Practical, hands-on learning provides them with new tools, refines their existing skills, and satisfies their intrinsic desire to become more effective.
- **Leading the charge:** Professional development that offers voice, choice, and pathways for teacher leadership empowers Believers to share their expertise. This not only honors their contributions but also expands their impact, positioning them as natural leaders within the school's professional learning culture.

Conversely, generic, passive sit-and-get professional development can make even the most dedicated Believers feel their time is undervalued, which risks dimming their crucial light.

Supporting Tweeners

For Tweeners navigating their pivotal early years, professional development is a primary tool for socializing and building efficacy. The quality of their professional development experiences can lead to the following benefits, significantly influencing whether they trend toward the Believer path or the Fundamentalist path following their inevitable moment of truth.

- **Competence and confidence building:** For new teachers, active learning experiences with immediate practical applications are vital. Well-designed professional development provides the mastery experiences needed to build both skills and the self-efficacy to use them.
- **Positive culture induction:** Engaging, respectful, and genuinely helpful professional development socializes Tweeners into a culture that values learning, collaboration, and continuous improvement. It shows them "how we do things here" in a constructive way.
- **Modeling of best practices:** When professional development models the principles of active learning, differentiation, and respect for learners, it provides a powerful lesson in effective pedagogy that Tweeners can then take back to their own classrooms.

Irrelevant, one-size-fits-all professional development does the opposite, leaving Tweeners lost, overwhelmed, and unsupported and making them more susceptible to the cynical narratives of the informal networks.

Flipping Fundamentalists

High-impact professional development directly challenges the core tenets of Fundamentalists' resistance. It systematically dismantles their common objections by being genuinely useful, respectful of adult learners, and grounded in collaborative problem solving. The familiar refrain "This is a waste of time; just let us work in our rooms" loses its power when the professional learning is engaging, practical, and directly applicable to their work.

Level One (Need Clarity): Supporting the Why

Level One resistance is often rooted in a perceived lack of purpose. When professional development targets authentic problems of practice and uses school data that teachers help analyze, the why becomes tangible and undeniable. Fundamentalists' argument that the initiative is confusing or pointless is neutralized when they are actively engaged in a sensible process that clearly demonstrates how a new approach benefits students.

Level Two (Need Trust): Building Agency

Level Two resistance stems from broken trust. By designing professional development that operationalizes teacher agency—offering voice and choice, respecting existing experience, and empowering credible peers to lead—you can systematically rebuild that trust. When the learning process itself feels respectful and valuable, Fundamentalists begin to trust the people and the process. Seeing Believers genuinely engaged and valued further softens their defensive stance.

Level Three (Need Capacity or Skills): Modeling the How

Level Three resistance is a fear of failure masked as defiance; these resisters retreat to the familiar because they don't feel capable of implementing the new. Active learning, modeling, and job-embedded support are the antidotes. Make-and-take sessions, collaborative curriculum adaptation, and coaching cycles directly build their skills. When Fundamentalists leave professional development feeling more competent, the urge to retreat to their classroom and shut the door lessens because the change feels possible.

Level Four (Resistant to the Core Mission): Isolating Resistance

While high-impact professional development may not fully convert a Level Four Fundamentalist, its quality and relevance make their persistent complaints ring hollow to others. Their "just let us work in our rooms" argument becomes transparently defiant when the alternative is a valuable, collaborative learning experience. When a professional development experience is designed using sound andragogy, it's genuinely collaborative, solves a real classroom problem that educators face, or creates a product that they find useful. Undeniably good professional development strengthens the school's positive core, isolates extreme negativity, and makes it clear that such resistance is an outlier, not the norm. Poorly designed professional development does the opposite: It validates every level of Fundamentalist resistance and actively hinders positive cultural change.

Saving Survivors

For educators struggling to stay afloat, professional development can feel like one more burden. However, when designed with their reality in mind, it can get them the support they need when they need it, giving them a chance to grow.

- **Practical and manageable professional development:** Survivors benefit most from professional development that offers immediately usable, practical strategies that can make their demanding jobs more efficient or effective without adding to their cognitive load.

- **Small successes:** A session that helps Survivors achieve even a small tangible win in their classroom can provide a much-needed boost to their morale and efficacy, potentially renewing their desire for professional engagement.
- **Gentle engagement:** Differentiated options that allow Survivors to participate at a comfortable entry level are key. The goal is to reduce their feeling of overwhelm, not add to it.

Chapter 5 Tools

When leaders design professional development with teachers in mind, they do more than just deliver content. By fostering agency, tailoring professional development to teachers' needs, and grounding professional development in classroom realities, they build collaborative capacity and create a learning environment where every adult feels valued, supported, and equipped to grow. This is how leaders cultivate a culture of continuous improvement that benefits every student and makes school a more positive and productive place for all. We suggest starting with tool 5.1 as the instrument to collect real perspectives and determine what other tools collaborative teams need to engage with.

Figure 5.1 breaks down this chapter's tools.

Tool Number	Title of Tool	Purpose
Tool 5.1	Survey: Dissonance of Traditional Professional Development	Gather teachers' feedback on their experiences with traditional professional development and identify areas where current professional development practices may misalign with teacher needs or be perceived as ineffective. Use these insights to inform the design of more relevant, engaging, and impactful professional learning opportunities.
Tool 5.2	Guiding Coalition Teacher Agency Reflection	Support the guiding coalition in reflectively assessing and systematically building the conditions and practices that foster teacher agency.
Tool 5.3	My Professional Growth and Efficacy Plan	Provide a structured yet personal framework for teachers to reflect on their practice, set a meaningful professional goal, and intentionally plan for a mastery experience that builds self-efficacy.
Tool 5.4	The High-Impact Professional Development Design Rubric: From Compliance to Transformation	Help school teams, the guiding coalition, and leaders evaluate the current state of their professional development offerings against the principles of high-impact, adult-centered learning.

Figure 5.1: *Chapter 5 tools.*

Tool 5.1: Survey—Dissonance of Traditional Professional Development

Purpose

Gather teachers' feedback on their experiences with traditional professional development, and identify areas where current professional development practices may misalign with teacher needs or be perceived as ineffective. Use these insights to inform the design of more relevant, engaging, and impactful professional learning opportunities.

Instructions

Anonymously administer this survey to all teaching staff. Encourage honest and thoughtful responses. The data should be compiled and reviewed by the guiding coalition or school leadership team to facilitate discussion and action planning.

Survey

Rate your level of agreement with the following statements based on your typical experiences with professional development in our school or district. Please note that questions 3 and 9 list the selections in reverse order.

Relevance and Practical Application

1. Professional development sessions you attend are directly relevant to your daily classroom challenges and student needs.

4	3	2	1
Strongly agree	Agree	Disagree	Strongly disagree

2. You are usually able to immediately apply the knowledge and skills you gain from professional development sessions to your teaching practice.

4	3	2	1
Strongly agree	Agree	Disagree	Strongly disagree

3. The content covered in traditional professional development often feels theoretical and disconnected from the practical realities of your classroom.

4	3	2	1
Strongly disagree	Disagree	Agree	Strongly agree

Teacher Voice and Personalization

4. You have sufficient opportunities to provide input into the topics and formats of professional development offered.

4	3	2	1
Strongly agree	Agree	Disagree	Strongly disagree

5. Professional development offerings generally cater to a wide range of teacher experience levels and diverse learning needs.

4	3	2	1
Strongly agree	Agree	Disagree	Strongly disagree

6. You would benefit from more choice in selecting professional development activities that align with your specific growth areas and interests.

4	3	2	1
Strongly agree	Agree	Disagree	Strongly disagree

Engagement and Learning Methods

7. Professional development sessions typically involve active participation, collaboration, and hands-on learning.

4	3	2	1
Strongly agree	Agree	Disagree	Strongly disagree

8. The delivery methods used in professional development sessions are generally engaging and motivating.

4	3	2	1
Strongly agree	Agree	Disagree	Strongly disagree

9. A significant portion of professional development time is spent on passive sit-and-get presentations.

4	3	2	1
Strongly disagree	Disagree	Agree	Strongly agree

Support and Impact

10. You receive adequate ongoing support and follow-up to effectively implement new strategies or concepts introduced in professional development.

4	3	2	1
Strongly agree	Agree	Disagree	Strongly disagree

11. You believe that the professional development you have participated in has led to meaningful and sustained improvements in your teaching practice.

4	3	2	1
Strongly agree	Agree	Disagree	Strongly disagree

12. You have observed a clear positive impact on student engagement and learning outcomes as a result of professional development initiatives.

4	3	2	1
Strongly agree	Agree	Disagree	Strongly disagree

Scoring

Calculate your scores for each category using the following chart.

Category	Statements	Score
Relevance and Practical Application	Add your scores for statements 1, 2, and 3.	
Teacher Voice and Personalization	Add your scores for statements 4, 5, and 6.	
Engagement and Learning Methods	Add your scores for statements 7, 8, and 9.	
Support and Impact	Add your scores for statements 10, 11, and 13.	

Interpret your scores for each category.

- **Low dissonance, strong alignment (score of 10–12):** This indicates general satisfaction. Professional development practices in this area are perceived positively and meet teacher needs well.
- **Moderate dissonance, some misalignment (score of 7–9):** This suggests some concerns or inconsistencies. While there might be positive aspects, there are clear opportunities for improvement in this area.
- **High dissonance, significant misalignment (score of 4–6):** This indicates substantial dissatisfaction. Professional development practices in this area are largely perceived as ineffectively meeting teacher needs.
- **Critical dissonance, severe misalignment (score of 3):** This signals serious issues and a critical need for immediate attention. Professional development practices in this area should be overhauled.

Team Reflection and Discussion

As a guiding coalition or leadership team, use the compiled survey data to facilitate a discussion.

- What are the overall scores for each of the four categories? Which areas show the highest levels of dissonance? Which show the lowest?
- Looking at individual statements, which specific aspects of traditional professional development are causing our staff the most concern? Are there any surprising results?
- How do these findings align with the characteristics of effective professional development discussed in chapter 5 (such as teacher agency, active learning, collaboration, and ongoing support)?
- What potential consequences could the identified areas of dissonance have on teacher morale, staff's willingness to engage in future professional development, implementation of new practices, and ultimately, student learning?
- Do we have any anecdotal evidence or previous feedback that corroborates or contrasts with these survey results? If so, how do we respond?

Action Plan

Based on your reflection and discussion, develop an action plan.

- **Prioritize areas for improvement:** Identify the one or two categories (or specific statements) with the highest dissonance that your team will address first.
- **Brainstorm solutions and strategies:** For each priority area, brainstorm specific, actionable changes that you could make to professional development design and delivery. How can you increase relevance, teacher voice, active engagement, and impactful support? (Refer to chapter 5 for ideas.)
- **Involve teachers in the redesign:** Decide how you will ensure teacher voices are central to redesigning professional development (for example, focus groups, professional development planning committees with teacher representation, and further surveys on preferred topics and formats).
- **Establish first steps and a timeline:** Determine the next step your team will take. Who is responsible? What is the timeline?
    - Next step—

      ____

      ____

      ____

    - Responsible party—

      ____

      ____

      ____

    - Timeline—

      ____

      ____

      ____

page 5 of 5

Tool 5.2: Guiding Coalition Teacher Agency Reflection

Purpose

Support the guiding coalition in reflectively assessing and systematically building the conditions and practices that foster teacher agency. This tool helps operationalize a shift from top-down mandates to a teacher-centered approach, recognizing educators as active agents in their learning journey.

Teacher Agency Defined

Teacher agency is the capacity of teachers to purposefully act and constructively direct their professional growth and contribute to that of their colleagues.

Part 1: Assessment of the Foundational Conditions for Agency

For teacher agency to flourish, certain conditions are necessary. Use the following checklist to assess our school's current reality and identify areas for improvement.

Foundational Condition	Guiding Question	Response	Evidence and Notes
Leadership and Support	Do we actively build trust and a supportive culture where risk taking is viewed as part of learning?	☐ Yes ☐ Partially ☐ No	
	Is leadership distributed, empowering teacher leaders to facilitate professional development and other initiatives?	☐ Yes ☐ Partially ☐ No	
	Are sufficient time, resources, and clear structures provided for teacher-led learning and collaboration?	☐ Yes ☐ Partially ☐ No	
Quality and Coherence	Are our professional development offerings high quality, research based, and inclusive of practical application and reflection?	☐ Yes ☐ Partially ☐ No	

page 1 of 7

	Is our professional development coherent and aligned with school goals and teacher beliefs, rather than representative of fragmented initiatives?	☐ Yes ☐ Partially ☐ No	
	Do we ensure teachers understand the connections between different professional development activities to avoid confusion?	☐ Yes ☐ Partially ☐ No	
Sustained and Embedded Learning	Is our professional learning sustained and ongoing, not just a series of isolated workshops?	☐ Yes ☐ Partially ☐ No	
	Is our professional learning job embedded with consistent support and feedback (such as coaching and postobservation conferences)?	☐ Yes ☐ Partially ☐ No	
	Do we provide professional development in the presence of students, such as through model classrooms, for contextualized learning?	☐ Yes ☐ Partially ☐ No	

Action Plan

Based on the preceding assessment, what are our top one or two priorities for strengthening the conditions for agency?

1. ______________________________

2. ______________________________

Part 2: A Nuts-and-Bolts Action Plan for Fostering Agency

Use part 2 to plan the concrete actions our school will take to build teacher agency.

Strategy 1: Operationalize Voice, Choice, and Personalization

Teachers overwhelmingly prefer having more say in selecting professional development activities. This increases relevance and intrinsic motivation. Answer the questions for each actionable step.

Actionable Step	Our Plan for Implementation
Conduct Needs Assessments How will we regularly survey teachers and analyze data with them to inform professional development offerings (for example, using Google Forms or focus groups)?	
Offer a Menu of Professional Development Options What will our varied menu of learning opportunities include? (See the following sample menu to get started.)	
Support Teacher-Proposed Professional Development What is the pathway for teachers to propose and lead their own professional development? What resources will we provide?	
Provide Flexible Formats and Pacing How can we offer professional development in different formats (in person, blended, and online) with flexible scheduling and pacing?	

Sample Menu of Professional Learning Opportunities

Professional Learning Choices		
Professional Development Focus	☐ Systems connector ☐ Educator wellness ☐ Culture transformation ☐ Student and staff learning	
☐ Create proficiency scales.	☐ Check dashboard.	☐ Create lessons for more time and support.
☐ Prepare lessons.	☐ Study assigned professional development.	☐ Read books of choice.
☐ Create an exemplary classroom environment.	☐ Create a behavior action plan.	☐ Create a data action plan.
☐ Read *The New Art and Science of Teaching* (Marzano, 2017) or *Learning by Doing* (DuFour et al., 2024).	☐ Create formative assessments and common formative assessments.	☐ Work on grades with your team.
☐ Work with special education plans.	☐ Prepare a special education slideshow.	☐ Work on special education behavior intervention plans and functional behavioral assessments.
☐ Train a special education paraeducator.	☐ Create Tier 2 supports.	☐ Create Tier 1 scaffolds.
☐ Create grade-level assignments and reflect on Depth of Knowledge levels.	☐ Create exemplars of grade-level work.	☐ Learn from a colleague.
☐ Study the curriculum.	☐ Create anchor charts that capture key points from a minilesson.	☐ Call as many families as possible for positive reasons.

Summary of Your Learning

Thoughts for Your Future Learning

Strategy 2: Systematize Empowerment Through Goal Setting and Reflection

Agency is fueled when teachers set their own goals and reflect deeply on their practice. Answer the questions for each actionable step.

Actionable Step	Our Plan for Implementation
Facilitate Individual Goal Setting What structured yet flexible process will we use for teachers to set meaningful, student-focused professional growth goals?	
Embed Reflective Practices How and when will we integrate regular opportunities for individual and collaborative reflection (for example, meeting protocols or digital tools like Socrative)?	

Coach Peers for Goal Attainment How will we establish peer-coaching partnerships to support goal attainment and reflection?	

Strategy 3: Build Robust Collaborative Structures for Shared Inquiry

Collaboration is a key component of agency building as networks of relationships become where learning takes place. Answer the questions for each actionable step.

Actionable Step	Our Plan for Implementation
Establish Effective Collaborative Teams How will we ensure our collaborative teams are authentic and provide the best professional development, as noted in chapter 4?	
Support Teacher-Led Action Research What frameworks, resources, and time will we provide for teams to engage in collaborative action research on problems of practice they identify?	
Facilitate Cross-Grade and Department Collaboration What opportunities will we create for teachers from different areas to collaborate on shared challenges?	

Part 3: Individual Reflection and Next Steps

Have individual members of the guiding coalition respond to these questions.

- **Summary of your learning:** What is your biggest takeaway from our discussion about teacher agency?
- **Connection to your practice:** How does a stronger sense of professional identity ("Who am I?" and "Who do I want to be?") influence your personal engagement in professional learning?
- **Thoughts for future learning:** Based on our school's needs and your own practice, what is one area of professional growth on this tool that you want to pursue? What support would help you?

References

DuFour, R., DuFour, R., Eaker, R., Many, T. W., Mattos, M., & Muhammad, A. (2024). *Learning by doing: A handbook for Professional Learning Communities at Work* (4th ed.). Solution Tree Press.

Marzano, R. J. (2017). *The new art and science of teaching*. Solution Tree Press.

Source: Adapted from Cabeen, J. (2018). Hacking early learning: 10 building blocks to success in preK–3 that all teachers and school leaders should know. *Times 10; Clark, S., & Duggins, A. (2016).* Using quality feedback to guide professional learning: A framework for instructional leaders. *Corwin; Hall, S. L. (2018).* 10 success factors for literacy intervention: Getting results with MTSS in elementary schools. *ASCD; Hooper, J. W. (2025).* Improving perceptions and practices of teacher professional learning: A collaborative action research study *(Publication No. 31939074). ProQuest Dissertations & Theses Global; Hose, J. C. (2022).* Elementary teachers' perceptions of professional development effectiveness *(Publication No. 29060872) [Doctoral dissertation, Walden University]. ProQuest Dissertations & Theses Global. www.proquest.com/docview/2644421464; McClusky, S. L., Goddard, R. D., & Yoon, I. (2021). Exploration of the relationship between professional development quality and teacher sense of self-efficacy in urban Ohio elementary schools.* Leadership and Research in Education, 6*(1), 49–78; Nicklas, A. (2025).* Andragogy and professional learning: Rethinking internal structures *(Publication No. 31997057). ProQuest Dissertations & Theses Global; Omare, E. (2021). Teacher qualification, experience, capability beliefs and professional development: Do they predict teacher adoption of 21st century pedagogies?* International Journal of Curriculum and Instruction, 13*(2), 1161–1192; Partin-Dunn, R. L. (2020).* The impact of research-based professional development on teacher self-efficacy and collective efficacy beliefs with respect to applying techniques from *Teach Like a Champion 2.0 [Doctoral dissertation, Gardner-Webb University]. Digital Commons @ Gardner-Webb University. https://digitalcommons.gardner-webb.edu/education-dissertations/66; Roche, K. R. (2021).* A qualitative case study of the influence of student presence in teacher professional development *[Doctoral dissertation, Duquesne University]. Duquesne Scholarship Collection. https://dsc.duq.edu/etd/2024; Rodman, A. (2019).* Personalized professional learning: A job-embedded pathway for elevating teacher voice. *ASCD.*

Tool 5.3: My Professional Growth and Efficacy Plan

Teacher: ______________________________ School Year: ______________

Purpose

Provide a structured yet personal framework for teachers to reflect on their practice, set a meaningful professional goal, and intentionally plan for a mastery experience that builds self-efficacy. This process is designed to foster agency, resilience, and belief in one's ability to positively impact student learning.

Instructions

Use this tool for individual reflection and planning. Work through the three parts sequentially. Begin by honestly assessing your current practice in part 1. Use those reflections to create a focused, actionable growth plan in part 2. Do not do part 3 yet. At a later meeting, after implementing your plan, complete part 3 to reflect on the plan's impact on your practice and your own sense of efficacy.

The Why Behind This Tool

As chapter 5 outlines, high-quality, teacher-driven professional development provides mastery experiences that boost teachers' self-efficacy. High self-efficacy, in turn, makes them more open to new ideas, more resilient in the face of challenges, and more eager to continue their professional growth. This tool helps you intentionally engage in that positive feedback loop.

Part 1: Where Am I Now? (Self-Assessment and Professional Identity)

The first step is to reflect on your current practice and connect it to your professional identity—your sense of "Who am I?" and "Who do I want to be?" as an educator.

- **Celebrating success:** Describe a recent moment, lesson, or interaction where you felt particularly effective and proud of your impact on student learning. What did you do? What was the result?

- **Identifying a growth area:** What is a current challenge in your practice where you feel less confident or would like to see greater student success? (This is not a deficit but an opportunity for growth.)

- **Connecting with your identity:** What skills, knowledge, or dispositions would help you move closer to the kind of educator you aspire to be?

Part 2: How Will I Grow? (Planning for a Mastery Experience)

Now, you will turn reflection into a concrete plan. This step involves designing a learning experience that will give you a tangible success to build on.

- **Your professional growth goal:** Based on your preceding reflections, what is one specific, student-focused goal you want to work on? (Here's an example: "I want to increase student engagement and ownership during the independent practice portion of my mathematics block by implementing learning stations.")

- **Visualization of mastery:** What would a mastery experience for this goal look and feel like? If you were successful, what would you see your students doing? How would you feel about your practice in that moment?

- **Your agency-driven learning plan:** What professional learning activities will best support you in achieving this mastery experience? Choose the support you need.
    - ☐ *Collaborative discussion*—Meet with your team or a colleague to discuss the goal and success criteria.
    - ☐ *Peer observation*—Visit a colleague who is strong in this area to observe their practice.
    - ☐ *Instructional coaching*—Work with a coach for planning, observation, and feedback cycles.
    - ☐ *Action research*—Engage in a small-scale inquiry cycle to test a new strategy.
    - ☐ *Book study or online course*—Deepen your knowledge on the topic.
    - ☐ *Video reflection*—Record your own practice to observe it, reflect on it, and discuss it with a trusted colleague.
    - ☐ *Other (teacher-proposed)*—______________________________

Part 3: What Was the Impact? (Reflection on the Feedback Loop)

Save part 3 for a later meeting after the professional development. After engaging in your learning plan, complete this section to reflect on its impact on your practice and your self-efficacy.

- **Impact on practice and student learning:** What did you try? What happened? What was the impact on your students?

- **Impact on self-efficacy:** How did this experience (even if imperfect) affect your confidence and belief in your ability to tackle this challenge? Did you have a mastery experience?

- **Resilience building:** How did this experience better prepare you to handle future challenges in your practice?

- **Next steps:** What is your biggest takeaway? What will you continue to do, and what new questions do you have for your next growth cycle?

page 3 of 3

Tool 5.4: The High-Impact Professional Development Design Rubric—From Compliance to Transformation

Purpose

Help school teams, the guiding coalition, and leaders evaluate the current state of their professional development offerings against the principles of high-impact, adult-centered learning. This rubric serves as a diagnostic tool to identify strengths, pinpoint areas for growth, and facilitate shared understanding of what transformative professional learning looks like in practice.

Instructions

Complete the following process.

1. **Group discussion:** As a guiding coalition or leadership team, review the descriptions of the four stages: (1) static, (2) fragmented, (3) purposeful, and (4) transformative.
2. **Collaborative assessment:** For each of the six principles of andragogy, discuss where your school's typical professional development plan currently falls on the rubric. Use specific examples from recent professional development experiences to justify your placement.
3. **Identification of evidence:** Identify what tangible evidence or feedback from staff supports your assessment. What might staff members with different perspectives say?
4. **Calibration and planning:** Come to a consensus on your school's current stage for each principle. Use the insights gained to identify one or two priority areas and brainstorm actionable steps to move toward a more transformative model.

	Static Stage (Compliance-Driven Plan)	Fragmented Stage (Emerging Plan)	Purposeful Stage (Strategic Plan)	Transformative Stage (Embedded Plan)
Principle 1: The Need to Know (the Why)	The plan dictates the why or assumes it's understood. The topic is presented without a clear connection to staff-identified needs or school data.	The plan attempts to explain the rationale, but the connection to classroom problems is inconsistent or feels like an afterthought in the agenda.	The plan explicitly targets an authentic schoolwide problem. The design uses data to establish a clear why for the learning.	The plan is designed for teachers to co-construct the why by solving problems of practice they have identified. The rationale is intrinsic to the planned activities.
Principle 2: The Learner's Self-Concept (the Who)	The plan prescribes a one-size-fits-all agenda for all teachers, regardless of role or experience. It lacks options for teacher voice.	The plan offers some choice (for example, a few elective sessions), but the core learning activities remain mandated and undifferentiated.	The plan incorporates regular opportunities for differentiation, such as tiered activities or different pathways, and it includes mechanisms to gather teacher voice.	The plan is built on personalization. It includes structures for significant teacher voice and choice, such as developing personalized learning plans and proposing or leading sessions.

page 1 of 2

Principle 3: The Role of Experience (the What)	The plan positions teachers as isolated learners and the presenter as the sole expert. It includes no structure to leverage teacher experience.	The plan encourages discussion but lacks clear protocols or purposeful tasks to structure peer-to-peer learning and leverage collective wisdom.	The plan intentionally structures peer-to-peer learning with clear protocols for activities like analysis of student work, peer observation, or collaborative inquiry.	The plan's primary vehicle for learning is collaboration. It is designed around the PLC process, action research, or instructional rounds, positioning expertise as distributed among staff.
Principle 4: Readiness to Learn (the When)	The plan presents theoretical content disconnected from daily classroom work. It's designed as a stand-alone event with no planned follow-up.	The plan attempts to connect to practice but provides little time or structure for teachers to plan for actual application in their classrooms.	The plan is designed for immediate application. It includes modeling and dedicates time for teachers to create action plans or adapt materials for their students.	The plan is designed to be job embedded. It outlines a process for ongoing support (for example, coaching or co-teaching) during the implementation phase.
Principle 5: Orientation to Learning (the How)	The plan outlines a passive sit-and-get session dominated by lectures with little planned interaction for participants.	The plan includes basic engagement (for example, turn-and-talks) but doesn't build the core experience around deep, hands-on, problem-centered learning.	The plan's agenda is consistently designed around active tasks where teachers solve problems or create materials relevant to their work.	The plan outlines an experience where teachers are constantly engaged in simulations, peer teaching, or cocreation of usable products, blurring the line between learning and working.
Principle 6: Motivation (the Drive)	The plan focuses on delivering information. It does not consider how the experience will impact teacher motivation or efficacy.	The plan might include a positive closing message but lacks any systematic design intended to connect the learning to increased teacher confidence or competence.	The plan includes activities that are likely to build teacher self-efficacy. It may incorporate sharing success stories to inspire participants.	The plan explicitly states the goal of building individual and collective efficacy. It includes structures to celebrate mastery and reinforce a shared sense of professional purpose.

CHAPTER 6

Implementing Skillful Leadership and Focus

THE CURSOR BLINKED, A rhythmic pulse at the top of the blank document. For the first time in a decade, Mrs. Nguyen was building a résumé. She typed her name, then stared at the Professional Experience heading. What was she supposed to write—"turned Clark Elementary from the district's punchline to its poster child in three years"? That was the truth.

Her mind flashed back to a typical Tuesday at Northwood once she had gotten the building humming. At 7:45 a.m., she was a whirlwind of productive energy, greeting students with high fives while simultaneously using her shoulder microphone to speak to the custodian about a spill in the west hall. At 9:15 a.m., she was in the classroom of a new teacher (a classic Tweener struggling with transitions), offering a quick, in-the-moment coaching tip that settled the class instantly. At 11:30 a.m., she was navigating a tense parent conference with the calm of a seasoned diplomat. By lunch, she had solved three logistical problems, reviewed a draft of the school-improvement plan, and received a glowing email from the superintendent about the school's latest test scores. She was the hero. She had all the answers. She was the system.

But the system was fragile. Mrs. Nguyen remembered another day months later, when she was sitting in her office at 9:00 p.m. under the harsh fluorescent lights, the remains of a sad takeout salad pushed to the side. Her screen was a dizzying grid of student data, each red cell a personal failing. Her phone buzzed with a text from her husband: "Kids are asleep. Missed you again." Things weren't going so well at home.

The weight of it all, the five hundred students and forty staff members, felt like a physical pressure on her chest. Earlier that day, in the lounge, a veteran teacher (a classic Fundamentalist who resisted every new initiative) had watched her pass and muttered to a colleague, "Must be nice to have the energy to save the world every day." It wasn't a compliment. It was a barb laced with resentment about her celebrated success. The reality was that Mrs. Nguyen felt utterly alone in making this school work.

Then came the phone call that shattered everything. There was a family crisis, immediate and unignorable. She needed to be gone for weeks, maybe longer. Panic seized her as she looked at her calendar, at the initiatives she was single-handedly driving. There was no one to delegate to. There was no robust guiding coalition to carry the work forward. There was just her.

The final gut punch came six months after she'd stepped away. She received an email from that same new teacher she had coached, who had blossomed under her mentorship. It read, "Mrs. Nguyen, hope you're well. I have to be honest, it's slipping around here; the meetings are just not really running now. The old guard is saying 'I told you so' about the intervention block. It feels like we're going backward."

That still stung, even though it was months ago.

Mrs. Nguyen looked back at the blinking cursor. The success at Northwood wasn't the school's; it was hers. And when she'd left, she'd taken it with her. She deleted the Professional Experience heading and instead typed a new professional objective: "to build a culture of shared leadership where success is a system, not a single person, and the work endures." Now, she was ready to write.

The opening of this chapter focuses on principal leadership. If you are on a guiding coalition, this leadership still has a lot to do with you, as you will quickly find out. Additionally, if you aspire to lead a school, this may be the most important part of the book for you. As Mrs. Nguyen illustrated in the preceding vignette, being a superhero principal is not sustainable; acting in ways that grow collaborative leadership is. Furthermore, school-level leadership is critical to a healthy school culture. In all the school culture audits that Alex has performed, he has never found a truly healthy school culture with a superhero principal.

One of the first leadership steps for growing a healthy school culture is to make sure that you understand what culture is and how it forms and changes. Edgar H. Schein (2004), a significant voice on organizational culture, clarifies that culture emerges and transforms through three primary forces: (1) the founders, (2) the new leaders, and (3) the new members of the organization. We add that new information learned by the leaders can be transformative as well, but information alone doesn't change culture. Changing the leaders' behaviors as a result of new information does change culture. Culture essentially is about how schools solve their problems, and if your school has the principal solve every problem, that situation is unsustainable. If you want to change your culture, change how you and your team solve your problems.

The question you must ask is socially structural: "How did we get this way, and how do we redesign our school to systematically empower Believers, support Tweeners, flip Fundamentalists, and save Survivors to forge a new and more effective way of working for students' success?" Answering this question begins with dismantling the most pervasive and damaging myth in this profession—that of the solo superhero principal.

Like in the preceding vignette, there are exceptional leaders who help turn schools around, but when they do so, two byproducts are common: (1) they experience burnout and (2) they build a system that relies too much on the principal. Sometimes, when a school is in this situation, its culture can feel healthy. It may, in fact, become a healthy culture, but to truly have a lasting impact, collaborative leadership is paramount. Sadly, educators' socialization about what a principal is supposed to do, say, and be has built into something that might be unhelpful. To portray this, we describe the history of school leadership in this chapter. Then we explore the role of the guiding coalition in transforming school culture before we circle back to the principal's critical need to find the right balance between tight and loose leadership. Then, as always, we detail the meaning of this work for each of the school culture players.

A Timeline of an Impossible Job Description

The history of the principalship has often cast the leader in the role of the solitary hero expected to ride in and single-handedly save the day. This image is not just a caricature; it is a deeply ingrained expectation that many principals feel in their bones, born from a profound sense of personal responsibility for every student who walks through the doors. Those expectations didn't emerge in a vacuum; they were built over more than a century of evolving demands. A core skill of a focused leader is the ability to step back and apply this historical perspective because knowing this background can help them understand their own and others' expectations, and it can help them forge a new path toward collaborative leadership.

The cultural image of the principal as the singular force for change is the result of decades of layering new responsibilities onto the role without ever taking any away. Understanding the following history is the first step in giving yourself permission to build a new, more sustainable model.

- **The principal teacher (1800s):** Educational leadership began simply as the principal teacher, an experienced educator who handled administrative duties like recordkeeping, discipline, and basic logistics in addition to their own full teaching load (Graf, 2019).
- **The manager (early 1900s):** Influenced by the Industrial Age and factory-line efficiency, the principalship transformed into a management position. The principal became the building manager, focused on creating a smooth-running, efficient, and standardized operation. This era established the top-down, hierarchical structure of schools and planted the seed of the principal as the sole person responsible for the institution's success (Graf, 2019).
- **The instructional leader (1970s–1990s):** Following a wave of research on effective schools, expectations shifted dramatically. A principal was now expected to be the chief instructional leader as well as an expert in curriculum, teaching strategies, and assessment for all subjects and grade levels. This monumental layer was added on top of all existing managerial duties. The release of *A Nation at Risk* (National Committee on Excellence in Education, 1983) amplified this, shifting the principal from the building manager to the person held publicly responsible for the school's success or failure (Graf, 2019; Hanks, 2023).
- **The accountable superhero (2000s–present):** With the rise of the high-stakes accountability movement, the final crushing layer was added. Principals became the single point of accountability for student test scores and school performance ratings, solidifying the solo superhero myth (Graf, 2019).

This historical trajectory has socialized people into believing that the principal must be the singular heroic figure who possesses the vision, answers, and stamina to save the school. A 2013 MetLife survey confirmed this, finding that a staggering 89 percent of principals agree that they "should be held accountable for everything that happens to the children in [their] school" (p. 27). While altruistic, this mindset is a crushing weight to bear alone, and it comes at a significant cost. The same survey revealed that 57 percent of principals in low-performing schools "feel under great stress several days a week or more" (MetLife, 2013, p. 32). They quite literally make themselves sick by chasing an impossible expectation.

Both of us (Bo and Alex) have experienced this weight; it feels like a constant, low-grade hum of anxiety that spikes with every parent phone call, every budget meeting, and every struggling student whose story you know by heart. It's the mental calculus you do at 3:00 a.m., wondering if you've done enough, planned enough, and anticipated enough for the next day. It's the loneliness of being the final stop—the person everyone looks to for the answer, the solution, or the decision even when you're just as uncertain as they are. The weight comes from not the tasks themselves but the belief that if anything fails, it is a personal failure. For anyone, this is not a sustainable pattern.

Operating under such intense pressure inevitably leads to burnout and attrition, robbing the most challenged schools of the very leaders they need. Even more critically, the superhero model is a flawed strategy for creating lasting change. A charismatic and tireless principal can certainly make a difference, but when that success is tied to their individual presence, the improvements are often fragile. If that principal leaves, the positive culture and improved outcomes are likely to go with them. And a healthy school culture can become a toxic culture if the principal is the center of all change from the status quo. This model fails to build the one thing that ensures sustainable improvement: the collective capacity and shared ownership of the people who remain. In other words, "leadership for learning is not a solo act; it is shared and widely dispersed" (Kramer & Schuhl, 2017, p. 5).

There is also a significant dark side to the superhero principal; sometimes, they can become the supervillain. The immense pressure of sole accountability often gives rise to fear-driven leadership (Noble, 2021). This style, born from an understandable fear of failure, defaults to top-down mandates and a rigid focus on compliance as a way to control outcomes. However, this approach actively disengages the very people needed to make change happen: the teachers. A fear-based approach is essential to a Fundamentalist factory. It removes teachers' professional agency and input, breeding resentment, passivity, and even resignation.

Think back to Alex's soul story in the introduction. As a new teacher, after his new principal disallowed classroom animals, he became disenfranchised and disengaged. Every leader needs to know the impact of their words on the staff zeitgeist, sometimes one interaction at a time. This plays out the other way as well: When leaders have student-focused, rational, ethical, and non-fear-based interactions with the teachers, they help build commitment. As leadership authority Stephen R. Covey (1989) famously noted, with "no involvement, there is no commitment" (p. 143). A lack of involvement systematically erodes the relational trust that is the bedrock of any productive collaboration (Russell et al., 2025).

The fear-based, go-it-alone approach is a tempting trap. When a transformational leader enters a new system, they often feel compelled to make unilateral decisions to fix pressing issues immediately (Tait & Faulkner, 2019). Indeed, sometimes this is necessary, but be careful. That level of autocratic behavior establishes a routine in which teachers look to the principal to solve all problems. While you absolutely need to make unilateral decisions in a true emergency (O'Day & Marsden, 2022), it is critical to recognize this as a temporary measure. The skillful leader must pivot from initial decisive actions to collaborative leadership. Additionally, abusing the *emergency* label for situations that don't warrant it will produce only distrust. The hard reality is that the very issues requiring immediate, autocratic fixes were likely created by that autocratic style of decision making in the first place.

Therefore, the principal's isolation is not just a personal burden; it is a structural barrier that prevents the formation of a healthy, trusting, and collaborative culture. A skillful leader demonstrates the courage to be vulnerable, replacing fear with an intentional focus on building trust and psychological safety. This shift fosters emotional wellness, reduces fear and resentment, and increases job satisfaction (Mitterer & Mitterer, 2023). All of these quiet the adult drama that can poison a school's atmosphere. The key to leaving a place better than you found it is not to be the hero who does it all but to be the leader who builds the leadership of others. This is not about abdicating responsibility; it is about distributing it. Healthy school cultures are built through shared leadership. The skill of a leader in this context is *systems thinking*: the ability to see the architecture of the school's problem solving and deliberately redesign it.

The decision to move from going it alone to following a shared leadership model is more than a stylistic choice; it is a fundamental shift in the architecture of your school's culture. This shift will be a challenge, but the best and quickest way to make that happen is the establishment of a guiding coalition. That is the first deliberate act of dismantling toxic architecture and rebuilding your school around communication, trust, capacity building, and collective responsibility (Hall, 2022; Muhammad & Cruz, 2019; Noble, 2021).

Are you interested in reflecting on whether your current leadership is collaborative or solo? Use "Tool 6.1: Principal's Collaborative Leadership Self-Assessment" (page 218) to see where you can grow.

What a Guiding Coalition Is (and Isn't)

Now that you know that solo leadership isn't as effective or sustainable as collective leadership, the question becomes, How do leaders transfer authority, and who do they transfer it to? As you read this, you might be thinking, "I already have a leadership team." You're not wrong. Most schools have some form of leadership or school-improvement team. In fact, if your school receives Title I funding, you are required to have one (Every Student Succeeds Act, 2015). These teams are a familiar part of the educational landscape. They meet, they discuss, and they manage. To illustrate, we'll actually start with what a guiding coalition is not before defining what it is, who belongs on it and why, and the work it engages in.

What a Guiding Coalition Isn't

To understand the distinction between a leadership team and a guiding coalition, you must differentiate between a messenger and a missionary (Berg, 2018; Williams & Hierck, 2015).

Most traditional leadership teams operate with what has been termed a *messenger mentality* (Williams & Hierck, 2015). Their primary function is informational and managerial. The principal relays information and directives down to the team to disseminate them to the staff, or the team brings staff concerns up to the principal for them to solve. The conversations in these meetings are dominated by logistics and compliance. They sound like this:

> *"How is our bus duty schedule going to work?"*
>
> *"When will the assembly on Wednesday take place?"*
>
> *"Can you please convey this timeline representing the latest mandates on assessment compliance from the state?" (Noble, 2021, p. 115)*

While this information is necessary, it is not the work of transforming the most important part of your culture. Questions like these stay on the outside of real conversations about two crucial responsibilities of a guiding coalition: (1) instructional practices and (2) the effectiveness of teachers' collaboration in their grade-level or department meetings (DuFour et al., 2024).

Figure 6.1 provides a clear at-a-glance summary of the fundamental differences between the team most schools have and the team your school needs.

	Traditional Leadership Team	**Guiding Coalition**
Primary Responsibilities	The team manages multiple areas: facilities, discipline, community relations, and compliance. It is a jack-of-all-trades team (Hall, 2022).	The coalition is singularly responsible for leading the collaborative team process and school improvement. It focuses on the right work of learning (Hall, 2022; Noble, 2021).
Member Selection	Team membership is often based on having longevity, being willing to volunteer, or being the only person available. Members may be handpicked by the principal (Hall, 2022).	Coalition members are strategically selected based on a balance of position power, expertise, credibility, and leadership. Selection often involves a transparent application process (Cuddemi, 2021; Hall, 2022).
Core Focus	The team focuses on managerial tasks: meeting deadlines, creating schedules, allocating resources, and sharing information. Its focus is on things and logistics (Hall, 2022).	The coalition focuses on the three big ideas of a PLC: (1) a focus on student learning, (2) a collaborative culture, and (3) a results orientation. Its focus is on people and learning (Hall, 2022; Noble, 2021).

Decision-Making Authority	The team's authority is primarily advisory. It gives input and opinions, but the principal often makes the final decision alone (Hall, 2022).	The coalition members share in the decision-making process as equals with the principal. The coalition aims for consensus, where all points of view are heard and the will of the group is evident (Cuddemi, 2021; Hall, 2022).
Organizational Structure	The team structure is often hierarchical, with the principal acting as the boss. This team tends to operate with a "do as we say" mentality (Hall, 2022).	The coalition has a flat structure with no positions of power. All members are equals. This coalition models the expected collaborative behaviors for the entire school ("We will model the way"; Hall, 2022; Noble, 2021).

Figure 6.1: *Traditional leadership team versus guiding coalition.*

Does your team need to reflect on whether it functions as a traditional leadership team or a guiding coalition? Use "Tool 6.2: Guiding Coalition Reality Check—Aligning Practice to Purpose" (page 221) to reflect on and plan for the best practices listed in figure 6.1.

So what does an effective guiding coalition actually look like?

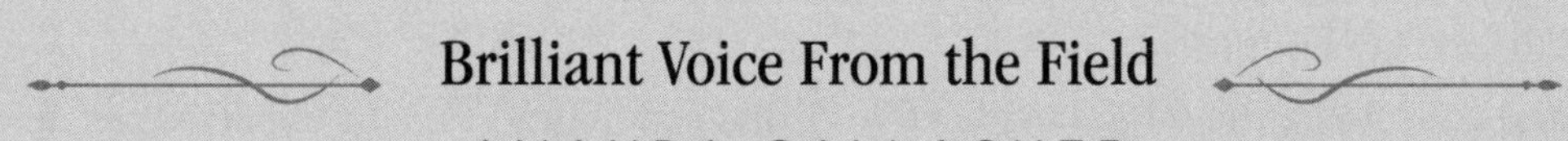

Brilliant Voice From the Field

AMANDA GALLAGHER

Principal, Belshaw Elementary School, Antioch, California

Our work as a professional learning community began with an honest acknowledgment that our previous system was not producing the level of academic and behavioral success our students deserved. For years, our leadership team functioned primarily as a logistical group—managing calendars, events, and routines—with little meaningful use of data to drive instruction or intervention. While well intentioned, the structure lacked clarity, purpose, and collective ownership for student learning.

The turning point came in March 2024, when I attended the RTI at Work™ conference. I saw a clearer, research-based pathway for how schools improve: through a true PLC process grounded in collaboration, data, and collective responsibility. I returned knowing that this was the direction our site needed in order to effect real change.

At first, we slipped back into old habits. Meetings felt admin-led, and we unintentionally recreated the hierarchy we were trying to move away from. Midway through the 2024–2025 school year, it finally clicked—this is a team, not a council with one person in charge. We restructured our time to focus on the four PLC questions, instructional priorities, and data-based action steps instead of updates and logistics.

> *To launch the 2025–2026 school year, we formalized our commitment with an application process. Although new on paper, the work itself wasn't new—we had already begun learning what it meant to be a guiding coalition. Throughout this process, I was transparent that I, too, was learning. The results have been a stronger shared purpose, clearer systems for intervention, and a unified team that leads with data and collective efficacy. We are now building momentum, together, for students. (A. Gallagher, personal communication, September–October 2025)*

What a Guiding Coalition Is

A guiding coalition is the school's engine for change. It is not a "dictatorship committee" but rather a team that "learns deeply about best practices, assesses candidly the school's current reality, determines potential next steps to improve the school, identifies possible obstacles and points of leverage, and plans the best way to create staff consensus and ownership" (Buffum, Mattos, & Weber, 2012, p. 20). Its members are not mere messengers; they are *missionaries* who understand, believe in, and champion the why behind the change (Berg, 2018; Williams & Hierck, 2015). This missionary role is directly linked to the work of building a collective focus on purpose, discussed in chapter 1; they are the champions of the collaboratively built mission, vision, and values that define the school. Their purpose is to "unite and coordinate the school's collective efforts across grade levels, departments, and subjects" and to forge a "culture of collective responsibility" (Williams & Hierck, 2015, p. 18).

Their conversations sound fundamentally different, centered on learning and results:

> *"Is what we are currently doing working schoolwide to improve student learning?"*
>
> *"What is our evidence?"*
>
> *"What do we need to create, do, or adapt to ensure our students are increasing their learning outcomes?" (Noble, 2021, p. 116)*

A core skill of a focused leader is the ability to facilitate this discourse shift, moving conversations from the merely urgent to the truly important. The guiding coalition is responsible for leading this transformation by example (Hall, 2022). This means modeling core PLC concepts, including the three big ideas: (1) a focus on student learning, (2) a collaborative culture with collective responsibility, and (3) a results orientation. The guiding coalition also models engagement with the four critical questions that drive collaborative teams (DuFour et al., 2024).

1. What are students supposed to learn?
2. How do we know if they learned it?
3. How will we respond if they don't learn it?
4. How do we extend learning for those who are proficient?

The guiding coalition, however, should view these questions through a slightly different lens than a teacher team does—a lens focused on leading the process.

1. How should our teams collaborate?
2. How will we know if they are collaborating well?
3. What will we do if they need support collaborating?
4. How will we celebrate and learn from those teams that collaborate well?

Are you interested in a protocol for addressing these questions? "Tool 6.3: Guiding Coalition Work Analysis—Focusing Our Force" (page 224) provides that.

Brilliant Voice From the Field

JESSECA STONE

Principal, Turner Elementary School, Antioch, California

Before transitioning to a guiding coalition, our school operated under a traditional leadership model focused largely on administrative matters and adult-centered concerns—such as playground rules, field trip logistics, and personal preferences. The emphasis on operational issues overshadowed our true purpose: ensuring that all scholars achieve at or above grade level.

This perspective shifted dramatically after attending a Solution Tree conference in March 2024. The keynote and breakout sessions illuminated how collaborative practices and strategic changes could directly enhance student learning. Inspired by these insights, I returned to my school determined to realign our focus toward scholar success.

One of the first initiatives implemented was the adoption of block scheduling, allowing all grade levels to teach language arts and mathematics simultaneously. Aligning prep times provided additional opportunities for collaboration and collective planning. As the leadership team evolved into a guiding coalition, we engaged in professional readings to deepen our understanding of the purpose and impact of these structural changes.

Together, we established "guaranteed standards," with each grade level selecting one math and one language arts standard that all scholars would master at or above grade level. Vertical alignment across grades ensured continuous academic progression.

After the first year of implementing the PLC process and RTI process, our scholars demonstrated significant academic growth. Teachers reported increased confidence among students and deeper conceptual understanding through reteaching and reassessment. State assessment results confirmed this progress, with achievement gains ranging from 9 percent to 26 percent—the highest in a decade.

> *This transformation reflects a profound cultural shift: from completing lessons by a fixed timeline to ensuring that every scholar achieves genuine mastery through collaboration, reflection, and collective responsibility. (J. Stone, personal communication, September–October 2025)*

To elevate this concept further, think of your guiding coalition as your school's hub for improvement, a term drawn from research on networked improvement communities (Russell et al., 2025). A *hub* is a leadership group that actively "recruits and coordinates the work of diverse members" and "creates organizational structures and routines that support network members as they develop, test, and refine interventions and practice changes" (Russell et al., 2025, p. 8). This framing gives the guiding coalition a more powerful and strategic identity than a simple committee.

The transition from a messenger team to a missionary hub represents a profound shift in your school's underlying theory of change (Noble, 2021). A *messenger team* operates on a compliance model: The principal decides, the team disseminates, and success is measured by whether people follow the rules (Noble, 2021). A *missionary hub*, however, operates on an inquiry model. It begins with the fundamental question "Is what we're doing working?" (Noble, 2021). Answering this question requires a different kind of work. It demands looking at evidence, engaging in disciplined inquiry, and being vulnerable enough to admit that current practices may not be effective (Russell et al., 2025). This moves the locus of control from external ("Am I doing what I'm told?") to internal ("Are we figuring out what works for our students?"; Cuddemi, 2021). Therefore, creating a guiding coalition is not just about renaming a team; it requires consciously deciding to abandon a simplistic, compliance-based theory and embracing a more complex but far more powerful theory: collective learning and problem solving. This requires the leadership skill of conceptual clarity, defining and communicating this crucial distinction for the entire staff. This is the essential first step in building what researchers call a *scientific-professional learning community*, a PLC in which the community continually verifies learning (Russell et al., 2025).

The Who and Why of the Guiding Coalition

In his seminal work *Good to Great*, Jim Collins (2001) offers a powerful metaphor for organizational transformation: First, get the right people on the bus, then get the right people in the right seats, and then figure out where to drive it (Hall, 2022). This principle of *who before what* is the most important strategic consideration when forming your guiding coalition. The composition of this team is not an administrative detail; it is the foundation on which all future success is built (Berg, 2018). A powerful, aligned, and trusted team can navigate any challenge, while a "misaligned, ill-fitting, uncaring team can cause the entire [program] to flounder or grind to a halt" (Ferrabee, 2016).

So, who are the right people? The research provides a clear, multifaceted strategy for selection.

To be effective, the coalition must be more than the principal's inner circle. It must have strategic representation from the wider school population, including teacher leaders from different grade levels, subject areas, and departments. It must also include representatives of support areas such as counselors, special education staff, and instructional coaches. This broad representation ensures that insights from all corners of the school are considered and that the shared understandings and actions developed by the coalition can be effectively implemented across the entire school community (Noble, 2021).

To create a balance of power and competencies, the principal must employ the skill of strategic talent assessment to look beyond titles and identify true influence and expertise. Look for a team that collectively embodies four essential types of power and competence (Mattos et al., 2025).

1. **Positional power:** Include key managers and formal leaders whose authority and commitment are necessary to prevent the work from being blocked (Hall, 2022).
2. **Expertise:** Seek out individuals with deep knowledge of content, pedagogy, data analysis, or the PLC process itself. Someone who has been part of a successful PLC at another school can be an invaluable asset (Hall, 2022; Noble, 2021).
3. **Credibility:** Identify the informal opinion leaders. These are the staff members who are so respected and trusted that others will follow their lead. Their influence is critical for building consensus and investment (Hall, 2022; Noble, 2021).
4. **Leadership ability:** Look for individuals with proven leadership and management skills who can help structure the process and drive the work, turning vision into sustained action (Hall, 2022).

Next, look for the change-ready mindset. According to Everett M. Rogers's (2003) research on the diffusion of innovations, about 15 percent of any organization is composed of innovators and early adopters. These are the individuals who are naturally drawn to new ideas, are willing to take risks, and are excited by the prospect of change (Hall, 2022). Educational leadership consultant Ian Jukes, in his now-defunct blog, likens them to the *committed sardines* in a large school of fish; when this critical mass of 10 to 15 percent turns, the rest of the school instantly follows (Hall, 2022). Your guiding coalition should be built primarily from this group of dreamers and promoters of change—in other words, your Believers.

Finally, just as important as who to get on the bus is who to keep off. Leadership expert John Kotter (1996) warns against including two types of people on a change-leading team: (1) those who have egos that "fill up a room, leaving no space for anybody else," and (2) those who create so much mistrust that they destroy any chance of genuine collaboration (p. 59). In the language of this book, this requires a more nuanced approach to Fundamentalists—those who resist change.

While it is crucial to listen to and understand all perspectives, Level Four Fundamentalists, specifically, should not be given leadership seats on the guiding coalition. This group's resistance is rooted in the belief that not all students deserve success, and these resisters actively work to maintain an inequitable status quo. In contrast, other levels of resistance often stem from a lack of clarity, trust, or skills, and these individuals can often be brought on board through clear communication, trust building, and guided implementation support. Therefore, the role of most resisters is not to lead the change but to engage in it. You require the difficult but essential leadership skill of setting ideological boundaries, protecting the mission by strategically excluding those who fundamentally oppose it.

Are you planning to find members of your guiding coalition, or do you need a new tool so people can apply for membership? "Tool 6.4: Guiding Coalition Application and Self-Reflection" (page 228) can help you.

But what happens when, despite your best efforts in selection, an attack comes from within the guiding coalition? This is a critical test of the team's health and the principal's leadership. When a member uses defamation or other undermining tactics against a colleague on the team, the issue must be addressed directly and immediately. The first line of defense is the coalition itself, revisiting the established norms of trust and professional dialogue that are the price of admission for membership. If the behavior persists, the principal has a non-negotiable duty to intervene to protect the psychological safety of the team and the integrity of the work, which may include removing the individual from the coalition. Disagreements are allowed (and even expected), but leaders have to be able to name the three Ds when they are being employed among them. Make sure to review the three Ds (chapter 1) as a first step to identifying if there is a problem. A guiding coalition cannot function as an engine for positive change if it is a source of personal attacks.

The Work of the Coalition, From Isolated Problems to Collective Solutions

One of the greatest challenges to meaningful school improvement is the education profession's deeply ingrained culture of isolation. As Dan Lortie (1975) describes in his concept of the apprenticeship of observation, people learn how to be teachers by spending thirteen years as students, watching their own teachers work alone in their classrooms. This experience socializes them to believe that teaching is a private act and that problems are to be solved individually, behind a closed classroom door. That traditional culture pushes problem solving into silos, such as the teacher's classroom and the principal's office (Noble, 2021). The guiding coalition is designed to systematically dismantle these silos. Collaborative cultures foster seamless problem solving, innovation, and effective interventions when educators work together to leverage their collective experiences and knowledge for sustained improvement (Hanks, 2023; Kiral, 2025; Valera, 2023).

To see the power of this shift, consider a common scenario: the implementation of a new district-mandated literacy curriculum.

In a school with a traditional isolated culture, the process is predictable and often painful. The principal announces the new curriculum at a staff meeting. Boxes of materials are delivered to classrooms. Teachers are then left to figure it out on their own. Some, through heroic effort, will make it work. Others will struggle, growing frustrated and demoralized. A few may simply close their doors and continue teaching the way they always have. This approach inevitably leads to wildly inconsistent implementation, negative feelings toward the new initiative, and a culture of blame. Teachers blame the curriculum ("This is junk"), the district ("Another top-down mandate"), or the students ("The kids just can't do this work"). This is the very culture that burns out good teachers and creates what we call Survivors.

Now, consider the same challenge in a school where a guiding coalition leads the process. The work looks entirely different. The guiding coalition members do the following.

- **They learn deeply and collectively:** The guiding coalition members don't just distribute the materials; they become the lead learners. They study the new curriculum, the research behind it, and the instructional shifts it requires (Hall, 2022).
- **They anchor the work in the four critical questions of a PLC:** Instead of just asking, "How do we implement this?," the coalition asks the questions that matter: "What is it we want our students to know and be able to do? How will we know if each student has learned it? How will we respond when some students do not learn it? How will we extend the learning for students who have demonstrated proficiency?" (DuFour et al., 2024, p. 67).
- **They engage in disciplined inquiry:** The coalition members model and lead a process of experimentation. A skillful leader guides them to use continuous improvement methods like action research, which cultivate a systemwide mindset for school improvement (Durden, 2024). Utilizing structures like the plan-do-study-act cycle, they test specific strategies from the new curriculum on a small scale (Russell et al., 2025). They use practical measures, or short and simple assessments, to gather real-time data on what is and isn't working in their specific context (Russell et al., 2025). This is the skill of designing and managing improvement processes.
- **They build collective teacher efficacy:** This is the crucial outcome. By analyzing the data from their small tests together, the teams identify which strategies are most effective for their students. They build common formative assessments to monitor student learning across grade levels (Cuddemi, 2021; Hall, 2022). Success is no longer isolated in one classroom; it becomes a shared, collective achievement. A skillful leader doesn't hope this happens; they use the skill of intentionally cultivating collective teacher efficacy. This process builds the unshakable belief that by working together, teachers can ensure all their students succeed. Research by John Hattie (2023) shows that collective teacher efficacy is one of the most powerful influences on student achievement, more powerful than the effects of poverty.
- **They attend to the human side of change:** A high-functioning guiding coalition has a finger on the pulse of the staff. Coalition members recognize that change is stressful, and they work with the principal to balance the pressure for results with authentic support, ensuring that teachers feel capable and not overwhelmed (Noble, 2021). Leaders must be intentional about their feedback process to manage cognitive dissonance and avoid ill-fated decisions (Brown & McGill, 2025).

Finally, and most importantly, educators reading this section will ask, "When?" A guiding coalition cannot become a team of experts by simply adding more to an already overflowing workload. This deep learning requires dedicated time. That may mean paid summer work, dedicated time over breaks, or focused weekly meetings before or after school. Sometimes, this is done with substitutes, interventionists, or coaches spending routine time in the classrooms of a small work group as they jigsaw the work for the meeting. While district-level support for this guiding coalition learning time is very helpful (and what we advocate for), its absence isn't a reason to abandon the work if the focus remains on student success. The minutes are there, but the team and the principal may need to use creative ways to compile them.

This chapter is your road map for moving from isolated problems to collective solutions. The tools we have shared are the very instruments your team will use to do this work. Once a guiding coalition is formed and understands its purpose, its primary function is to lead change. "Tool 6.5: Time for Change—A Guiding Coalition Framework" (page 231) provides a structured process for the team to use whenever a new initiative or change to policy or practice is considered. It ensures that any proposed change is thoughtfully vetted, aligned with research, and planned with the school's unique culture in mind. It was built to help a school's guiding coalition move the needle and make a difference for the students.

The Principal's Non-Negotiable Clarity on Tight and Loose

Let's get back to the principal's role in the complex work of school improvement. Effective leaders must be clear about what is tight and what is loose (Noble, 2021). *Tight* refers to the few critical, non-negotiable elements that must be implemented with fidelity across the organization. *Loose* refers to the areas where professionals have the autonomy and creative freedom to determine how best to achieve shared goals.

Schools have many important tight elements. Student safety is tight, and adherence to a guaranteed and viable curriculum is tight. But the ultimate tight practice, the principal's most important non-negotiable responsibility for improving student learning, is the development and maintenance of a high-functioning guiding coalition (Noble, 2021). This is not just a recommendation; it is a structural necessity for building a sustainable, healthy school culture and ensuring the leader is not viewed as a superhero (or supervillain).

Educators know guiding coalitions are important, so why can't every school just get started tomorrow? The reality is that initiating formal collaborative leadership is unequivocally the leader's job because it cannot work the other way around. The history of the role and educators' socialization in the field work against this concept. This is a critical point and an essential skill of modern leadership: No matter how influential, passionate, or credible a teacher leader is, without the active partnership and structural support of the building's principal, any grassroots effort to form such a team will remain on the periphery at best. The principal holds the formal authority to allocate time, provide resources, and legitimize the team's work in the eyes of the entire staff. As educational consultant Robin Noble (2021) states unequivocally, "Setting up a guiding coalition must be your number-one priority as a school leader" (p. 112).

Your job is to be the leader of the hub, not the sole source of answers (Russell et al., 2025). This requires a specific set of leadership actions and a relentless focus on what matters most.

- **Strategic knowledge management:** You must ensure that the valuable learning generated by individual teams does not stay locked in those teams. Your role as hub leader is to create systems to harvest that learning, manage it, and make it visible to everyone. This is how a network accelerates improvement, ensuring that promising practices spread effectively across all classrooms (Russell et al., 2025). This is a critical skill for scaling success.
- **Relational trust:** You are the chief architect of your school's culture. You must intentionally cultivate an environment of psychological safety where coalition members feel they can have honest conversations, disagree respectfully, and take risks without fear of reprisal (Russell et al., 2025). This starts with you. When you genuinely welcome different opinions and model being a good listener, you teach your team that all voices are critical to the process (Noble, 2021). Skillful leaders know that trust is the currency of change.
- **Fidelity to the process:** Your tightest hold must be on the process of collaboration itself. Your most important skill is maintaining a laser-like focus, constantly ensuring that the guiding coalition members—and by extension, all collaborative teams—stay true to the three big ideas of a PLC (a focus on learning, a collaborative culture, and a results orientation) and consistently anchor their work in the four critical questions (Hall, 2022).

This is how you leave a legacy. The guiding coalition is the fertile ground where you nurture the next generation of leaders from within your own staff. It is the engine that creates a culture of continuous improvement that does not depend on any single individual, including you. By making the guiding coalition your non-negotiable priority, you are not just improving your school for today but building a system that can learn, adapt, and thrive long after you are gone. That is how you truly leave a place better than you found it.

The School Culture Players

The shift from a top-down, principal-centric model to one driven by a guiding coalition fundamentally alters the school landscape for every school culture player. It changes the nature of influence, the channels of communication, and the pathways to professional growth. Understanding how this structural change impacts each group is key to navigating the transition successfully. Here is how it directly impacts the school culture players.

Empowering Believers

For Believers, establishing a guiding coalition is like opening the floodgates. These educators have always been committed to student success but may have felt their influence was limited to their own classrooms or informal conversations. The guiding coalition provides them with a formal, legitimized structure to channel their passion and expertise. It shifts them from isolated advocates to core drivers of the school's improvement engine. They are no longer just hoping for change; they are actively designing and leading it. This structure empowers them to share their effective practices more broadly, mentor colleagues, and contribute to decisions that affect the entire school, amplifying their positive impact exponentially.

Supporting Tweeners

For Tweeners, a visible and effective guiding coalition provides a powerful, positive model of professional life in the school. Instead of being socialized primarily through the informal networks, where they might be swayed by the cynicism of Fundamentalists, they see a clear alternative. They observe respected teachers leading, collaborating, and solving problems together. This communicates a powerful norm and expectation for a newer staff member. The guiding coalition represents a career pathway and a vision of what it means to be an empowered professional in the building, encouraging Tweeners to align with the forces of positive change and aspire to one day be part of that engine themselves.

Flipping Fundamentalists

A guiding coalition is perhaps the most powerful tool for flipping Fundamentalists because it systematically dismantles the conditions in which their resistance thrives. As this chapter's opening vignette shows, savvy Fundamentalists know that a lone superhero leader is temporary—that such a leader will eventually burn out. Their strategy often is simply to wait them out, knowing the system will likely revert to the status quo. A guiding coalition, however, represents a permanent structural shift, making the wait-and-see approach obsolete. It acts as a supercharger for addressing the core needs of each level of resistance.

Level One (Need Clarity): Supercharging Communication

For Level One Fundamentalists, whose resistance stems from a lack of clarity, the guiding coalition is a communication powerhouse. It moves beyond simply having the principal as a single source of information and establishes a formal, multifaceted communication plan. This means information is now communicated, discussed, and championed by a team of respected peers from across the building. This multivoiced, consistent messaging makes the why behind initiatives clearer and harder to dismiss as one person's agenda.

This formal communication system includes several key components. First, the coalition members leverage modern technology like texting apps and social media alongside traditional newsletters and meetings to ensure messages reach diverse audiences (Graf, 2019). Second, they professionalize meetings by sending agendas in advance; allowing staff time to process content and come prepared for discussion makes for more effective use of time (Ford, 2023). Third, they use structured protocols to guide conversations, ensuring all voices are heard and helping teams build consensus (Cuddemi, 2021). They might also use a data wall in a shared, accessible space as a leadership strategy because this empowers teachers to collectively analyze patterns and make instructional decisions (Fisher & Nepote, 2025). Finally, staff meetings themselves become collaborative, with guiding coalition members presenting and facilitating to turn a passive event into an active learning experience. This robust communication structure ensures the misinformation that might fester in the informal networks is quickly countered by credible colleagues who are part of the process.

Level Two (Need Trust): Supercharging Trust in Leadership

For Level Two Fundamentalists, who resist due to broken trust, a guiding coalition changes the dynamic of decision making. It's no longer just the principal making decisions; it's a team of their peers. When they see colleagues they respect grappling with data, debating solutions, and sharing leadership, it builds trust not just in individuals but in the process itself. The transparency of the coalition's work demonstrates a commitment to shared power, which can begin to heal past wounds caused by top-down mandates.

Level Three (Need Capacity or Skills): Modeling Capacity Building

For Level Three Fundamentalists, who resist because they feel they lack the skills to succeed, the guiding coalition serves as a living model of professional learning. The coalition doesn't just mandate change; it engages in the messy work of learning, experimenting, and problem solving out in the open. This demonstrates that it's OK not to have all the answers and that support is available. The coalition's focus on building systems of support shows these resisters how the work will be done and that they won't be left to figure it out on their own.

Level Four (Resistant to the Core Mission): Mitigating Resistance

The guiding coalition fundamentally neutralizes the tactics of Level Four Fundamentalists. Their primary weapons of *defame*, *disrupt*, and *distract* become largely ineffective against a collective leadership body.

1. **Defame:** It is much harder to personally defame an entire team of respected colleagues than it is to target a single principal. The rest of the staff are more likely to see attacks on the group as unreasonable and out of touch.
2. **Disrupt:** The disruption tactic, often used to derail meetings or initiatives with last-minute objections, is also blunted. Because the guiding coalition has developed a thoughtful, data-informed plan, a sudden disruption is less likely to succeed. Furthermore, a healthy coalition is willing to listen to logical concerns, so if there is a legitimate issue, the coalition addresses it constructively, robbing the disruption of its power to simply stop progress.
3. **Distract:** In a one-on-one or top-down model, it's easy for a resister to disengage. However, in a collaborative team setting led by the guiding coalition, overt distraction becomes socially isolating and professionally untenable. When your peers are all engaged in focused, productive work, choosing to be the one on your phone or making side comments marks you as an obstacle to the team's success.

Saving Survivors

The existence of a guiding coalition can turn things around for Survivors. Instead of one helpful individual whose attention is split multiple ways (the principal), the guiding coalition can provide support across multiple avenues. Additionally, by distributing leadership and responsibility, the coalition lessens the individual burden on all teachers. More importantly, by focusing on creating effective systems of support, the coalition can address the root causes of a Survivor's struggles. When a Survivor sees a team of colleagues actively working to solve the systemic issues that make their job feel impossible, it can provide a glimmer of hope and a reason to reengage. The collective problem solving of the coalition can offer practical solutions that make the daily work feel more manageable and sustainable. There still is no guarantee this will rehabilitate these school culture players, but it does represent a hopeful opportunity.

 **Brilliant Voice From the Field** 

SHARON KOLLAR

Principal, Garden City High School, Garden City, Michigan

At Garden City High School, we are definitely a work in progress, but we are on the move. The journey to build an authentic collaborative culture and a dedicated intervention time for our students didn't happen overnight. It began in my seventh year as principal, and our first hurdles weren't just about school improvement—we had to navigate a difficult teacher contract and the immediate disruption of COVID.

The real story is about persisting and actually believing in what you are doing, rather than pushing a movement just for the sake of it. Our approach was about showing people what could be done, little by little. Like a sunrise or a sunset, gradual change is more amazing than if it suddenly appears or disappears. As more staff saw the value, they realized they really can be good with change. In fact, some of the people initially resistant are now encouraging others to join our journey.

We are still overcoming hurdles, but our why is clear and the payoff is visible: Our students are achieving more. We're seeing grades improve and celebrating growth on the SAT. Seeing the results for our kids proves that this persistent, gradual work is the right work. (S. Kollar, personal communication, September–October 2025)

Chapter 6 Tools

Shifting from the superhero model of leadership to a collaborative guiding coalition is a fundamental step for sustaining a healthy school culture. This takes a high level of reflection and bravery because you must open yourself up to the past. When you know better, you can do better. This is true for leaders as people and as teams. There are many places where a principal and guiding coalition could start with this chapter's selection of tools, but the most important thing is to take that first step of picking one. Be open, humble, and forward focused.

Figure 6.2 breaks down this chapter's tools.

Tool Number	Title of Tool	Purpose
Tool 6.1	Principal's Collaborative Leadership Self-Assessment	Provide the principal with a structured tool to reflect on their leadership practices, assess their alignment with a collaborative distributed leadership model, and identify specific areas for fostering a healthy school culture through a guiding coalition.
Tool 6.2	Guiding Coalition Reality Check: Aligning Practice to Purpose	Provide a structured process for the guiding coalition to reflect on its core purpose, analyze the alignment between its current practices and PLC best practices, and create a focused action plan for increasing its impact on instruction, collaboration, and results.
Tool 6.3	Guiding Coalition Work Analysis: Focusing Our Force	Provide the guiding coalition with a collaborative tool to reflect on its collective practices, assess its effectiveness in driving the school-improvement process, and identify areas for strengthening its leadership and impact.
Tool 6.4	Guiding Coalition Application and Self-Reflection	Provide a reflective application process for educators who are interested in joining the guiding coalition.
Tool 6.5	Time for Change: A Guiding Coalition Framework	Provide the guiding coalition with a structured framework for planning and leading any significant change initiative.

Figure 6.2: *Chapter 6 tools.*

Tool 6.1: Principal's Collaborative Leadership Self-Assessment

Purpose

Provide the principal with a structured tool to reflect on their leadership practices, assess their alignment with a collaborative distributed leadership model, and identify specific areas for fostering a healthy school culture through a guiding coalition.

Instructions

Rate yourself on each statement using the provided scale. Be honest in your reflection. In the Evidence and Notes column, jot down specific examples that support your rating. After completing the assessment, use the reflection questions to synthesize your thoughts and plan next steps.

Scale

1 = Rarely or never | 2 = Sometimes | 3 = Often | 4 = Consistently

Part 1: Adopting a Leadership Mindset—From Superhero to System Builder

Statement	Rating (1–4)	Evidence and Notes
1. You actively distribute leadership responsibilities rather than being the sole problem solver.		
2. You consciously model vulnerability and a learner stance, admitting when you don't have the answer.		
3. Your decisions are primarily driven by building long-term collective capacity, not finding short-term fixes.		
4. You resist the urge to make unilateral decisions in nonemergency situations, even when that would be faster.		

Part 2: Fostering the Guiding Coalition

Statement	Rating (1–4)	Evidence and Notes
5. You keep the development and maintenance of a high-functioning guiding coalition your top priority.		
6. You ensure the guiding coalition's work is focused on learning and the PLC process, not just managerial logistics.		

7. You empower guiding coalition members to share in decision making, treating them as equal partners.		
8. You protect the guiding coalition members' time and focus, ensuring they work on the right work of school improvement.		

Part 3: Cultivating a Culture of Trust and Safety

Statement	Rating (1–4)	Evidence and Notes
9. You intentionally foster an environment of psychological safety where staff feel they can take risks and speak openly.		
10. Your interactions with staff are characterized by trust-building behaviors (for example, listening and transparency) rather than fear-based compliance.		
11. You actively work to quiet adult drama by modeling and expecting professional, respectful dialogue.		
12. You create systems and opportunities that break down teacher isolation and promote collaboration.		

Part 4: Maintaining Focus and Accountability

Statement	Rating (1–4)	Evidence and Notes
13. You are clear and consistent about the few tight non-negotiables (for example, fidelity to the PLC process).		
14. You provide autonomy and flexibility on the loose elements, trusting your staff's professionalism.		
15. You act as the leader of the hub, creating systems to share and scale effective practices across the school.		
16. Your primary measures of your own success are the success and sustainability of the systems and the leadership of others.		

page 2 of 3

Scoring

Calculate your scores for each part using the following chart.

Part	Statements	Score
Adopting a Leadership Mindset: From Superhero to System Builder	Add your scores for statements 1–4.	
Fostering the Guiding Coalition	Add your scores for statements 5–8.	
Cultivating a Culture of Trust and Safety	Add your scores for statements 9–12.	
Maintaining Focus and Accountability	Add your scores for statements 13–16.	

Interpret your scores for each part.

- **Area of strength (score of 13–16):** Your practices in this area consistently align with a collaborative, system-building leadership model. How can you leverage this strength to support other areas?
- **Area of practice (score of 9–12):** You are actively working on this, but there is room for more consistency. What specific actions can make these practices more routine?
- **Area for growth (score of 5–8):** This is an area that presents a significant opportunity for your leadership development. What is one small change you can make to begin improving?
- **Critical priority (score of 4):** This area requires your immediate and focused attention. What support do you need to begin redesigning your approach here?

Individual Reflection

Consider your strengths as revealed by the preceding results. Analyzing the data, identify which parts match your perceptions and which don't.

- Based on your scores, which area is your greatest strength as a collaborative leader?
- Which area presents the biggest opportunity for your growth?
- What is one specific, actionable step you can take this month to move from a superhero mindset to a system-builder mindset?
- How can you better empower your guiding coalition to lead the work of school improvement?

Tool 6.2: Guiding Coalition Reality Check—Aligning Practice to Purpose

Purpose

Provide a structured process for the guiding coalition to reflect on its core purpose, analyze the alignment between its current practices and PLC best practices, and create a focused action plan for increasing its impact on instruction, collaboration, and results.

Instructions

Work through the four parts of this tool as a team. Part 1 is a foundational check-in on your team's identity. Part 2 is a collaborative brainstorming activity to map your work. Part 3 guides a deep-dive reflection that will lead directly to the action plan in part 4. You will need access to all your old agendas.

Part 1: Foundational Check-In—"Are We a Guiding Coalition?"

As a team, review the five tight practices of a high-functioning guiding coalition. Place a check mark in the Yes column for each practice that consistently describes your team and a check mark in the No column for each practice that doesn't consistently describe your team.

Tight Practice	Yes	No
1. Our primary responsibilities are to focus on learning, create a culture of collaboration, and be results driven.		
2. Our members are selected based on their expertise, credibility, and leadership, and we act as relentless learners.		
3. We consistently focus our meetings on improvement of student learning and outcomes, not just managerial tasks.		
4. We operate as a team of equals without positional power influencing our discussions or decisions.		
5. Our main focus is ensuring that all school policies, practices, and procedures support student learning.		

Part 2: Current Reality Versus Best Practice—A Venn Diagram Analysis

Access your old meeting agendas. As a team, identify specific actions, conversations, and agenda items from your meetings this year or last year, and record them on a poster that features the following categories. A Venn diagram works well for this, but you can choose whatever format you like.

1. **Our current practice (what we actually do):** List specific, recurring activities and topics from your meetings.
2. **PLC best practice (what a high-functioning coalition should do):**
    - Lead the development of a guaranteed and viable curriculum.
    - Analyze schoolwide instructional trends.

page 1 of 3

- Monitor the health of collaborative teams.
- Build systems for intervention (response to intervention or multitiered system of supports).
- Use data to drive all decisions.
- Model and support the four critical questions.

3. **Where we align (the overlap):** Determine what from your current practice list also fits in the best practice list.

Part 3: Deep-Dive Reflection

Discuss the following questions as a team based on your analysis in part 2.

Focus on Instruction and Learning

- Based on our meeting agendas and minutes, what percentage of our time is dedicated to discussing and improving Tier 1 instruction?
- What specific actions that we have taken this year have directly led to measurable improvements in classroom instruction across the school?
- How do we ensure that our work on curriculum and assessment (the *what* and *how we know*) translates into more effective teaching (the *how we teach*)?

Focus on Collaboration

- Beyond scheduling meetings, how do we actively monitor and support the effectiveness of our school's collaborative teams?
- What is our process for identifying and assisting a team that is struggling with conflict, a lack of focus, or inconsistent follow-through?
- How do we model the norms of a high-functioning collaborative team in our own work together?

Focus on Results

- What are the top two or three data points that we track relentlessly to measure our school's progress?
- Can we draw a direct line from a specific action we took as a coalition to a positive change in our school's results? What is it?
- How do we celebrate our successes and use our results (both positive and negative) to inform our next cycle of work?

Part 4: Focused Action Plan

Based on your reflections, identify one key area for improvement and create a plan to address it.

Our Goal What is the one thing we want to improve about our coalition's practice?
Key Actions What are the two or three specific steps we will take to achieve this goal?
1.
2.
3.
Who and When Who is responsible for each action, and what is the timeline?
Evidence of Success How will we know if we have succeeded? What will be different?

page 3 of 3

Tool 6.3: Guiding Coalition Work Analysis—Focusing Our Force

Purpose

Provide the guiding coalition with a collaborative tool to reflect on its collective practices, assess its effectiveness in driving the school-improvement process, and identify areas for strengthening its leadership and impact. This tool is designed to help the team distinguish between high-leverage, transformational work and low-leverage, managerial tasks.

Instructions

As a team, discuss and rate your guiding coalition's performance on each statement using the provided scale. Be candid and use specific examples from your work together. After completing the assessment, use the reflection questions to guide a discussion about your team's strengths, areas for growth, and future actions.

Scale

1 = Rarely or never | 2 = Sometimes | 3 = Often | 4 = Consistently

Part 1: The Work of Instructional Leadership

Statement	Rating (1–4)	Evidence and Notes *Meeting agendas, data reviewed, actions taken, and so on*
1. We analyze schoolwide data to identify trends in instructional strengths and weaknesses.		
2. We lead the development and monitoring of a guaranteed and viable curriculum for all students.		
3. We actively promote and support the implementation of high-quality, research-based instructional practices.		
4. We ensure that instructional decisions and schoolwide initiatives are driven by equity.		
Part 1 Total:		

page 1 of 4

Part 2: The Work of Fostering Effective Collaboration

Statement	Rating (1–4)	**Evidence and Notes** *Team protocols, support provided, feedback from teams, and so on*
5. We model the norms and practices of a high-functioning collaborative team in our own meetings.		
6. We have a clear system for monitoring the health and effectiveness of grade-level and department teams.		
7. We provide targeted support, coaching, and resources to teams that are struggling with the collaborative process.		
8. We ensure that collaborative team time is protected and focused on the right work (the four critical questions of a PLC).		
Part 2 Total:		

Part 3: The Nature of Our Work—Transformation Versus Management

This part is for reflection, not scoring. Discuss as a team where the balance of your time and energy falls.

Our Work Tends to Be More . . .	Evidence and Examples	What Shifts We Need to Make
Transformational (missionary work): Analyzing learning data, designing improvement cycles, building teacher capacity, leading professional learning, and challenging the status quo		
Managerial (messenger work): Discussing bus duty, planning assemblies, reviewing calendars, disseminating information from the principal, and solving immediate logistical problems		

page 2 of 4

Part 4: Our Momentum—Analysis of Our Force and Distance

This section is for reflection. Think of your work like this physics equation: work = force × distance. Your force is the quality and focus of your effort. Your distance is the tangible progress you make.

Reflection Prompt	Team Discussion and Notes
Our force (time and effort): How much time do we dedicate to guiding coalition work? Is that time protected and highly focused, or is it often interrupted or diluted by lower-leverage tasks?	
Our distance (impact and progress): Looking back at our work this year or in past years, what is the most significant distance that we have moved the school? What tangible, measurable progress can we point to as a result of our plans?	
Our friction (obstacles): What consistently holds us back or slows our momentum (for example, lack of time, competing initiatives, resistance from specific groups, unclear data, or lack of follow-through)?	

Scoring

Calculate your scores for parts 1 and 2 using the following chart.

Part	Statements	Score
Part 1: The Work of Instructional Leadership	Add your scores for statements 1–4.	
Part 2: The Work of Fostering Effective Collaboration	Add your scores for statements 5–8.	

Interpret your scores for parts 1 and 2.

The Work of Instructional Leadership

- **Score of 14–16:** Exemplary leadership
- **Score of 11–13:** Strategic impact
- **Score of 8–10:** Developing focus
- **Score of 6–7:** Foundational work needed
- **Score of 4–5:** Work just getting started

The Work of Fostering Effective Collaboration

- **Score of 14–16:** Synergistic team
- **Score of 11–13:** Connected collaborators
- **Score of 8–10:** Building momentum
- **Score of 6–7:** Foundational work needed
- **Score of 4–5:** Work just getting started

Team Reflection and Discussion

As a team, discuss the aggregated results of the survey.

- Based on our analysis, are we truly a guiding coalition, or are we operating more like a traditional leadership team? What is our evidence?
- Looking at our friction, what is the biggest obstacle we need to address to increase our momentum and impact?
- What is one specific change we will make to our meeting structures or work processes to ensure we spend more time on transformational, high-leverage activities?

Tool 6.4: Guiding Coalition Application and Self-Reflection

Purpose

Provide a reflective application process for educators who are interested in joining the guiding coalition. This tool is designed to help candidates assess their alignment with the mindset and responsibilities of a missionary leader and provide the selection committee with deeper insight into each applicant's readiness to lead change.

Instructions

Read the call-to-lead letter first. Then, thoughtfully complete the self-reflection sections that follow. Your candid responses will help both you and the selection committee determine whether this leadership role is the right fit at this time.

Part 1: The Call to Lead

Dear Colleague,

We are seeking to form our school's guiding coalition, and we are looking for a small group of dedicated missionaries to lead this team's work.

This is not a traditional leadership team. As guiding coalition members, we will not be messengers who simply manage logistics or disseminate information. Our purpose is singular and profound: to serve as the engine for our school's continuous improvement. We will be the lead learners, the chief strategists, and the unwavering champions for a culture where every student succeeds.

Our work will focus on what matters most: strengthening instructional practice and ensuring every collaborative team is effective. We will engage in disciplined inquiry, using data to ask hard questions and work together to build systems that support all teachers and students. This role requires courage, a collaborative spirit, a relentless focus on student learning, and the belief that we, collectively, can make a profound difference.

If you are passionate about building a sustainable system of success and are ready to lead this transformational work, we invite you to complete the following self-reflection.

Part 2: Applicant Self-Reflection

Section A: Your Leadership Mindset and Core Beliefs

Reflection Prompt	Your Response
1. **Your why:** Why are you drawn to this specific leadership work? What experiences have shaped your belief in the need for a collaborative, system-focused approach to school improvement?	

page 1 of 3

2. **Your view on change:** Describe your comfort level with challenging the status quo. When you see a practice or system that is not serving students, what is your typical response?	
3. **Your role in collaboration:** Do you see yourself more as a lone wolf who gets things done efficiently on your own or as a pack member who believes the best solutions come from the group? Explain your reasoning.	

Section B: Your Understanding of the Right Work

Reflection Prompt	Your Response
4. **Instructional practice:** From your perspective, what area of instructional practice does our school most need to strengthen? Why is this area critical?	
5. **Teacher collaboration:** What do you believe is the most significant factor that determines a collaborative team's effectiveness?	
6. **Missionary versus messenger work:** In your own words, what is the most important difference between the missionary work of a guiding coalition and the messenger work of a traditional leadership team?	

Section C: Your Capacity to Lead and Influence

Reflection Prompt	Your Response
7. **Your credibility:** Why do you believe your colleagues would trust you to help lead a significant change process? What have you done to build that trust?	
8. **Your expertise:** What specific skills, knowledge, or expertise do you have that would help the guiding coalition lead the PLC process?	
9. **Your approach to resistance:** Imagine a colleague expressed strong resistance to a new initiative that the guiding coalition is leading. How would you approach having a conversation with them to build understanding and seek common ground?	

Section D: Your Commitment to the Process

Reflection Prompt	Your Response
10. **Your role as a learner:** This work requires being a lead learner. Describe your willingness to engage with data, research, and new ideas, even if they challenge your current thinking.	
11. **Your commitment:** The work of a guiding coalition requires significant time, focus, and emotional energy. What makes you confident you can make and sustain this commitment for the school year?	

Tool 6.5: Time for Change—A Guiding Coalition Framework

Purpose

Provide the guiding coalition with a structured framework for planning and leading any significant change initiative. This tool is grounded in the four essential skills of transformational leaders—(1) communicating the rationale, (2) establishing trust, (3) building capacity, and (4) getting results—as described by Anthony Muhammad and Luis F. Cruz (2019). It is designed to help the team move from isolated problem solving to collective, systemwide solutions.

Instructions

When considering a new initiative (for example, implementing a new curriculum or changing a schoolwide practice), use this tool to guide your planning process. Work through each part as a team to ensure your plan is comprehensive and strategic and attends to the human side of change.

Part 1: Defining the Change Initiative and Its Purpose

Guiding Questions	Our Response
The proposed change: What, specifically, are we proposing to change?	
The problem of practice: What specific problem is this change intended to solve? What data tells us this is a problem?	
The desired outcome: If we are successful, what will be different for our students and our staff? How will we know it is different?	

Part 2: Applying the Four Essential Skills to Lead the Change

As a team, use the following sections to plan how you will apply each of the four essential skills to your initiative. These skills are your levers for moving from an isolated, compliance-based culture to one that is collaborative and effective.

Skill 1: Communicating the Rationale (the Why)

This skill counters the top-down mandate problem by ensuring everyone understands the purpose.

Guiding Questions	Our Plan and Actions
Clarity: How will we clearly and consistently articulate the why behind this change, connecting it with our school's mission and students' needs?	
Evidence: What specific data and research will we use to make a compelling and undeniable case for this change?	
Communication channels: What multiple pathways (such as staff meetings, newsletters, team meetings, and one-on-one conversations) will we use to ensure the message is heard and understood by everyone?	

Skill 2: Establishing Trust (the Who)

This skill addresses the human side of change by fostering psychological safety and collective ownership.

Guiding Questions	Our Plan and Actions
Collaboration: How will we involve staff in the planning and decision-making process to ensure their voices and expertise are valued?	
Vulnerability: How will we, as coalition members, model being lead learners who don't have all the answers and are open to feedback and adjustments?	
Support: How will we demonstrate that we understand the challenges this change presents and that we are committed to supporting our colleagues through the process?	

Skill 3: Building Capacity (the How)

This skill prevents the "figure it out on your own" problem by providing the necessary learning and support to build collective teacher efficacy.

Guiding Questions	Our Plan and Actions
Skill identification: What new knowledge or skills will our colleagues need to implement this change successfully?	
Professional learning: What specific, ongoing professional learning (for example, workshops, coaching, and peer observations) will we provide? How will it be job embedded and practical?	
Resources: What materials, time, and structural supports need to be in place for teachers to succeed?	

Skill 4: Getting Results (the Do, or the What—Accountability and Momentum)

This skill ensures the change initiative is anchored in disciplined inquiry and leads to measurable improvement.

Guiding Questions	Our Plan and Actions
Measurement: How will we measure the impact of this change? What are our short-term practical measures and our long-term success indicators?	
Monitoring: What is our timeline for checking progress? How will we use data in our collaborative team and coalition meetings to monitor implementation and results?	
Accountability and celebration: How will we hold ourselves accountable for the results? How will we celebrate progress and small wins along the way to build momentum and reinforce the work?	

Source: Adapted from Muhammad, A., & Cruz, L. F. (2019). Time for change: Four essential skills for transformational school and district leaders. *Solution Tree Press.*

CHAPTER 7

Navigating From the Status Quo to Action and Hope

The journey of a thousand miles begins with a single step.

—LAO TZU

This chapter won't be starting with an opening narrative. That's because you, your guiding coalition, and your school are actually writing that narrative. Whether you have used this book to plan ahead, adjust your path, or move forward in developing a healthier school culture with your team, the story that begins this chapter is the one you are living right now. It is an honor to walk that path with you!

Throughout this book, we have explored the socially intricate and profoundly rewarding work of transforming school culture. We began this journey with the foundational wisdom of Anthony Muhammad and have sought to build on it, offering new perspectives, the latest research, and strategies to meet the evolving demands of our field. Each chapter of this book is built around one of the key areas of action he identified in the healthiest and most effective school cultures. We have journeyed through the importance of a systematic focus on learning, the power of celebration, the necessity of supporting new colleagues, the work of breaking down isolation, the need for intensive professional development, and the impact of skillful, focused leadership.

Now, as we arrive at this final chapter, we are faced with the most important questions of all: Where do we go from here? How do we translate information into action?

The work of cultural transformation is not a sprint; it is a marathon. It is a continuous cycle of learning, reflection, and courageous action. It is about choosing to see the potential in every student and every colleague and then building the systems and structures that will allow that potential to flourish. You tinker your way to utopia, knowing that while every step of the journey is not easy, it makes a difference in young people's lives. You can continue to make future lives better and help society, doing a little bit of good that tilts the world ever so slightly toward intelligence, peace, and happiness.

This final chapter is designed to be your compass to get things started or reflect on next steps. It will help you and your team determine where to begin, or perhaps more importantly, it will help you evaluate the cultural work you have already done to determine next steps. Healthy school culture is not a one-size-fits-all prescription. Every school community has unique strengths, challenges, and starting points. The key is to begin the work with intention, clarity, and shared understanding of your current reality.

Before we turn to the diagnostic tools, let us pause and reflect on the most essential ingredient of this work: hope. The book *Transforming School Culture* (Muhammad, 2018) is, at its core, a message of hope. Hope is the radical belief that schools can be places of profound equity and excellence and that educators are the agents of that transformation. Hope is not passive optimism; it is an active stance. It is the courage to confront the *brutal facts* of your current reality, as Jim Collins (2001) would say, while maintaining unwavering faith that you will prevail in the end.

Hope is found in the teacher who sees the missing piece of the learning puzzle in a student's thinking. It is found in the collaborative team that finally breaks through a difficult instructional challenge. It is found in the principal who chooses to trust and empower their staff, even when it feels risky. And it is found in the collective commitment of a school community that refuses to accept the status quo.

As you embark on the next phase of your journey, hold on to that hope. Let it be the fuel that sustains you through the difficult conversations and the inevitable setbacks. Let it be the light that guides you toward a more just and effective future for the students you serve. The road is long, but you do not walk it alone.

A Diagnostic Approach

To start or to recalibrate your journey of cultural change, a tool or map can be very helpful. You probably already have an idea about where to begin, but when you ask your entire team, that starting point becomes a collective decision. "Tool 7.1: Transforming School Culture—Diagnostic Survey" (page 240) is a tool for diagnosis, not judgment. This survey is designed to be taken by your entire staff to create a snapshot of your school's current cultural health across the key areas discussed in this book. The goal is not to achieve a perfect score but to identify two items: (1) your greatest area of strength, which is a foundation on which to build, and (2) your most pressing area for growth, which is a clear and focused starting point for your work. You can use this survey to get started right away, or you can use it after developing your culture. You can also use the survey yearly to gauge the growth of your school culture.

To implement the survey, leaders can use the following process.

1. **Administer the survey:** Share the survey with all staff members. Ensure anonymity to encourage candid responses.
2. **Analyze the results:** Tally the scores for each of the six sections. Identify the section with the highest average score (your area of strength) and the section with the lowest average score (your area for growth).

3. **Share and discuss the results:** Present the aggregated anonymous results to the staff. Lead a discussion based on the following prompts.
    - What do you notice about our results? What surprises you?
    - Let's celebrate our area of strength. What are we doing in this area that is working so well? How can we continue to build on this success?
    - Let's look at our area for growth. Why do we think this is our most challenging area? What barriers are we facing?
4. **Determine your starting point:** Based on the discussion, determine which chapter corresponds to your greatest area for growth, and use that as your starting point. For example, if your lowest collective score is in creating systems of support for Tweeners, you will begin your focused work with chapter 3.
5. **Revisit and remeasure:** After a dedicated period of focusing on your chosen area (for example, a semester or a full school year), administer the survey again to measure progress and determine the next focus area. This creates a continuous cycle of improvement.

From Diagnosis to Action by Leveraging Strengths and Attacking Weaknesses

The data from this survey is not an end point; it is a starting line. It provides the clarity needed to focus your collective energy where it will have the greatest impact. Here, you'll discover your greatest strengths and weaknesses or areas for growth.

Attending to Your Strengths

Your area of strength (highest score) is your cultural bedrock. Build on it. It is the engine of your school and can be a source of pride. This is not an area to ignore but one to amplify.

- **Celebrate the area of strength and make it visible:** Publicly celebrate this strength. Ask the staff, "What does it look like and sound like when we are at our best in this area?"
- **Leverage your leaders:** The people who are champions of this strength are your internal experts. Empower them to share their practices and lead others. If your strength is celebration, have those staff members lead a committee to make your celebrations even more powerful. If it is collaboration, have them model effective team practices for others. Use your strength to pull up your areas for growth.

Attacking Your Weaknesses (Areas for Growth)

Your area of weakness (lowest score) is not a failure; it is your next great opportunity. It is the next chapter in your school's improvement story. This is where you will direct your collective effort.

- **Read and reflect:** We strongly recommend that your guiding coalition and relevant teams read the chapter in this book that corresponds with your identified growth area.

- **Use the tools for deeper diagnosis:** The tools within each chapter are designed to move you from a general feeling to a specific analysis. Use them in your team meetings to dig deeper into the why behind your challenges.
- **Plan and reassess:** After engaging with the chapter and its tools, create a focused, collaborative action plan. Commit to working on this area for a sustained period. Then, come back to this survey, reassess your progress, and celebrate the growth you have made before identifying your next area of focus. This is the cycle of continuous improvement.

The School Culture Players

Engaging with the concepts and tools in this book does more than change systems; it changes people. It creates a ripple effect that transforms the mindset and behavior of every player in your school's culture.

Empowering Believers

For Believers, the elements in this book provide a language and a structure for what they have always known in their hearts. It moves their passion from isolated acts of heroism to a systematic and schoolwide movement. The tools give them ways to channel their energy productively, engage their colleagues in rational and data-informed dialogue, and build coalitions. This work prevents Believer burnout by creating a system of shared responsibility, ensuring the Believers are no longer fighting for students alone.

Supporting Tweeners

For Tweeners, this book and its processes provide a clear and positive road map to the school's intended culture. Instead of being socialized primarily by the loudest voices in the staff lounge, they receive a constructive framework to understand their experiences. The focus on collaboration, support, and professional growth gives them a safe harbor during their moment of truth, making them far more likely to anchor themselves to the Believer-led mission of the school.

Flipping Fundamentalists

This work holds up a mirror to the Fundamentalists, revealing the profound inconsistency between their actions and their professional identity. The tools and processes in this book are not an attack; they invite Fundamentalists to be more effective in the following ways.

- **The end of plausible deniability:** The processes outlined in this book systematically remove the classic excuses for resistance. When leaders clarify the why with data (addressing Level One), build trust through collaboration (addressing Level Two), and grow capacity with practical tools (addressing Level Three), Fundamentalists can no longer claim the change is confusing, untrustworthy, or impossible.

- **The identity crisis:** The ultimate aha moment is a crisis of professional identity. Fundamentalists often see themselves as defenders of what works or tradition. However, when they are invited to engage with tools that demonstrably focus on improving student learning, and they refuse, their identity shifts. They are forced to confront a new reality: Their resistance is no longer about defending a pedagogical stance; it's about explicitly choosing to opt out of a process designed to help students. This reframes them, in their own and their colleagues' eyes, from guardians of tradition to obstacles to student success. This difficult but transformative realization can be their first step toward finally choosing to drop their stance.

Saving Survivors

For those in survival mode, a structured, transparent, and collaborative plan to address systemic issues can be the first glimmer of hope they have seen in a long time. The tools in this book are designed to create more effective and supportive systems. When a Survivor sees a real plan to improve collaboration, provide better support, or make professional development truly useful, it can catalyze them to move from simply coping to cautiously reengaging. It shows them that the organization is finally working to fix the problems that pushed them into survival mode in the first place.

These terms of the school culture players that we learned from *Transforming School Culture* allowed us to see the interworkings of people's thoughts and behaviors. It is our hope that you take these concepts and use them to make a difference for your students, teachers, and community.

Tool 7.1: Transforming School Culture—Diagnostic Survey

Instructions

Reflect on your experiences in our school over the past year, and honestly answer the following questions. Your individual responses will be kept confidential.

Developing a Systematic and Schoolwide Focus on Learning (Chapter 1)

1. Our school has one or two clear, universally understood academic goals that guide all our instructional decisions.

4	3	2	1
Strongly agree	Agree	Disagree	Strongly disagree

2. Our school's mission, vision, and collective commitments are living documents that we refer to and use to make decisions.

4	3	2	1
Strongly agree	Agree	Disagree	Strongly disagree

Celebrating the Success of All Stakeholders (Chapter 2)

3. We consistently and authentically celebrate the academic and personal growth of *all* students, not just the highest achievers.

4	3	2	1
Strongly agree	Agree	Disagree	Strongly disagree

4. Our school culture intentionally celebrates the hard work and contributions of all staff members (teachers, support staff, and so on), fostering a sense of appreciation and high morale.

4	3	2	1
Strongly agree	Agree	Disagree	Strongly disagree

Creating Systems of Support for Tweeners (Chapter 3)

5. Our school has a structured, comprehensive, and effective mentoring and support system for new teachers that goes beyond a single assigned mentor.

4	3	2	1
Strongly agree	Agree	Disagree	Strongly disagree

page 1 of 3

6. New teachers are intentionally socialized into a positive, supportive culture and are protected from negativity and isolation.

(4)	(3)	(2)	(1)
Strongly agree	Agree	Disagree	Strongly disagree

Removing the Walls of Isolation (Chapter 4)

7. Our collaborative team meetings are consistently focused on the right work (analyzing student learning and improving instruction).

(4)	(3)	(2)	(1)
Strongly agree	Agree	Disagree	Strongly disagree

8. There is a high level of trust and psychological safety on your collaborative team, allowing for open, honest, and sometimes difficult conversations about our practice.

(4)	(3)	(2)	(1)
Strongly agree	Agree	Disagree	Strongly disagree

Providing Intensive Professional Development (Chapter 5)

9. Our professional development is relevant and engaging, and it provides us with practical strategies we can use to improve student learning.

(4)	(3)	(2)	(1)
Strongly agree	Agree	Disagree	Strongly disagree

10. Teachers have a genuine voice and choice in their professional learning, which fosters a sense of agency and ownership over their growth.

(4)	(3)	(2)	(1)
Strongly agree	Agree	Disagree	Strongly disagree

Implementing Skillful Leadership and Focus (Chapter 6)

11. Our school leadership team (guiding coalition) operates as a cohesive missionary force that effectively leads the school-improvement process.

(4)	(3)	(2)	(1)
Strongly agree	Agree	Disagree	Strongly disagree

12. Our school is led with a focus on building collective capacity and shared ownership, rather than a top-down superhero model of leadership.

4	3	2	1
Strongly agree	Agree	Disagree	Strongly disagree

Reflection

Consider your survey results.

- What area is a clear strength? Where do you see this happening in our school?
- What one or two areas are the biggest needs or opportunities to improve? How should we use this book to help us (for example, to do a book study, give a presentation, or gather additional resources)?

EPILOGUE

The Transformational Promise

As we close this book, we invite you to consider this quote from Anthony Muhammad (2018):

> *My greatest hope is that educators . . . universally dedicate themselves to creating schools that provide adequate guidance and support for all students and that schools aspire to become the transformational institutions that make the community a better place to live in and our world a better place. (p. 156)*

This quote is the North Star for our work. It is a call that transcends policy, pedagogy, and politics, speaking directly to the profound moral purpose of our profession. For us, these words are a constant reminder that our work is not just about improving test scores or managing buildings; it is about cultivating environments of hope. It is about building systems where every single student feels seen, valued, and capable of greatness. This book, with its tools and elements, was born from that hope. It is our attempt to provide the practical *how* to Muhammad's powerful *why*. Every tool, every strategy, and every chapter are designed to help you and your team dedicate yourselves to this transformational promise.

In the introduction, we shared our soul stories, the personal experiences that define us. Bo was "that kid" who needed a different system to thrive. Alex's teaching career was almost snuffed out by poor leadership. We approach this work from two different directions, but our stories are the reasons we wrote this book. As you navigate your own path with these tools, know that your commitment to developing a healthy school culture is the very catalyst that will help "that kid" make it and that will build caring, skilled, and happy teachers.

Our greatest hope is that you take these words and the tools in this book and make them your own. We hope you use them to spark the courageous conversations, to build the bridges of trust, and to forge the collective commitments necessary to transform your school. The journey is not easy, but it is the most important work you can do. It is the work that changes lives, strengthens communities, and truly makes our world a better place.

Go forth. Take those steps, be the hope, and build the culture your students deserve.

REFERENCES AND RESOURCES

Archbald, D. (2016). System-level instructional leadership: A district-level leadership case—Implementing PLCs in schools. *International Journal of Educational Leadership Preparation, 11*(2), 116–151.

Armstrong, T. (2018). *Multiple intelligences in the classroom* (4th ed.). ASCD.

Audrain, L., Ingersoll, R., & Laski, M. (2025, June). *How team-based staffing models relate to teacher decision-making influence and turnover.* Center on Reinventing Public Education. Accessed at https://crpe.org/how-team-based-staffing-models-relate-to-teacher-decision-making-influence-and-turnover on October 23, 2025.

Aungst, G. (2016). *5 principles of the modern mathematics classroom: Creating a culture of innovative thinking.* Corwin.

Baatz, J., & Wirzberger, M. (2025). Resilience as a professional competence: A new way towards healthy teachers? *Social Psychology of Education, 28*(1), Article 56.

Bailey, K., & Jakicic, C. (2017). *Simplifying common assessment: A guide for Professional Learning Communities at Work.* Solution Tree Press.

Barber, D. (2019). *How to make it matter: Teacher professional development* [Doctoral dissertation, Northeastern University]. Digital Repository Service. https://repository.library.northeastern.edu/files/neu:m044hg002

Barker, R., Hartwell, G., Egan, M., & Lock, K. (2023). The importance of school culture in supporting student mental health in secondary schools: Insights from a qualitative study. *British Educational Research Journal, 49*(3), 499–521.

Barnes, M. (2015). *Assessment 3.0: Throw out your grade book and inspire learning.* Corwin.

Barnes, M., & Gonzalez, J. (2015). *Hacking education: 10 quick fixes for every school.* Times 10.

Bayar, A., & Karaduman, H. A. (2021). The effects of school culture on students' academic achievements. *Shanlax International Journal of Education, 9*(3), 99–109.

Bayewitz, M. D., Cunningham, S. A., Ianora, J. A., Jones, B., Nielsen, M., Remmert, W., et al. (2020). *Help your team: Overcoming common collaborative challenges in a PLC at Work.* Solution Tree Press.

Bendikson, L., Broadwith, M., Zhu, T., & Meyer, F. (2020). Goal pursuit practices in high schools: Hitting the target? *Journal of Educational Administration, 58*(6), 713–728.

Berg, J. H. (2018). *Leading in sync: Teacher leaders and principals working together for student learning.* ASCD.

Bliven, A., & Jungbauer, M. (2021). The impact of student recognition of excellence to student outcome in a competency-based educational model. *Journal of Competency-Based Education, 6*(4), 195–205.

Boogren, T. H. (2018). *Take time for you: Self-care action plans for educators.* Solution Tree Press.

Boogren, T. H. (2021). *Coaching for educator wellness: A guide to supporting new and experienced teachers.* Solution Tree Press.

Boogren, T. H. (2022). *Supporting beginning teachers* (2nd ed.). Marzano Resources.

Boogren, T. H., & Turner, A. (2026). *The beginning teacher's field guide: Embarking on your first years* (2nd ed.). Solution Tree Press.

Briese, P., Dirkx, M., Mueting, J., & Wiemers, E. (2016). Curriculum and professional development practices transformed through the AIW framework. In M. B. King (Ed.), *How schools and districts meet rigorous standards through authentic intellectual work: Lessons from the field* (pp. 71–87). Corwin.

Brown, B. (2012, June 14). *Brené Brown's top 4 life lessons.* Accessed at www.oprah.com/spirit/Life-Lessons-We-All-Need-to-Learn-Brene-Brown on March 17, 2026.

Brown, J., & McGill, C. M. (2025). Exploring principals' process of gathering, reflecting upon and implementing feedback from their teachers: A grounded theory. *School Leadership and Management, 45*(1), 84–104.

Buckman, M. M., Lane, K. L., Common, E. A., Royer, D. J., Oakes, W. P., Allen, G. E., et al. (2021). Treatment integrity of primary (Tier 1) prevention efforts in tiered systems: Mapping the literature. *Education and Treatment of Children, 44*(3), 145–168.

Buffum, A., Mattos, M., & Malone, J. (2018). *Taking action: A handbook for RTI at Work.* Solution Tree Press.

Buffum, A., Mattos, M., & Weber, C. (2012). *Simplifying response to intervention: Four essential guiding principles.* Solution Tree Press.

Cabeen, J. (2018). *Hacking early learning: 10 building blocks to success in preK–3 that all teachers and school leaders should know.* Times 10.

Charner-Laird, M., Szczesiul, S., Kirkpatrick, C. L., Watson, D., & Gordon, P. (2016). From collegial support to critical dialogue: Including new teachers' voices in collaborative work. *Professional Educator, 40*(2), 1–17.

Clark, S., & Duggins, A. (2016). *Using quality feedback to guide professional learning: A framework for instructional leaders.* Corwin.

Cobbin, B. F. (2025). *Integrating technology with literacy: K–3 teachers' perception of training effectiveness* (Publication No. 31995592). ProQuest Dissertations & Theses Global.

Coder, K. R. (2024). *A strength-based collaborative team approach for supporting twice-exceptional students in a public school setting* (Publication No. 31635591) [Doctoral dissertation, Bridges Graduate School of Cognitive Diversity in Education]. ProQuest Dissertations & Theses Global. www.proquest.com/docview/3145163756

Collins, J. (2001). *Good to great: Why some companies make the leap—and others don't.* HarperBusiness.

Cone, E. A. (2024). *Mentoring: A pathway to teacher retention* [Doctoral dissertation, University of Georgia]. UGA Open Scholar. https://openscholar.uga.edu/record/2146?ln=en&v=pdf

Covey, S. R. (1989). *The seven habits of highly effective people: Powerful lessons in personal change.* Simon & Schuster.

Cuddemi, J. (2021). Focusing on collective responsibility. In S. V. Kramer (Ed.), *Charting the course for leaders: Lessons from priority schools in a PLC at Work* (pp. 93–109). Solution Tree Press.

Daly, B. D., Rao, A., Dixon, R. J., & Krach, S. K. (2025). Caring for ourselves: A survey of school psychology faculty well-being and implications for recruitment and retention. *Contemporary School Psychology, 29*(1), 153–167.

Darling-Hammond, L., Hyler, M. E., & Gardner, M. (2017). *Effective teacher professional development.* Learning Policy Institute.

Deal, T. E., & Kennedy, A. A. (1982). *Corporate cultures: The rites and rituals of corporate life.* Addison-Wesley.

Deal, T. E., & Kennedy, A. A. (1999). *The new corporate cultures: Revitalizing the workplace after downsizing, mergers, and reengineering.* Perseus Books.

Deal, T. E., & Peterson, K. D. (1994). *The leadership paradox: Balancing logic and artistry in schools.* Jossey-Bass.

DeJesus, J. M. (2021). *Enhancing professional learning communities to improve student achievement at a Title I elementary school* [Doctoral dissertation, University of Georgia]. UGA Open Scholar. https://openscholar.uga.edu/record/5085?v=pdf

DeMatthews, D. E., & Wang, Y. (2023). How can principals lead in the school improvement planning process? Reducing biases in shared decision making. *The Clearing House: A Journal of Educational Strategies, Issues and Ideas, 96*(2), 43–51.

Drago-Severson, E., & Blum-DeStefano, J. (2018). *Leading change together: Developing educator capacity within schools and systems.* ASCD.

DuFour, R., DuFour, R., Eaker, R., Many, T. W., Mattos, M., & Muhammad, A. (2024). *Learning by doing: A handbook for Professional Learning Communities at Work* (4th ed.). Solution Tree Press.

DuFour, R., DuFour, R., Eaker, R., Mattos, M., & Muhammad, A. (2021). *Revisiting Professional Learning Communities at Work: Proven insights for sustained, substantive school improvement* (2nd ed.). Solution Tree Press.

DuFour, R., & Marzano, R. J. (2011). *Leaders of learning: How district, school, and classroom leaders improve student achievement.* Solution Tree Press.

Durden, M. E. (2024). *Building leadership capacity in grade-level chairs* [Doctoral dissertation, University of Georgia]. UGA Open Scholar. https://openscholar.uga.edu/record/2190?ln=en&v=pdf

Dweck, C. S. (2006). *Mindset: The new psychology of success.* Random House.

Eaker, R., DuFour, R., & DuFour, R. (2002). *Getting started: Reculturing schools to become professional learning communities.* Solution Tree Press.

Eaker, R., Hagadone, M., Keating, J., & Rhoades, M. (2021). *Leading PLCs at Work districtwide: From boardroom to classroom.* Solution Tree Press.

Eaker, R., & Marzano, R. J. (Eds.). (2020). *Professional Learning Communities at Work and High Reliability Schools: Cultures of continuous learning.* Solution Tree Press.

Elmore, T. (2022). *A new kind of diversity: Making the different generations on your team a competitive advantage.* Maxwell Leadership.

Escobedo, A. (2012). *Teacher perceptions of the effects of school celebrations of success on collective efficacy beliefs* (Publication No. 3533407) [Doctoral dissertation, University of Virginia]. ProQuest Dissertations & Theses Global. www.proquest.com/dissertations-theses/teacher-perceptions-effects-school-celebrations/docview/1221034113/se-2

Esqueda, D. (2024). *From data-driven to data-informed: How principals, counselors, and teachers use collaborative practices to support student achievement in an urban high school* [Doctoral dissertation, University of California, Los Angeles]. UCLA Electronic Theses and Dissertations. https://escholarship.org/uc/item/29c4c5nx

Every Student Succeeds Act of 2015, Pub. L. No. 114-95, 20 U.S.C. § 1177 (2015).

Falcone, A. L. (2021). *A study on the relationship between elementary teacher engagement and collective teacher efficacy* (Publication No. 28773069) [Doctoral dissertation, University of Nebraska at Omaha]. ProQuest Dissertations & Theses Global. www.proquest.com/docview/2637315179

Ferrabee, D. (2016, February 29). *5 change management rules for building a world-class guiding coalition.* Accessed at www.managers.org.uk/insights/news/2016/february/change-management-5-rules-for-building-a-world-class-guiding-coalition on January 27, 2021.

Fisher, D., Frey, N., & Pumpian, I. (2012). *How to create a culture of achievement in your school and classroom.* ASCD.

Fisher, R., & Nepote, S. (2025). Best bets for building a culture of shared leadership. *Learning Professional, 46*(1), 48–51.

Flanagan, T., Grift, G., Lipscombe, K., Sloper, C., & Wills, J. (2021). *Transformative collaboration: five commitments for leading a professional learning community.* Solution Tree Press.

Ford, E. (2023). *Benches in the bathroom: Leading a physically, emotionally, and socially safe school culture.* Solution Tree Press.

Freelander, K. (2024, December 18). *Teacher morale: What school leaders need to know in 2025* [Blog post]. Accessed at https://moreland.edu/resources/blog-insights/teacher-morale on October 23, 2025.

Gallagher, A., & Thordarson, K. (2018). *Design thinking for school leaders: Five roles and mindsets that ignite positive change.* ASCD.

Gartner, A. R. (2024). *The relationship between social learning theory and teacher perceptions of professional development* [Doctoral dissertation, University of Nebraska at Omaha]. Digital Commons @ UNO. https://digitalcommons.unomaha.edu/edleadstudent/50

Graf, K. (2019). *Understanding principles of sustainable leadership: An examination of stress factors which challenge urban high school principals* (Publication No. 13858843) [Doctoral dissertation, Southern Connecticut State University]. ProQuest Dissertations & Theses Global. www.proquest.com/docview/2268642215

Grant, D. G., & Drew, D. E. (2024). Reimagining instructional leadership: Integrated leadership functions predicting teacher effectiveness and teacher morale. *Leadership and Policy in Schools, 23*(1), 138–161.

Gruenert, S., & Whitaker, T. (2019). *Committing to the culture: How leaders can create and sustain positive schools.* ASCD.

Gulamhussein, A. (2013, September). *Teaching the teachers: Effective professional development in an era of high stakes accountability.* Center for Public Education.

Guskey, T. R., & Yoon, K. S. (2009). What works in professional development? *Phi Delta Kappan, 90*(7), 495–500.

Hall, B. (2022). *Powerful guiding coalitions: How to build and sustain the leadership team in your PLC at Work.* Solution Tree Press.

Hall, S. L. (2018). *10 success factors for literacy intervention: Getting results with MTSS in elementary schools.* ASCD.

Hanks, S. A. (2023). *School administrator instructional leadership self-efficacy influence on work engagement: A qualitative descriptive inquiry* (Publication No. 30424640) [Doctoral dissertation, Grand Canyon University]. ProQuest Dissertations & Theses Global. www.proquest.com/openview/dd93e72703e3175f20d5da6e7f116a47/1?pq-origsite=gscholar&cbl=18750&diss=y

Hanson, H., Torres, K., Yoon, S. Y., Merrill, R., Fantz, T., & Velie, Z. (2021, August). *Growing together: Professional Learning Communities at Work generates achievement gains in Arkansas.* Education Northwest. Accessed at https://educationnorthwest.org/sites/default/files/plc-at-work-impact-evaluation.pdf on March 19, 2026.

Hattie, J. (2023). *Visible learning: The sequel—A synthesis of over 2,100 meta-analyses relating to achievement.* Routledge.

Hejazi, E., Lavasani, M. G., Amani, H., & Was, C. A. (2012). Academic identity status, goal orientation, and academic achievement among high school students. *Journal of Research in Education, 22*(1), 291–320.

Hemi, A., Madjar, N., & Rich, Y. (2024). Perceptions of peer and teacher goals predict academic achievement goals among adolescents. *Journal of Experimental Education, 92*(4), 692–712.

Hierck, T. (2017). *Seven keys to a positive learning environment in your classroom.* Solution Tree Press.

Holloway, J., & Brass, J. (2018). Making accountable teachers: The terrors and pleasures of performativity. *Journal of Education Policy, 33*(3), 361–382.

Hooper, J. W. (2025). *Improving perceptions and practices of teacher professional learning: A collaborative action research study* (Publication No. 31939074). ProQuest Dissertations & Theses Global.

Hose, J. C. (2022). *Elementary teachers' perceptions of professional development effectiveness* (Publication No. 29060872) [Doctoral dissertation, Walden University]. ProQuest Dissertations & Theses Global. www.proquest.com/docview/2644421464

Ismail, M., Khatibi, A. A., & Azam, S. M. F. (2022). Impact of school culture on school effectiveness in government schools in Maldives. *Participatory Educational Research, 9*(2), 261–279.

Jensen, E. (2019). *Poor students, rich teaching: Seven high-impact mindsets for students from poverty* (Revised ed.). Solution Tree Press.

Johnson, J. R. (2016). *An evaluation of implementation and effectiveness of professional learning communities in Minnesota Public Schools* [Doctoral dissertation, St. Cloud State University]. The Repository @ St. Cloud State. https://repository.stcloudstate.edu/edad_etds/14

Jorgensen, R. R. (2025). *Why I stay: A qualitative appreciative inquiry study exploring teacher longevity in an urban educational setting* [Doctoral dissertation, Bethel University]. Spark Repository. https://spark.bethel.edu/etd/1149

Joyce, B., & Showers, B. (2002). *Student achievement through staff development* (3rd ed.). ASCD.

Kanold, T. D. (2021). *SOUL! Fulfilling the promise of your professional life as a teacher and leader.* Solution Tree Press.

Kiral, B. (2025). Creating collective responsibility at school: Principals' roles, faced challenges, and solution strategies. *Education and Urban Society, 57*(2), 147–167.

Knowles, M. S. (1980). *The modern practice of adult education: From pedagogy to andragogy* (Revised and updated ed.). Follett.

Kohn, A. (2018). *Punished by rewards: The trouble with gold stars, incentive plans, A's, praise, and other bribes* (25th anniversary ed.). HarperOne.

Kotter, J. P. (1996). *Leading change.* Harvard Business School Press.

Kramer, S. V. (Ed.). (2021). *Charting the course for collaborative teams: Lessons from priority schools in a PLC at Work.* Solution Tree Press.

Kramer, S. V., & Schuhl, S. (2017). *School improvement for all: A how-to guide for doing the right work.* Solution Tree Press.

Kwok, A., & Macfarlane, K. O. (2025, February). *Strengthening early-career teachers: Effective components of teacher induction programs* (Overview Brief No. 32). EdResearch for Action.

Lane, K. L., Kalberg, J. R., & Menzies, H. M. (2009). *Developing schoolwide programs to prevent and manage problem behaviors: A step-by-step approach.* Guilford Press.

Learning Policy Institute. (2025). *An overview of teacher shortages: 2025* [Fact sheet]. Author.

Lortie, D. C. (1975). *Schoolteacher: A sociological study.* University of Chicago Press.

Lowry, K. L. (2021). *A case study of the leadership styles a highly effective principal employed to cultivate teacher collective efficacy* [Doctoral dissertation, Texas A&M University]. OAKTrust. https://oaktrust.library.tamu.edu/items/aec18f85-34f5-4a28-94a7-ff652b4a4fe6

Mansell, K. E., & Kirksey, J. J. (2025). *Exploring the effectiveness of the PLC at Work process in Texas elementary and middle schools: Part 2—Evaluating the effectiveness of the PLC at Work process and student achievement in Texas* (PLC Model School Report No. 2). Center for Innovative Research in Change, Leadership, and Education, Texas Tech University. Accessed at https://files.eric.ed.gov/fulltext/ED675138.pdf on December 3, 2025.

Marcolini, J. P. (2022). *The impact of STEM professional development on teacher self-efficacy: A phenomenological mixed methods study* (Publication No. 29208556) [Doctoral dissertation, Florida Gulf Coast University]. ProQuest Dissertations & Theses Global. www.proquest.com/docview/2666520613

Maready, B., Cheng, Q., & Bunch, D. (2021). Exploring mentoring practices contributing to new teacher retention: An analysis of the beginning teacher longitudinal study. *International Journal of Evidence Based Coaching and Mentoring, 19*(2), 88–99.

Marzano, R. J. (2017). *The new art and science of teaching.* Solution Tree Press.

Mattos, M., Buffum, A., Malone, J., Cruz, L. F., Dimich, N., & Schuhl, S. (2025). *Taking action: A handbook for RTI at Work* (2nd ed.). Solution Tree Press.

Mavi, D., Tuti, G., & Ozdemir, M. (2025). How does teacher academic optimism affect teacher self-efficacy: Mediating role of teacher professional development and teacher subjective well-being? *Psychology in the Schools, 62*(4), 1013–1025.

McBride, C., & Duncan-Davis, B. (2021). *Ready for the workforce: Engaging strategies for teaching secondary learners employability skills.* Solution Tree Press.

McClure, P. A., Jr. (2024). *The role of psychological safety in teacher retention at Title 1 middle schools* [Doctoral dissertation, Southwest Baptist University]. https://libguides.sbuniv.edu/ld.php?content_id=83852701

McClusky, S. L., Goddard, R. D., & Yoon, I. (2021). Exploration of the relationship between professional development quality and teacher sense of self-efficacy in urban Ohio elementary schools. *Leadership and Research in Education, 6*(1), 49–78.

McCormick, M. (2025, August 5). *Spotlight on evidence: Reimagining the teaching role by investing in strategic staffing.* Overdeck Family Foundation. Accessed at https://overdeck.org/news-and-resources/article/spotlight-on-evidence-reimagining-the-teaching-role-by-investing-in-strategic-staffing on October 23, 2025.

McNeece, A. (2019). *Launching and consolidating unstoppable learning.* Solution Tree Press.

McNeece, A. (2020). *Loving what they learn: Research-based strategies to increase student engagement.* Solution Tree Press.

McNeece, A., & Sheppard, C. (2025). Empowering Believers to speak up: The Fundamentalist playbook. In A. Muhammad (Ed.), *Culture champions: Teachers supporting a healthy classroom culture* (pp. 23–37). Solution Tree Press.

Mertler, C. A., & Charles, C. M. (2011). *Introduction to educational research* (7th ed.). Allyn & Bacon.

MetLife. (2013, February). *The MetLife survey of the American teacher: Challenges for school leadership.* Author. Accessed at www.metlife.com/content/dam/microsites/about/corporate-profile/MetLife-Teacher-Survey-2012.pdf on February 10, 2020.

Middleton-Cox, B. (2025). *Strong foundations: Building resilience in early career teachers* [Doctoral dissertation, Northeastern University]. Digital Repository Service. https://repository.library.northeastern.edu/files/neu:ms37fn39v

Mieliwocki, R., & Fatheree, J. (2019). *Adventures in teacher leadership: Pathways, strategies, and inspiration for every teacher.* ASCD.

Miller-Bailey, C. S. (2016). *Reciprocal accountability and capacity building: The influence of distributed leadership on collective teacher efficacy and professional learning communities* (Publication No. 10246360) [Doctoral dissertation, Russell Sage College]. ProQuest Dissertations & Theses Global. www.proquest.com/openview/0beae4fceda071994f72f70577b7cb86/1?pq-origsite=gscholar&cbl=18750

Mitterer, D. M., & Mitterer, H. E. (2023). The mediating effect of trust on psychological safety and job satisfaction. *Journal of Behavior and Applied Management, 23*(1), 29–41.

Moir, E. (1999). The stages of a teacher's first year. In M. Scherer (Ed.), *A better beginning: Supporting and mentoring new teachers* (pp. 19–23). ASCD.

Muhammad, A. (2009). *Transforming school culture: How to overcome staff division.* Solution Tree Press.

Muhammad, A. (2015). *Overcoming the achievement gap trap: Liberating mindsets to effect change.* Solution Tree Press.

Muhammad, A. (2018). *Transforming school culture: How to overcome staff division* (2nd ed.). Solution Tree Press.

Muhammad, A. (2023, June 23–24). *Transforming School Culture training.* Bloomington, IN.

Muhammad, A. (Ed.). (2025). *Culture champions: Teachers supporting a healthy classroom culture.* Solution Tree Press.

Muhammad, A., & Cruz, L. F. (2019). *Time for change: Four essential skills for transformational school and district leaders.* Solution Tree Press.

Muhammad, A., & Hollie, S. (2012). *The will to lead, the skill to teach: Transforming schools at every level.* Solution Tree Press.

National Committee on Excellence in Education. (1983, April). *A nation at risk: The imperative for educational reform.* U.S. Department of Education. Accessed at https://files.eric.ed.gov/fulltext/ED226006.pdf on December 16, 2025.

Newman, R. (2012). Goal setting to achieve results. *Leadership, 41*(3), 12–16, 38.

Nicklas, A. (2025). *Andragogy and professional learning: Rethinking internal structures* (Publication No. 31997057). ProQuest Dissertations & Theses Global.

Noble, R. (2021). Leveraging shared leadership in the priority school. In S. V. Kramer (Ed.), *Charting the course for leaders: Lessons from priority schools in a PLC at Work* (pp. 111–129). Solution Tree Press.

Noddings, N. (2005). *The challenge to care in schools: An alternative approach to education* (2nd ed.). Teachers College Press.

Nohe-Dirk, A. (2024). *The constructs of teacher well-being: A phenomenological study* [Doctoral dissertation, Indiana State University]. Sycamore Scholars. https://scholars.indianastate.edu/etds/3716

O'Day, J., & Marsden, D. (2022, January). *Educational leadership in crisis: Reflections from a pandemic* [Policy brief]. California Collaborative on District Reform.

Omare, E. (2021). Teacher qualification, experience, capability beliefs and professional development: Do they predict teacher adoption of 21st century pedagogies? *International Journal of Curriculum and Instruction, 13*(2), 1161–1192.

Partin-Dunn, R. L. (2020). *The impact of research-based professional development on teacher self-efficacy and collective efficacy beliefs with respect to applying techniques from* Teach Like a Champion 2.0 [Doctoral dissertation, Gardner-Webb University]. Digital Commons @ Gardner-Webb University. https://digitalcommons.gardner-webb.edu/education-dissertations/66

Pelletier, D. N. (2024). *The impact of working conditions on special education teacher attrition* [Doctoral dissertation, University of Maine]. DigitalCommons@UMaine. https://digitalcommons.library.umaine.edu/etd/4019

Pelton, K. S. L., Lane, K. L., Oakes, W. P., Buckman, M. M., Lane, N. A., Allen, G. E., et al. (2024). Re-examining the relation between social validity and treatment integrity in CI3T models. *Assessment for Effective Intervention, 49*(3), 159–170.

Perryman, J., Bradbury, A., Calvert, G., & Kilian, K. (2025). "A tipping point" in teacher retention and accountability: The case of inspection. *British Journal of Educational Studies, 73*(2), 181–200.

Peterson, K. D. (2002). Positive or negative. *Journal of Staff Development, 23*(3), 10–15.

Pi, Y., Ma, M., Hu, A., & Wang, T. (2024). The relationship between professional identity and professional development among special education teachers: A moderated mediation model. *BMC Psychology, 12*, Article 570.

Radford, C. P. (2017). *Mentoring in action: Guiding, sharing, and reflecting with novice teachers—A month-by-month curriculum for teacher effectiveness* (2nd ed.). Corwin.

Reeves, D. B. (2020). *The learning leader: How to focus school improvement for better results* (2nd ed.). ASCD.

Rhode Island Department of Education. (2025, June). *Research-based practices for educator retention*. Author. Accessed at https://ride.ri.gov/sites/g/files/xkgbur806/files/2025-07/Research-based%20Practices%20for%20Educator%20Retention.pdf on October 23, 2025.

Richardson, S. (2014). *Individual sense of efficacy, collective teacher efficacy and student achievement in high achieving and low achieving urban public schools* [Doctoral dissertation, Pepperdine University]. Pepperdine Digital Commons. https://digitalcommons.pepperdine.edu/etd/429

Roche, K. R. (2021). *A qualitative case study of the influence of student presence in teacher professional development* [Doctoral dissertation, Duquesne University]. Duquesne Scholarship Collection. https://dsc.duq.edu/etd/2024

Rock, M. L. (2019). *The eCoaching continuum for educators: Using technology to enrich professional development and improve student outcomes*. ASCD.

Rodman, A. (2019). *Personalized professional learning: A job-embedded pathway for elevating teacher voice*. ASCD.

Rogers, E. M. (2003). *Diffusion of innovations* (5th ed.). Free Press.

Russell, J. L., Bryk, A. S., Peurach, D. J., Sherer, J. Z., Duff, M., Sherer, D., et al. (2025). Catalyzing scientific-professional learning communities: A framework for conceptualizing the health and development of educational improvement networks. *Peabody Journal of Education, 100*(1), 7–27.

Ryan, B. (2023). *The brilliance in the building: Effecting change in urban schools with the PLC at Work process*. Solution Tree Press.

Ryan, R. M., & Deci, E. L. (2000). Intrinsic and extrinsic motivations: Classic definitions and new directions. *Contemporary Educational Psychology, 25*(1), 54–67.

Sanfelippo, J., & Sinanis, T. (2016). *Hacking leadership: 10 ways great leaders inspire learning that teachers, students, and parents love*. Times 10.

Santia, S., Astuti, B., & Syafitri, D. (2024). The relationship between school culture and student achievement in high school. *Journal of Innovation in Educational and Cultural Research, 5*(4), 693–701.

Savage, B. J. (2023). *The role of communities of practice in a professional learning community (PLC): Case study* (Publication No. 30818343) [Doctoral dissertation, Southern Nazarene University]. ProQuest Dissertations & Theses Global. www.proquest.com/docview/2919539939

Schein, E. H. (2004). *Organizational culture and leadership* (3rd ed.). Jossey-Bass.

Schleifer, D., Rinehart, C., & Yanisch, T. (2017). *Teacher collaboration in perspective: A guide to research*. Public Agenda. Accessed at https://publicagenda.org/wp-content/uploads/PublicAgenda_TeacherCollaborationInPerspective_AGuideToResearch_2017.pdf on March 18, 2026.

Scoresby, A. (2024). Show up for yourself to keep showing up. *English in Texas, 54*(1), 68–74.

Shakespeare, W. (n.d.). As you like it (B. Mowat, P. Werstine, M. Poston, & R. Niles, Eds.). *The Folger Shakespeare*. Accessed at www.folger.edu/explore/shakespeares-works/as-you-like-it/read on February 4, 2026.

Simms, J. A. (2024). *The Marzano synthesis: A collected guide to what works in K–12 education*. Marzano Resources

Sims, R. L., & Penny, G. R. (2015). Examination of a failed professional learning community. *Journal of Education and Training Studies, 3*(1), 39–45.

Smith, J. R., & Smith, R. L. (2015). *Evaluating instructional leadership: Recognized practices for success*. Corwin.

Snyder, R. R. (2017). Resistance to change among veteran teachers: Providing voice for more effective engagement. *International Journal of Educational Leadership Preparation, 12*(1), 1–14.

Szabo, Z. (2023). *Building a collaborative culture: Study of a high school cross-curricular professional learning community* (Publication No. 30420908) [Doctoral dissertation, Arizona State University]. ProQuest Dissertations & Theses Global. www.proquest.com/docview/2813836441

Tait, A., & Faulkner, D. (2019). *Dream team: A practical playbook to help innovative educators change schools.* ASCD.

Talbert, J. E. (2009). Professional learning communities at the crossroads: How systems hinder or engender change. In A. Hargreaves, A. Lieberman, M. Fullan, & D. Hopkins (Eds.), *Second international handbook of educational change* (pp. 555–571). Springer.

Tan, J. P. I. (2015). Examining the socialisation of new teachers through the lenses of positioning theory and micropolitical theory. *Asia-Pacific Education Researcher, 24*(1), 177–188.

Thornton, K. (2024). Mentoring preparation in educational contexts: A review of the literature. *International Journal of Mentoring and Coaching in Education, 13*(4), 441–456. https://doi.org/10.1108/IJMCE-07-2023-0069

Toll, C. A. (2023). *The effective facilitator's handbook: Leading teacher workshops, committees, teams, and study groups.* ASCD.

Trice, H. M., & Beyer, J. M. (1993). *The cultures of work organizations.* Prentice Hall.

Valera, C. C. (2023). *An integrative literature review of collaborative school culture: Basis for a proposed model.* ScienceOpen Preprints.

Van Soelen, T. M. (2021). *Meeting goals: Protocols for leading effective, purpose-driven discussions in schools.* Solution Tree Press.

Weinstein, J., Raczynski, D., & Peña, J. (2020). Relational trust and positional power between school principals and teachers in Chile: A study of primary schools. *Educational Management Administration and Leadership, 48*(1), 64–81.

Weisling, N. F., & Gardiner, W. (2018). Making mentoring work. *Phi Delta Kappan, 99*(6), 64–69.

Wiesner-Groff, A. J. (2023). *Middle school teachers' perceptions of principal practices which influence collective teacher efficacy in a highly efficacious, high achieving middle school* (Publication No. 30814747) [Doctoral dissertation, Saint Louis University]. ProQuest Dissertations & Theses Global. www.proquest.com/docview/2900126809

Wilcoxen, C., Newman, R., & Wulff, M. (2025). A coaching and mentoring tool anchors support and collaboration. *Educational Process: International Journal, 14*, Article e2025001.

Wiley, C. (2024). *How leaders cultivate effective collaborative environments for teachers: An investigation of the role site leaders play in creating teacher collective efficacy* [Doctoral dissertation, San Diego State University]. SDSU Digital Collections. https://digitalcollections.sdsu.edu/do/c75bf7b6-24b1-438a-acd3-534952991be4

Williams, K. C., & Hierck, T. (2015). *Starting a movement: Building culture from the inside out in professional learning communities.* Solution Tree Press.

World Population Review. (n.d.). *Poorest cities in the United States.* Accessed at https://worldpopulationreview.com/us-city-rankings/poorest-cities-in-america on March 18, 2026.

York-Barr, J., Sommers, W. A., Ghere, G. S., & Montie, J. (2016). *Reflective practice for renewing schools: An action guide for educators* (3rd ed.). Corwin.

Young, A. K., Julien, A. B., & Osborne, T. (2023). *The instructional coaching handbook: 200+ troubleshooting strategies for success.* ASCD.

Zepeda, S. J., Goff, L. R., & Steele, S. W. (2019). *C.R.A.F.T. conversations for teacher growth: How to build bridges and cultivate expertise.* ASCD.

INDEX

R

S

T

U

V

W

Z